Sex, Lies, and Autobiography

Sex, Lies, and Autobiography

The Ethics of Confession

James O'Rourke

UNIVERSITY OF VIRGINIA PRESS

Charlottesville and London

University of Virginia Press
© 2006 by the Rector and Visitors of the University of Virginia
All rights reserved
Printed in the United States of America on acid-free paper
First published 2006
1 3 5 7 9 8 6 4 2
Library of Congress Cataloging-in-Publication Data
O'Rourke, James L.
  Sex, lies, and autobiography : the ethics of confession / James O'Rourke.
  p. cm.
  Includes bibliographical references and index.
  ISBN 0-8139-2512-6 (cloth : alk. paper)
  1. English literature—19th century—History and criticism. 2. Self in literature.
3. Nabokov, Vladimir Vladimirovich, 1899–1977. Lolita. 4. Rousseau, Jean-Jacques, 1712–
1778. Confessions. 5. Autobiographical fiction—History and criticism. 6. Autobiography
in literature. 7. Confession in literature. 8. Ethics in literature. 9. Sex in literature.
10. Autobiography. I. Title.
PR468.S43O76 2006
820.9'384—dc22   2005016401

This is one of the laws of life.
The shadows of our past actions stalk beside us
during our existence, and never cease to torment
or to soothe, according as they are ill or good,
that mysterious portion of mind termed conscience.
—Mary Shelley, "Rousseau"

Contents

⋮

Acknowledgments

⋮

I would like to thank the members of the faculty committees at Florida State University who provided a sabbatical semester and a summer research grant in support of my work on this book. I appreciate the vigorous readings given to the manuscript by the anonymous readers for the University of Virginia Press; their spirited responses helped to make this a better book. Portions of chapter 3 appeared in ELH and *Studies in Romanticism*, and I thank the editors of those journals, and the Johns Hopkins Press, for permission to reprint that material.

I am very happy to express my gratitude to Cathie Brettschneider at the University of Virginia Press, whose support and advice have been indispensable to me, and to my colleagues in the English Department at Florida State University, especially those whose contentiousness has helped me to hone the more ambitious parts of this manuscript.

As always, I owe the most to Helen Burke, who fixed most of what was wrong with this book during our perpetual walk in the woods. And if our silent companions on that walk were any more patient and devoted, I would have to revise my opinion about the difficulty and the rarity of truly ethical behavior.

Abbreviations

⋮

AR   Paul de Man, *Allegories of Reading.* New Haven: Yale University Press, 1979.

CL   Samuel Taylor Coleridge, *Collected Letters,* ed. Earl Leslie Griggs. Oxford: Clarendon Press, 1956–1971.

EST   Michel Foucault, *Ethics: Subjectivity and Truth,* trans. Robert Hurley et al., ed. Paul Rabinow. New York: New Press, 1997.

HS   Michel Foucault, *The History of Sexuality. Volume One: An Introduction,* trans. Robert Hurley. New York: Vintage, 1980.

Journals   Dorothy Wordsworth, *The Grasmere Journals,* ed. Pamela Woof. Oxford: Clarendon Press, 1991.

LB   William Wordsworth and Samuel Taylor Coleridge, *Lyrical Ballads* (1798), ed. W. J. B. Owen. Oxford: Oxford University Press, 1969.

Letters1   William and Dorothy Wordsworth, *The Letters of William and Dorothy Wordsworth: The Early Years,* arr. and ed. Ernest de Selincourt. 2nd ed. rev. by Chester L. Shaver. Oxford: Clarendon Press, 1967.

Letters2   William and Dorothy Wordsworth, *The Letters of William and Dorothy Wordsworth: The Middle Years,* arr. and ed. by Ernest de Selincourt. 2nd ed. rev. by Chester L. Shaver. Oxford, Clarendon Press, 1967.

MWSJournals   *The Journals of Mary Shelley 1814–1844.* Ed. Paula R. Feldman and Diana Scott-Kilvert. Baltimore: Johns Hopkins University Press, 1987.

OG   Jacques Derrida, *Of Grammatology,* trans. Gayatri Chakravorty Spivak. Baltimore: Johns Hopkins University Press, 1974.

PW   William Wordsworth, *Poetical Works*, ed. Thomas Hutchinson, rev. ed. Ernest de Selincourt. Oxford: Oxford University Press, 1978.

"Rousseau"   Mary Shelley, "Rousseau," in *Mary Shelley's Literary Lives and Other Writings. Volume 3: French Lives.* Ed. Clarissa Campbell Orr. London: Pickering & Chatto, 2002.

SE   Sigmund Freud, *The Standard Edition of the Complete Psychological Works of Sigmund Freud*, trans. James Strachey et al. London: Hogarth, 1955.

UP   Michel Foucault, *The Use of Pleasure. The History of Sexuality: Volume Two*, trans. Robert Hurley. New York: Vintage, 1985.

Sex, Lies, and Autobiography

Introduction

⋮

THE study of ethics in literature has generally been conducted along lines developed in the field of moral philosophy, with one procedural difference. Philosophers typically invent examples of ethical choices as test cases for general principles so that the validity of a principle depends on the range of cases in which it seems to provide a desirable outcome. In literary studies, the examples are already given, and critics attempt to derive general ethical principles from literary instances. One enabling premise of this methodology is that ethics is intuitive. Critics who have focused on the ethical dimensions of literature, from Aristotle to Martha Nussbaum, have generally presumed it is possible to pass directly from the aesthetic to the ethical principles of literary works. Critics often gesture toward the necessity of taking the complexities of literary form into account before venturing on summary ethical judgments, but there is a general presumption that some degree of analytic tact can enable critical work to be both morally edifying and simultaneously responsive to the aesthetic qualities of literary texts. Even when a skilled and experienced critic such as Wayne Booth takes up the novels of Henry James as an example of the ambiguities that literature can pose to straightforward ethical analysis, Booth is eventually willing to specify "the defensible moral or ethical stances" brought into "conflict" (26) in James's novels.

In *Sex, Lies, and Autobiography*, I argue that the most compelling ethical work that literary texts can do is counterintuitive. Literary works are uniquely capable of challenging the narratives that give our lives a sense of ethical coherence when their polysemic qualities—their ironies, ambiguities, and indeterminacies—falsify the central premise of moral philosophy, the presumption of a discernible continuity from ethical principle to practice in everyday life. Furthermore, I contend that the genre that best exemplifies this discontinuity is the confessional autobiography. In the modern form of the confession initiated by Rousseau, the controlling ethical principle of the dominant narrative is either directly stated or clearly implied: It is the claim that the autobiographer is a good person. This story of the good self is a narrative of interiority that centers on the feelings and intentions of the autobiographer. In the more literary instances of autobiography, this narrative of the good self is shadowed by an account of acts and consequences in which the autobiographer profits from the misfortunes of others and plays some role in the production of those misfortunes. The principle of indeterminacy in the confessional autobiography rests on the impossibility of reconciling these two narratives.

Before entering into the specific ways in which confessional autobiographies rupture the ethical fabric of everyday life, let me illustrate the difference between the philosophical and the literary construction of ethical examples by comparing a case study from a contemporary philosophical text with the most compelling ethical crux in contemporary literature, Sethe's "rough choice" in Toni Morrison's *Beloved*. In "A Critique of Utilitarianism," Bernard Williams offers a hypothetical example to demonstrate the limits of utilitarian reasoning. Williams tells the story of a chemist named George who is offered a job in a chemical weapons factory. In this scenario, George's career options are limited, his children suffer as long as he is out of work, and George's scruples will make him a less enthusiastic worker, and hence less of a danger to the world, than the person who will take the position if he turns it down. Williams concludes that according to the utilitarian aspiration to maximize happiness for the greatest number of people, it seems "*obviously* the right answer" (99) that George should take the job. But Williams objects that the utilitarian answer overlooks the fact that a sense of moral conviction is one of the things that give our lives integrity and make them worthwhile. As a result, he argues that there are cases, like this one, in which the importance of one's own moral principles should override a straightforward utilitarian calculus.

Williams presents a case with an entirely prospective focus, in which it is presumed that it is possible for George to arrive at a justifiable basis for an ethical decision. In *Beloved*, Morrison forces the reader first to look retrospectively; the difficulty of deciding whether Sethe has made the right choice redirects the reader's focus from her action to the historical background that produces her harrowing decision. Sethe's choice then takes on broader and more problematic dimensions than George's decision calls

2 : Sex, Lies, and Autobiography

for. In a lucid and sensitive account of the ethics of *Beloved*, James Phelan shows how the inability to isolate Sethe's action within a definitive causal chain with a beginning and an end opens the enduring legacy of plantation slavery as a palpable and present reality. I see little to disagree with in Phelan's reading, apart from his suggestion that Morrison's construction of this ethical impasse is not only "somehow beyond the reach of standard ethical judgment" (106) but that it also deviates from a literary norm. When Morrison presents a character whose motives are not entirely transparent and the implications of whose actions are unknowable, she produces a quintessentially literary moment of undecidability. Sethe's choice cannot be properly read, in that it cannot be incorporated into a linear narrative of cause and effect that lends itself to summary judgment, but, as has been said in literary studies at least since the New Criticism, this is what literature does. It offers a density of experience and a resistance to interpretation that are not available in other forms of discourse.[1]

While Sethe's predicament is an exemplary literary formation, as an ethical case study it violates the norms of the genre of moral philosophy. If the validity of a principle (e.g., "thou shalt not kill") is in question, it makes perfect sense, from a methodological perspective, to choose examples that provide a recognizable continuity from the principle underlying a choice to the consequences of that choice. Thus the circumstances that might legitimize an act of killing are tested against a wide range of case studies in Jeff McMahan's recent book *The Ethics of Killing*, a work that has been praised both for the subtlety of its analyses and for the inventiveness of the examples deployed in order to examine such topics as abortion, suicide, and euthanasia. McMahan's construction of examples operates within disciplinary protocols so common that they are used without comment in virtually every modern academic study of ethics, but a recent textbook offers an explanation of these procedures. In the Blackwell *Companion to Ethics*, Dale Jamieson first outlines the difference between "hypothetical" examples (those that "could occur without requiring us to rewrite the laws of physics") and "imaginary" examples (those that "involve logical possibilities that could only occur in worlds very different from ours"). He then explains why hypothetical examples are to be preferred to imaginary ones: "In order to be valid, counterfactual reasoning must go on against a fixed background . . . [where] we have a relatively clear idea what will be different and what will be the same whatever we do. In imaginary cases, we do not really know what is up for grabs" (484–85). Jamieson thus suggests two ways of distinguishing the "hypothetical" from the "imaginary." At first, the hypothetical only has to remain within the laws of physics, but Jamieson goes on to say that in order for a hypothetical instance to provide a valid basis for a general inference, it should offer a "relatively clear idea" of the consequences of an ethical choice. As Jamieson's explanation shows, the next logical question—How often, in real life, do we know all that is at stake in our decisions?—is systematically excluded from the standard practice of moral philosophy.

It will undoubtedly occur to the literary critic that these two criteria for establishing the legitimacy of a particular example in ethical studies—compatibility with the laws of physics and predictable causality—correspond to the conventions of a particular literary genre: realism, a genre that claims to offer the material world as a transparent totality. Beloved, as it departs from realist conventions, offers no such clarity. The ethical problematic produced by Morrison is far more radical than her use of nonrealist representation. The figure of Beloved can be seen as a literary device for the representation of an explicable psychological phenomenon (what Freud calls melancholia, or the inability to complete the process of mourning), but Morrison's severing of any knowable connection between Sethe's intentions and the consequences of her action upsets the most fundamental principle of ethical philosophy. While Jamieson shows why the validity of an example as a useful ethical case study depends on our ability to identify the consequences of a moral choice, Morrison confronts her reader with an unbridgeable gap between principle and practice. She presents a character who is not only sympathetic but admirable—Sethe's action is a potent example of courage, a value that occupies a preeminent place in virtue ethics from Aristotle to the present day—without offering any guarantee that this is the virtue that her situation calls for.

Ethical philosophers look for iterative principles that can be transferred intact from one context to another. They identify these principles by constructing rhetorical laboratory conditions that allow for the specification of discrete variables and that measure success in terms of the repeatability of an experiment, but these are not the conditions of everyday life. We do not live our lives as the authors of novels who construct imaginary examples; we are more like the characters who inhabit, and only partly discern, the layers of narrative that surround us.[2] The impossibility of reconciling the motivating principles with the practical consequences of an ethical choice from within our embedded perspectives derives from what Derrida calls in his critique of Austin's speech-act theory the insaturation of context. Derrida argues that it is impossible to assign a univocal value to any speech act because it cannot be determined, in any principled way, how to limit the frames of context that are relevant to the interpretation of a particular event. It is presumed, in Williams's example of George the chemist, that the answer to his dilemma is not to say that he should go back to school, get a medical degree, and become a member of "Doctors Without Borders," but there is no reason in principle to judge that ethics calls for any less of a response to global inequalities. While Austin contends that ordinary language is adequate to our everyday communicative needs, Derrida objects that Austin "makes us accept as ordinary a teleological and ethical determination" (*Margins* 323). Although Austin offers an extensive survey of the ways in which performative utterances can fail to achieve their intended effects, he persistently identifies these failures as regrettable exceptions to the ordinary.

Austin describes a world that works; salt gets passed, people get married, and cities get built without excessive confusion over the intentions of speakers. Derrida focuses on the linguistic and "teleological" features of Austin's work, showing how every act of communication has the potential to misfire; in the metaphor he adopts in *The Post Card*, a letter can always not arrive. But the more significant challenge to Austin's description of the adequacy of ordinary language rests in Derrida's fleeting observation that there is also an "ethical determination" to Austin's work. There is an elided step in Derrida's critique of this ethical determination, which can be filled in with Foucault's observation that power "is everywhere" (HS 93). Every social interaction, every speech-act, activates a relation of power between a speaker and her interlocutors.[3] The structural condition of failure does not rest simply on the possibility that a listener will not understand a speaker; it results from the fact that there is no guarantee that the exercise of power in this exchange can be controlled or legitimated. When Austin answers a supposedly linguistic question (what is the nature of ordinary language?) with an ethical solution (performatives are ordinarily successful), he trivializes the possibility of failure by occluding the presence of power. Austin's central claim, that it is the ordinary condition of a performative speech act to succeed, is ethical in nature in that it functions as a legitimating narrative. Austin's description of a world that works implies that this world is relatively sound and is not a moral abomination. *Beloved*, in contrast, illustrates a gap between an incipient narrative of ordinary life, in which Sethe loves Paul D and tries to raise her surviving children, and a shadow narrative that impinges on that world and threatens to destroy it by depriving it of any value.

In historical discourse, the gap between legitimating narratives and their counterformations was delineated by Walter Benjamin when he said that every document of civilization was also a document of barbarism (256). In the modern form of the confessional autobiography initiated by Rousseau, the split structure of legitimating and counternarratives is stark. In the legitimating narrative, I, Rousseau, am a good person. The shadow narrative tells the story of acts and events in which, with something less than deliberate malice, I somehow—unconsciously, unintentionally, unwittingly, accidentally, carelessly, possibly negligently—harmed other people. While both of these stories are contained within the *Confessions*, Rousseau's critics have generally agreed with Jean Starobinski's confidence in the "anthropological optimism" of Rousseau's thought, which, Starobinski believes, shows that "Man is naturally good" and that Rousseau himself is a "man of nature" (295). Rousseau's own reflections on the *Confessions* are not so secure. In the "Fourth Walk" of the *Reveries of the Solitary Walker*, Rousseau puzzles over the fact that although he thinks of himself as a man who loves truth and abhors falsehood, he has to admit that not only has he lied frequently throughout his life, but he is not even sure that he was able to tell the truth about himself in the *Confessions*. The "Fourth Walk" begins with Rousseau trying to depict the lies he has told in his life as accidental responses to the pressures of the moment, but his realization that he has also lied in the *Confessions*, in a solitary and deliberative act of retrospective autobiography, presents a more formidable challenge to the persona of natural goodness.

Rousseau tries to recover the story of his good self by arguing (with himself) that the embellishments of reality in the *Confessions* are only innocent "fictions" as opposed to actual "lies," but as the essay unfolds he discovers that even in the essay he is currently writing—the "Fourth Walk"—he becomes evasive when he is forced to confront the ethical status of his own actions. In an essay which begins with the rueful admission that the Delphic imperative to "'know thyself' is not such an easy precept to observe as I thought in my *Confessions*" (63), Rousseau finally decides that there is a big difference between morals in books and morals in life. In books, one can say anything, since "the most austere morals cost the author nothing," but in real life, "the morals of books are seen as nothing but idle and impracticable chatter" (65). Working within the genre of autobiography, Rousseau finds that the exercise of personal retrospection imposes ethical demands that are far more stringent and overdetermined than any form of philosophical speculation. Rousseau can only conclude his essay with the rueful acknowledgment his enemies might be right to mock him for having adopted so presumptuous a motto as "to live for truth," since the principles of his philosophical texts have not enabled him to lead an ethical life, and he cannot understand, even in retrospect, why he has failed to do so.

The interior focus of confessional autobiography enables Rousseau to treat misstatements of empirical facts as unimportant mistakes, but it also compels him to judge every story he tells against an implicit standard of moral justice. The ethical aporia that results—Rousseau's inability to know whether, even in the moment of confessing, he is once again lying against "moral truth"—recurs in highly sophisticated forms in a series of post-Rousseauean, English-language texts that are virtually paradigmatic of their periods: William Wordsworth's *Prelude*, Mary Shelley's *Frankenstein*, Charlotte Brontë's *Jane Eyre*, and Vladimir Nabokov's *Lolita*. *The Prelude* and *Frankenstein* seem to epitomize the optimism of first-generation Romanticism and the disillusionment of its second generation, but both Wordsworth and Shelley operate in the near shadow of Rousseau. Wordsworth's autobiographical persona and Shelley's first-person narrators (Victor and the creature) produce Rousseauean narratives of explicit self-justification that are troubled by the realization of the harm that they have brought to others. Wordsworth embraces Rousseau's valorization of natural goodness as he imbues the character of the Poet with moral value, but Wordsworth can only claim his imaginative reunion with nature after he expunges from his autobiography his repetition of Rousseau's greatest fault: the abandonment of an illegitimate child. The ethics of *The Prelude* generally have been identified with the more sublime and declamatory sections of the work, but in other passages that have remained beneath the critical radar, Wordsworth, in supple and vernacular English, charts the cost to those closest to him—Coleridge, Dorothy, Mary Hutchinson, and Annette and Caroline Vallon—of his Poetic vocation. Shelley's depiction of a guilt-ridden parent-child relationship is very much about Rousseau's problematic ethical legacy. Both Victor Frankenstein and his creature re-enact Rousseau's obsessive puzzlement over the discrepancy between his originally benign intentions and the damage he has caused to others. Shelley's critique of Rousseau in an essay written late in her life—including the observation that "there is nothing more unnatural than his natural man" (337)—testifies to the importance of Rousseau's ideas as a source of Shelley's own "hideous progeny."

Jane Eyre and *Lolita* are among the most popular reference points for the realist Victorian novel and the high modernist novel, but they share a very different generic filiation that is revealed in their subtitles. When Brontë subtitles *Jane Eyre* "An Autobiography" and Nabokov subtitles *Lolita* "The Confession of a White Widowed Male," the generic markers "autobiography" and "confession" indicate that Brontë and Nabokov are engaged in the form of metadiscourse that Barbara Johnson describes in her account of *Frankenstein*: Autobiographical form is put in the service of a "theory of autobiography" (10). Shelley, Brontë, and Nabokov all, consciously and deliberately, use first-person fictional narrative in order to interrogate the legitimating narratives of autobiography. The metafictional level of each of these novels is produced in an ethical register that contests the self-justifying voice of the autobiographical narrator. Victor Frankenstein offers a Rousseauean gesture of self-exoneration when he tells us that "During these last days I have been occupied in examining my past conduct; nor do I find it blameable" (241), but when Victor dies with his creature—a universal victim turned into an indiscriminate terror—hovering over his lifeless body, *Frankenstein* opens into an infinitely expansive set of ethical questions that are not contained within Victor's calculus of individual responsibility. Jane Eyre's smug account of her arrival at the center of an insular conjugal utopia depends, as recent commentary on the novel instigated by Jean Rhys and Gayatri Spivak has shown, on the marginalizing of Bertha Mason. But the material conditions of Jane's utopia—the unhealthy air of Ferndean that recreates the debilitating atmosphere of Lowood, the stepchild sent off to boarding school who reenacts Jane's own expulsion from a blood-kin group at the outset of the novel, and the mutilated husband—register the human cost of this domestic ideal. In *Villette*, Brontë returns to the barely suppressed knowledge of *Jane Eyre*—that even a marriage of true minds is a game of power—and asks, once again, whether the triumph of the marriage plot inevitably strews some form of catastrophic harm. *Villette* offers no assurance that such devastation is escapable. In *Lolita*, Nabokov first compels his postwar, post-Holocaust readers to confront the possibility of the noncoincidence of aesthetic and moral values, and then he demonstrates how easily aesthetic resources can put such questions to rest. The figural doubles in these novels—the creature who pursues Victor Frankenstein like a malignant doppelganger, the madwoman in the attic, and the hallucinatory Quilty—are the personifications of the unresolved guilt of the primary narrators of these texts.

While guilt operates as an organizing principle in each of these texts, the dominant reception histories of these works regularly bypass their ethical conundrums by identifying their authors with simple and unequivocal values: Rousseau and Wordsworth with individual imagination and a cult of nature, Shelley and Brontë with domesticity, and Nabokov with aestheticism. W.J.T. Mitchell begins to break with the received critical wisdom on *The Prelude* when he suggests that not only did Wordsworth know of Rousseau's *Confessions*, but his suppression of that knowledge was also a suppression of his reenactment of Rousseau's paternal neglect. But Mitchell steers back into conventional waters when he judges of Rousseau and Wordsworth that "both of these sublime egotists" believe in "the subordination of [familial] ties to the interests of the egotists" (658). The soft illocutionary focus of Mitchell's prose, which almost suggests that there is some ethical deficit to this sublime egotism but finally refrains from personal criticism of Rousseau or Wordsworth, rests on the implicit premise that the actions of these authors can be excused because of their limited ethical competence. This is not the verdict that Rousseau passes on himself in the "Fourth Walk." In the case of Wordsworth, some of the densest and subtlest passages of *The Prelude* narrate Wordsworth's sexual history, which includes not only his abandonment of his first child but his rivalry with Coleridge over the erotic affections of Dorothy Wordsworth and Mary and Sara Hutchinson. The elliptical texture of these passages mirrors the opacity of the stories they tell, but to overlook these sections of *The Prelude* in favor of the more accessible portraits of the sublime Wordsworth or the sentimental Wordsworth underestimates the skill and the candor with which Wordsworth uses a language "really spoken by men" in order to dissect the powers that run through everyday life.

The critical blend of charity and condescension that informs Rousseau and Wordsworth studies operates in a similar fashion in the standard receptions of Shelley and Brontë. Two of the most profound revisions in the reception histories of canonical novels have taken place in recent years in the cases of *Frankenstein* and *Jane Eyre*. A newfound critical attention to the decentering force of the Other has made it possible to rehabilitate Shelley's "monster" as "the creature" and to recognize the humanity of the "mad" Bertha Mason. But even the most recent critical work on Shelley and Brontë generally presumes that these acts of ethical rebalancing run contrary to the intentions of the authors. The widespread return to the 1818 first edition of *Frankenstein* is based on the premise that once Shelley understood the radical implications of her youthful work she deliberately compromised its original force and that the editor's task is to save the innovative work of the young, semi-iconoclastic Shelley from her mature self. Gayatri Spivak's censure of the reduction of Bertha Mason to the status of an animal is accompanied by her disavowal that Spivak does not blame "Charlotte Brontë the named individual" for not understanding the "axiomatics of imperialism" (257). Rather than seeing Shelley and Brontë as oblivious or antagonistic to the ethical implications of their own works, I argue that their novels embed, in the parabolic form of literary language, challenges to the reader to confront his own implication in the structures of privilege that marginalize Shelley's creature and Brontë's madwoman. That it has taken so long for these questions to be recognized, even obscurely, indicates how deeply ingrained are the legitimating narratives that these novels deploy.

No similar transformation has occurred in the reception history of Lolita, even though the time should have come for a wider recognition that the ethical demands of the novel call for something more than a veneration of its aesthetic quality. While most of the current critical work on Lolita continues to ratify Nabokov's assertion of the value of "aesthetic bliss," there have been two notable recent departures from this critical tradition, both of which have sought to address the ethical status of the novel. The one point on which both agree, with each other and with the prior reception history, is that Lolita is not to be faulted for aestheticizing pedophilia. In the first instance, Richard Rorty offers a standard philosophical investigation of ethical themes in a literary text in which he echoes both Lionel Trilling's declaration that "Lolita is not about sex" (15) and John Ray's optimistic vision of a world in which "greater vigilance" (Lolita 6) triumphs over aberrant desire when Rorty concludes that "The moral is not to keep one's hands off little girls, but to notice what one is doing, and in particular to notice what people are saying" (164). Rorty crystallizes an interpretive tradition predicted in Nabokov's parodic Foreword to the novel, in which a story of child molestation is replaced with a narrative of governable interiority, as though the Humbert Humberts of the world could be reformed if they would just become better listeners. The displacement from a story of actions and consequences into a realm of defensible interiority is the Rousseauean shift, but it is not one that even Rousseau is ultimately able to legitimate.

In a more thorough defense of the pedophilic content of Lolita, Frederick Whiting proffers a Foucauldian analogy between pedophilia and homosexuality. Whiting cites Foucault's thesis that "the homosexual" only comes into existence as a form of identity in the nineteenth century through a transposition of "the practice of sodomy onto a kind of interior androgyny," and he concludes that this "description of the shift of emphasis from acts to identity is an accurate description of the pedophile . . . as a distinct form of sexual subjectivity" (837). Although Whiting's citation of Foucault is consistent with the dominant reception of Foucault's work, this conclusion—that an analogy can be drawn between the practice of same-sex sex and pedophilia—does not take into account the full implications of Foucault's thesis in *The History of Sexuality* that power is, at its origin, a local phenomenon that "comes from below" (HS 94). As Foucault elaborates the confessional theory of power of *The History of Sexuality* in a late interview (EST 281–301), he makes it clear that this theory of power allows for its reversibility, so that the figure who is confessing can upset the dominance of the surveillant authority. This contingent theory of power departs from the panopticon model of *Discipline and Punish*, which describes a far more unidirectional dispersal of power along predictable lines. The panopticon model, which is the basis of Whiting's analysis of *Lolita*, also informs such influential Foucauldian studies of subjectivity in the eighteenth- and nineteenth-century novel and autobiography as D. A. Miller's *The Novel and the Police*, Nancy Armstrong's *Desire and Domestic Fiction*, and Felicity Nussbaum's *The Autobiographical Subject*. Each of these works describes the power of what Miller calls the "regime of the norm" (viii) to produce uniform, properly disciplined subjects. The ethical implication of the panopticon model is that freedom, as an escape from disciplinary constraint, becomes an ethical goal in itself.[4] Thus, according to Miller, the only problem with the "subversion hypothesis," which claims that literary texts subvert the disciplinary power of normative forces, is that it does not work. In the panopticon thesis, the problem with literary texts is that they do not show us how to be free but only how to imagine ourselves to be freer than we really are.

The critical legacy of the panopticon thesis has been twofold. In practical terms, it has created a focus on the relation between individual subjects and what Foucault calls "terminal forms of power" (HS 92)—institutional forces and discursive norms—rather than on the power relations that arise "from below" (HS 94), from between individual subjects. Both pedophilia and homosexuality are delegitimated by a regime of heternormativity, but in terms of the circulation of power between two individuals in a sexual relation, there is no analogy between homosexuality and pedophilia. In a pedophilic relation, power is not reversible. At a conceptual level, the critical focus on institutional and discursive norms has thus had the effect of stabilizing a relation of power that "The Ethics of the Concern for Self" shows to be fluid and volatile.

Not only have Foucault's interpreters generally adopted the more straightforward panopticon model of power rather than the confessional theory of *The History of Sexuality*, but Foucault himself was liable to regress from this more innovative model of power in his construction of scenarios that describe a conflict between persecuted individuals and normative institutional and discursive forces. Foucault's case study in The History of Sexuality is the story of Jouy, the "simple-minded" itinerant farmhand who is apprehended for purchasing "a few caresses from a little girl" and consequently has the full force of state science brought to bear on him: "they went so far as to measure the brainpan, study the facial bone structure, and inspect for possible signs of degenerescence" (31). As Foucault shows, the explicit theory of power in The History of Sexuality, that power "is produced from one moment to the next, at every point, or rather in every relation from one point to another" (93), dictates that the primary question to be asked about the relation between sex and power is not "how and why is it that power needs to establish a knowledge of sex?" but "what were the most immediate, the most local power relations at work?" (97). Nevertheless, Foucault's account of the Jouy story is focused entirely on the relation between Jouy and the police and not on what takes place between Jouy and the little girl from whom he obtains the "few caresses." But the "most immediate, most local power relations" at work for those who wanted to exchange sex for money in nineteenth-century Lapcourt were not between the villagers and the police but among the villagers themselves. The most immediate power relations consisted of learning the local arrangements: where to go, what to say, the rate of exchange. Foucault's rhetoric in this anecdote is suffused with a pastoralism which suggests that before the intervention of the state authorities, Lapcourt was a world without power, in which everyone could enjoy "inconsequential bucolic pleasures," "timeless gestures," "barely furtive pleasures between simple-minded adults and alert children" (31–32). But this pastoral fantasy contradicts Foucault's own principle that power "is everywhere" (93). This pastoral rhetoric returns in the conclusion to the first volume of The History of Sexuality, where Foucault imagines a world that is very like his imaginary Lapcourt, in which "a different economy of bodies and pleasures" could overcome the disciplinary regime of "sex" (159). But this "different economy" could only offer a greater degree of freedom if power did not once again begin to emerge from everywhere, in every moment and every point of social interaction.

Foucault's late turn to the subject of ethics in the subsequent volumes of The History of Sexuality and in the interviews and essays that accompanied their publication marked a realization that the omnipresence of power requires an understanding of ethical obligation that does not depend on the existence of free agency. But in Foucault's study of ancient Greek and

Roman cultures, he never achieved the distanced critique of his materials that he had demonstrated throughout his studies of the emergence of modernity. Instead, he often assumed the ethical positions of classical texts without separating himself from the immediate power relations, or even the class and gender biases, that informed their production. In the most direct explication of the ethical position he adopted in his later work, Foucault cites Plutarch as a source of the wisdom that ethics consists of "mastering the appetites that threaten to overwhelm one," and he confidently asserts that "if you take proper care of yourself, that is, if you know ontologically what you are, you cannot abuse your power over others" (EST 285, 288). In formulating this classical ethic of "the care of the self," Foucault is curiously oblivious to the structural relations of power that are implicit in the subject positions he identifies throughout this interview: a free man, a magistrate, a philosopher, a counselor to the prince, a master of a household, a husband. Identifying power simply as something that is exerted "over others" rather than as a possibility that is in constant circulation, Foucault imagines ethical responsibility as something that originates within the self, so that if one becomes master of one's appetites, then the care of others follows as a natural by-product. But this conception of what Foucault calls an "ontological self" (287; as if one simply is, ontologically, a magistrate) is incompatible with the most fundamental insights of The History of Sexuality: that both power and subjectivity are, at their origins, effects generated in the friction between incipient subjects and that modern subjectivity is primarily constituted through the "especially dense transfer point" (103) of sex.

Foucault's confessional model of power, desire, and subjectivity in The History of Sexuality is directly pertinent to the relation between the writer and the reader of the confessional autobiography. In this dyadic structure, from the side of the reader comes the surveillant "power that questions, monitors, watches, spies, searches out, brings to light," while the writer enjoys the divided pleasure that is at once "animated by the attention" of this power but which also finds a "pleasure that kindles at having to evade this power, flee from it, fool it, or travesty it" (45). Foucault's account of the "spirals of power and pleasure" that envelop these subject positions takes the psychoanalytic pair of the voyeur and the exhibitionist and gives it a fluidity and a dramatic depth. The desire of the voyeur, Foucault shows, is not simply to possess the surface of the other but to consume her to the depths of her interiority, while the desire of the exhibitionist is always capable of becoming more than a submissive wish for the approval of a dominant other and of turning into a desire to overthrow that power. The game of truth that is played between these positions of surveillant power and exhibition-ist pleasure is not simply pedagogic and epistemological but, as Foucault argues, erotic; and because it is erotic, it is also inescapably ethical. If sex is not a liberation from power but is itself a site of power, and autobiography is the story of the self that emerges from these eroticized transactions of power, then the inevitable metadiscourse of autobiography is ethics. In Michel Leiris's metaphor (153), autobiography is distinguished from other genres in that it is like a bullfight. Other books are just games; the worst that can happen is that the reader judges that the writer has written a bad book, and she loses the game. But in autobiography, an author's real life can be damaged if her readers judge her to be an immoral person.

In these hypercanonic texts—the *Confessions*, *The Prelude*, *Frankenstein*, *Jane Eyre*, and *Lolita*—forceful and problematic ethical claims are made: that ends justify means, that great aesthetic achievements can subsume mundane moral side effects, that adherence to principle absolves one of responsibility for unintended consequences. The authors and narrators of these texts stake their moral standings on the legitimation of these claims, but the dangerous edge that Leiris calls "the bull's horn" (155) of autobiography is regularly blunted in critical commentary. When interpretation is displaced onto something other than these ethical claims (such as love of nature, domesticity, or aesthetic bliss), literary critics repeat what Austin describes as the common fault of philosophers: they remain at the constative surface of these texts and fail to recognize them as performative acts that solicit the reader's complicity in their legitimating narratives. Even when the ethical claims of these texts are at least partially engaged, the challenges they pose are easily defused through a rhetorical blend of charity and condescension which grants that Rousseau, Wordsworth, Shelley, Brontë, and even Nabokov are, forgivably, unable fully to grasp the ethical implications of their own work.

These authors are ill-served by this discretion, which does more to protect the readers than the authors from the ethical demands posed by these works. The study of ethics in literature is constituted by the same futurist orientation that characterizes ethical philosophy: Texts are studied as sources of examples that provide, in a prescriptive or a cautionary form, principles that will enable us to lead more ethical lives. But in the retrospective focus of autobiography, it can become clear that the specific contexts of intention and consequence, and the relation between these contexts, were unknowable in their moment, and may not be any more available in retrospect. Intentions are not always transparent, consequences are not always predictable, and responsibility—which depends on these two opaque, often uncontrollable, and sometimes incommensurate variables—is not always easy to assign. Breaking with the usual futurist orientation of moral philosophy, Geoffrey Harpham defines ethics as "the site of a desire for a clean conscience" (xiii). As a retrospective wish that the past should be comprehensible according to principles that have only become clear in the present, the desire of ethics is always unlikely to be fulfilled. The premise that power originates in microsites of interpersonal exchange suggests that the only way to see it at its origin is in the microscopic self-analysis of confessional autobiography. There is no guarantee, however, that this retrospective journey will produce a liberating truth.

1

Supplements

Rousseau, Libertinism, and Guilt

⋮

THE first empirical fact disclosed in Rousseau's autobiography, that "I was born at Geneva in 1712," does not appear until the fourth paragraph of the *Confessions*. In the three preliminary paragraphs with which the work begins, Rousseau explicates the rules of the genre that he claims to found, explaining that his autobiography will not be a record of the events of a life but the revelation of a singular self, "*moi seul*"; as a result, its standard of truth will not be mimetic fidelity but ethical candor. Rousseau's claim to have "no precedent" in such an enterprise is regularly refuted by his commentators, who point to the titular antecedent of Augustine's *Confessions*, but Rousseau's insistence on the uniqueness of his identity separates his *Confessions* from the tradition of spiritual autobiography. The spiritual autobiography offers its narrator as an exemplary model of fall and redemption, but Rousseau identifies his value with his inimitability. Not only has Rousseau "no precedent," he "will have no imitator" (5); the reader, Rousseau claims, cannot replicate his autobiographical endeavor.[1]

When Rousseau imagines himself appearing at his final judgment "with this book in my hand," he parodies the spiritual autobiography. The moral effect of the spiritual autobiography depends on a literal acceptance of the power of God, but Rousseau's judgment scene forces the reader to choose between a literal reading, which takes on a comic incongruity as the assignment of Rousseau's eternal destiny is delayed while God reads the *Confessions*, and a figurative reading that makes divine judgment into a metaphor for the judgment that will be passed on Rousseau by his reader. The three-paragraph prologue to the story of Rousseau's life ends with a challenge to the reader in which Rousseau dares anyone to offer an equally thorough self-revelation and still claim to be better than he is. For the second time in this prefatory passage, the relation between the confessional speaker and his imaginary listener is depicted as a scene of power. As Foucault argues in *The History of Sexuality*, the technology of the religious confession is easily adapted to the secular narrative of self-revelation; the reader of Rousseau's text is positioned as a "virtual . . . authority" (HS 61) who silently monitors and judges the speaker's confession. But at this moment of the origin of the modern autobiography, Rousseau destabilizes this power relation.[2] While the silent interlocutor seems to be positioned to exercise a judgmental authority, Rousseau repeatedly wrests discursive power to himself. He demands that God recognize the sufficiency of his self-exoneration, and he defies any reader to match his own standard of honesty and still emerge with a more attractive self-portrait.

Rousseau's autobiographical pact with the reader thus constructs the volatile power relation of the Foucauldian dyad: Rousseau displays the truth of his inner being to the surveillant authority of the reader, but the circulation of power between these positions is mobile and unstable. The elusive availability of power eroticizes the relation between the reader and the writer of autobiography; they become partners in a dialogue where "to wield power over the other in a sort of open-ended strategic game where the situation may be reversed is not evil; it is part of love, of passion and sexual pleasure" (EST 298). This erotic intensification of autobiography emerges from the context of the libertine "Confessions" that were being read and confiscated alongside Rousseau's *Emile* and *Social Contract* in mid-eighteenth-century France, texts like the *Confessions of a fop by the chevalier de la B**** (1749), *Confessions of a young girl (Confessions d'une jeune fille* [confiscated in 1771]), and *Confessions of a nun (Confessions d'une religieuse* [confiscated 1771] [see Darnton 38]). In his own *Confessions*, Rousseau compares himself to the author of a libertine confession, his friend Duclos, the author of *The Confessions of the Comte de **** (244). Rousseau's account of his masturbatory habits emerges from this libertine tradition, but Rousseau's *Confessions* replace the conventional pornographic representation of a series of erotic conquests with the candid psychological portrait of the interiority of a sexual history. This relation between Rousseau's *Confessions* and the libertine tradition has been largely obscured in modern critical studies, in which Rousseau's most influential biographers and critics have concentrated on the more respectable aspects of the *Confessions* in order to reconcile Rousseau's autobiographical persona with the central ideas of his political and educational works.[3]

Central to the modern reception of the *Confessions* is the belief that Rousseau's autobiography ratifies the familiar precept stated in the notes to the *Second Discourse* that "man is naturally good" (208). This "anthropological optimism," as Starobinski calls it (295), requires a distinction between one's actions and one's inner being, a distinction that has become central to Rousseau's place in western intellectual history. W.J.T. Mitchell's contention that Rousseau was able to believe that "his heart was always innocent no matter what his behavior might have been" (647) epitomizes this modern consensus. The effect that Foucault attributes to an expansion of the realm of power in the eighteenth century, its newfound ability to infiltrate bodies and to produce a "fictitious point" of interiority that carries the burden of being the "deeply buried truth" (HS 69) of our being, is considered in Rousseau studies to be just one more *faute de Rousseau*. As Christopher Kelly writes, Rousseau's "emphasis on the internal life of feelings is surely unprecedented and epoch-making. . . . Rousseau and his numberless imitators have won us over: we accept . . . that feelings are what count, much more so than thoughts, words, or deeds" ("Introduction," xvii).

The reconciliation of the "internal life of feelings" disclosed in the *Confessions* with the goodness of the "natural man" of the *Second Discourse* requires one more act of interpretation: It becomes necessary to accept Rousseau's distinction between feelings that are natural (*"veritable"*) and those that are unnatural (*"bizarre"*) (*Confessions*, 26). When the natural, or the *veritable*, is made into the cornerstone of Rousseau's philosophy, the principles of Rousseau's philosophical works are inevitably privileged over the more eccentric and erotic episodes of his autobiography. But as studies of Rousseau have marginalized the erotic elements of the *Confessions*, they have tended to obscure what is most innovative in this work. As Derrida argued in his examination of the supplementary structure of Rousseau's rhetoric, overlooking the centrality of masturbation in the *Confessions* has the pervasive rhetorical effect of foregrounding what Rousseau "declares" and obscuring what he "describes" (OG 229). Critical confidence in Rousseau's belief that he is a good person depends on giving an unequivocal value to Rousseau's declarations and on suppressing the descriptive elements of the *Confessions* that challenge Rousseau's rhetoric of excuses. But the rhetoric of description is as active a rhetorical strategy in the *Confessions* as the rhetoric of declaration. The *Confessions* ends with Rousseau in a state of paranoid insularity and unable to believe that he has in fact convinced his readers that he is a good person. His exculpatory declarations fail to accomplish a purgation of guilt because his self-justifying fictions do not absolve him of responsibility for the harm he has brought to others.

A less straightforward reading of the rhetoric of the *Confessions*, along the lines suggested by Derrida and de Man, can show that Rousseau's autobiography is structured not as an illustration of a set of optimistic ideas about human nature but by a self-regulating, supplementary structure in which an excessive candor about sexuality—i.e., a frankness that exceeds the conventions of the libertine genre from which it emerges—triggers a self-examination that is driven not by an epistemological quest for self-knowledge but by an ethical anxiety. When Rousseau acknowledges in the "Fourth Walk" of his *Reveries* that "the 'know thyself' of the temple of Delphi was not such an easy precept to observe as I had thought in my *Confessions*" (63), the examples that he brings forward in this reflection—the lie that doomed Marion and his continuing lies about his abandonment of his children—show that the primary obstacle to a truthful autobiography is not the fallibility of memory but the difficulty of confronting the moral consequences of one's actions.

In Derrida's reading of Rousseau, the insight that masturbation is not simply a marginal peccadillo in Rousseau's life but a central term in his account of representation becomes the occasion for a critique of representation; for Derrida, masturbation becomes nothing but a textual sign. But masturbation in the *Confessions* is neither just a sign nor just an act; it is the point at which sexuality is displaced from the natural economy of intercourse and procreation—what Rousseau calls *veritable* sexuality—into the imaginary, or *bizarre*, realm of sexual fantasy. Both the *veritable* and *bizarre* itineraries of desire depart from the principle of natural goodness; the *bizarre* does so through a psychological complexity at the level of motivation, while the *veritable* story of acts and consequences is ultimately more uncontrollable in terms of its ethical effects. Ultimately, even the most elaborate of Rousseau's fantasies cannot protect him from the responsibilities of material, *veritable* sexuality. The guilt that is produced there nullifies the efficacy of confession and severs Rousseau from any genuine human contact as it plunges him into a world of paranoid insularity.

In the First Part of the *Confessions*, masturbation operates as a pivotal term in Rousseau's separation of his unique "*moi seul*" from the identities constructed in the libertine confession. In the two most direct references in the *Confessions* to libertine literature, Rousseau first makes explicit the conventionally unspoken purpose of pornographic writing when he refers to "those dangerous works" that "can only be read with one hand" (34), and he later acknowledges that he himself was never able to live up to the standard of virility established in such works as Duclos's *Confessions* (244). The most intimate sexual revelations of the *Confessions* then describe Rousseau's indulgence in the supplementary vice that compensates for his failure as a ladies' man. Several of the erotic episodes in the *Confessions*, particularly the Basile and the de Graffenried/Galley stories, have the set-piece quality and implausibility of the sex scenes of pornographic literature, but the erotic scenes in the *Confessions* violate both pornographic conventions and their underlying libertine ideology. While the classic pornographic text offers only a minimal narrative scaffolding leading from one sex scene to another, Rousseau repeatedly offers the customary prologue to a sex scene but then withholds the payoff, as he substitutes for the graphic description of physical consummation a detailed account of his own feelings in the absence of that consummation. When these passages take a *bizarre* turn, they violate the pornographic contract that keeps the masturbatory purpose of the reader discreetly hidden. In Rousseau's repeated references to his own masturbation, he violates the homoerotic contract of pornography written by one heterosexual male for another and appropriates the reader's masturbatory pleasure for himself.

Rousseau's more significant challenge to the libertine tradition involves an understanding of the relation between sex and power that is far more sophisticated than the libertine equation of sex and freedom. While some passages in libertine literature might call for a qualification of Foucault's argument that the West has never had an *ars erotica* (HS 67), the libertine tradition generally viewed sexuality in terms that are perfectly in accord with Foucault's major thesis about "sex" in the modern period: Sex was depicted as a force of freedom that could be opposed to the repressive power of a quasi-theocratic state. The perception of a causal relation between libertine literature and the French Revolution has allowed this claim to enjoy a generally favorable reputation in modern academic criticism, but Rousseau depicts sexuality as itself a field of power. In Foucault's terms, power "comes from everywhere," and its nature, generated in the friction between subjects of desire, is always "local and unstable" (HS 93). And because sex is traversed by power, it always entails questions of ethics. As Rousseau reviews his sexual history with the awareness that power does not come to sex from the outside but comprises an inherent property of sex, he evaluates his sexual conduct not in terms of conformity to socially approved codes of conduct but through the debts he incurs in the reciprocal construction of sexual identities.

Rousseau's account of his autoerotic behavior begins with the frenzies of adolescence ("foolish fantasies, erotic furies, extravagant acts" [14]) and ends with his resigned acceptance of a sexual practice that he sometimes calls a "weakness" (401), sometimes a "vice" (672; Paris manuscript), but which he adopts on the pragmatic grounds that it protects Thérèse from the threat of pregnancy and himself from the exacerbation of his urinary dysfunction. This decision brings Rousseau into conformity on one point with the materialist values of eighteenth-century libertine literature. In one of the classics of the genre, *Thérèse Philosophe*, mutual masturbation is presented as morally and physiologically superior to intercourse. The Abbé T., who is involved in a masturbatory relationship with Madame C., denounces another priest who has intercourse with a nun as a "scoundrel" who is "going to rack and ruin" for running "the risk of impregnating her" (Darnton 264–65). The priest's sin, according to the Abbé, is not a violation of the sixth commandment but "an offense against the natural law which teaches us to love our neighbor as ourselves" (265). By placing the nun at risk of pregnancy, the Abbé argues, the priest violates that law.

Although *Thérèse Philosophe* declares that sexual relations should be governed by the "natural law" of mutuality, the novel participates in a tradition of gender asymmetry that pervades eighteenth-century libertinism in its willingness to describe, and prescribe, the solitary masturbation of women but not that of men. Thérèse discovers autoeroticism when she spies on the Abbé T. and Madame C. during their liaisons and mimics their actions on her own body, but as she listens to their conversations she finds that men do not always practice what they preach. Contrary to the Abbé's lectures on natural law, he attempts to seduce Madame C. by assuring her that he is unfailingly capable of coitus interruptus. When this same debate recurs in Thérèse's life, she finds herself negotiating with a count who offers to keep her in a chateau with a liberal allowance; the final point to be decided is whether their sex life will consist of mutual masturbation or coitus interruptus. Thérèse's fate is settled through a bet she makes with the count. He gives her access to his erotic library with the wager that she cannot remain abstinent for two weeks. If she can do so, she gets the entire library; if she succumbs to masturbation (and of course she does), he gets the right to coitus interruptus. The count turns out to be capable, like Abbé T., of controlling his ejaculation, so that at the time of her memoir Thérèse tells us that "we . . . have continued to renew our pleasures in the same manner for ten years, without a problem, without a worry, without children" (298).

Thérèse Philosophe thus describes the compulsive effects set into motion by erotic literature; not only cannot Thérèse resist masturbating in response to her reading, but once she starts reading she cannot even stop reading long enough to win the bet. This compulsive dynamic comes to a different end in Nicolas Restif de La Bretonne's pseudo-memoir *Monsieur Nicolas*, which claims to illustrate "the danger of such books as *Le Portier de Chartreux*, *Thérèse Philosophe*, [and] *La Religieuse en chemise*." As Nicolas begins reading the first work, he reports that "after a score of pages, I was on fire"; a servant brings his linen from the laundry, he throws himself on her, and he finds that "she did not put up very much resistance." This is the first of six such episodes in the ensuing three hours. After each encounter, several of which amount to rapes, Nicolas returns to reading until, like clockwork, another woman knocks on the door, until the last visitor is "submitted to a sixth triumph no less vigorous than the first." Nicolas presents the entire episode as a cautionary tale, concluding that "such is the effect of erotic literature" (342). In these two classic texts of the libertine age, *Thérèse Philosophe* is able to state that reading erotic texts leads Thérèse into compulsive masturbation, while *Monsieur Nicolas* claims that the effect on Nicolas is to make him capable of having sex with six women in quick succession.

The immediate progress from reading to rape could turn Restif's text into a point in a Mackinnonite brief, but the current academic consensus on eighteenth-century French pornography, which includes not only the influential work of Robert Darnton and Jean Marie Goulemot but such well-credentialed feminist critics as Lynn Hunt, Joan DeJean, and Margaret Jacob, insists that such condemnation severely misstates the impact of this literature. Darnton is confident that the modern concept of pornography, of which the "implicit purpose . . . is deemed to be the sexual arousal of the reader" is not the point of libertine texts, asserting that "Frenchmen in the eighteenth century did not think in such terms" (87). The terms in which they did think, according to Darnton, were "libertinism, a combination of freethinking and free living, which challenged religious doctrine as well as sexual mores" (90). The philosophical challenge to religion lay in the doctrine of materialism, so that the sex scenes of libertine literature showed that "Love" is only "a tingling in the epidermis, a surge of liquids, a rush of particles through the fibers, and nothing more." In such a world, Darnton argues, "all bodies are ultimately equal, whether noble or plebeian, male or female." Having control of one's body is thus the criterion of freedom, and in *Thérèse Philosophe* the heroine's sexual choices make this, for Darnton, a protofeminist text, in which Thérèse "takes charge of her life and lives it on her own terms, making her own decisions" (111–12).

The economic inequity of *Thérèse Philosophe*, in which the count controls the means of Thérèse's survival and she lives at his good will, does not trouble Darnton's reading of the text as liberatory literature. Darnton's study of clandestine literature is based on the principle that this literature contained the "intellectual origins of the French Revolution" (xix), and the focus on the Revolution as the telos of *dix-huitièmiste* study has given eighteenth-century French pornography a surprisingly good reputation among feminist critics. Joan DeJean agrees with Darnton's thesis of the indispensable role of pornography in producing the Revolution, arguing that "in France, the creation of pornography played an essential role in the formation of a new episteme" that "was necessary to make the Revolution possible" (118). Lynn Hunt gives pornography a comparative advantage over other contemporary discourses, contending that pornography "often valorized female sexual activity and determination more than did the prevailing medical texts," and she offers *Thérèse Philosophe* as an example of a text in which women "had much more control over their destinies than was apparent in other representations of women during that time" (44). Hunt subscribes to the thesis that as pornography showed that "all bodies were interchangeable" (44), it played a central role in the emergence of a materialist worldview. This thesis is also argued eloquently by Margaret Jacob, who places pornography at the center of an emerging urban sociability where "men and some women met as individuals" in a "freer, more anonymous" (159), always potentially subversive milieu where "the ethical and philosophical boldness expressed by pornography was what made the new cities and the new science so potentially dangerous" (161). Pornography gives the glamour and the edge to this new world where "materialism is the logical outcome when nature is abstractly mechanized and bodies in motion are made wholly sufficient" (161). As Foucault suggests, the ability to "link together enlightenment, liberation, and manifold pleasures" (HS 7) is a heady temptation for an academic critic.

Jean Marie Goulemot's treatment of early modern French pornography, which borrows its title from Rousseau (*Ces livres qu'on ne lit que d'une main*), is even more forcefully pro-porn than the work of the American *dix-huitièmistes*, but Goulemot departs from the American interpreters in that he makes no connection between eighteenth-century French pornography and the Revolution. Goulemot approaches Rousseau's level of candor about the purpose of pornography when he praises it for producing a heightened reality effect that creates "an immediate passage from reading to action" (52), and he locates pornography not at the dawn of a democratic, progressive history but in a "Golden Age of reading," the time "of adolescence," when "reading was something immediate and without distance, in forgetfulness of the outside world" (140). Given Goulemot's reverence for an adolescent sensibility and the solemnity with which he praises the ability of pornography to produce "a return to the real" (58), it is unclear whether Goulemot is being archly euphemistic or oddly ingenuous when he repeatedly equates "the real" with the "physical effects it [porn] provokes" (ix) in a book that rarely uses the word masturbation, and which, when it does so, usually cushions the reference for the male reader by immediately referring to women's masturbation.[4]

Goulemot's valorization of the erotic effect of pornographic literature results in some very different readings of libertine classics than those offered by their American defenders. Where Darnton judges that it is Part Three of Thérèse Philosophe that "does not harmonize well with the rest of the book, because it is merely a catalogue of . . . curious sexual practices" (97), Goulemot demurs that it is the other parts of the book that are at fault; when "the erotic novel . . . give[s] way to philosophical didacticism," Goulemot finds that this is "a flaw in quite a few pages of Thérèse Philosophe" (133). Goulemot's reading of the "astonishing extract" (36) of Restif's six sequential conquests presents that story as an exemplary case of the power of erotic literature, where the physical demand engendered by reading obliterates all other considerations: "The man under the spell of the erotic work knows neither remorse nor pity: he requires physical satisfaction" (40). Goulemot declares that he is unable to decide whether Restif intends "the degree of humour" (41) in this passage in which "the act of reading leads directly to the act of rape" (39); I am not sure whether Goulemot's reference to Restif's text as "allegorical" is meant to function as a marker of Goulemot's understanding of the reciprocal substitutability of rape and masturbation in Restif's text along the axis of the imaginary and the real (i.e., for the character of Nicolas, the literal plot event of a rape is a metaphor, or allegory, of his masturbation; for the male reader, his own actual masturbation is provoked by the imaginary participation in a rape), or if Goulemot just accedes to the pornographic contract of never actually saying that a text has been created for the purpose of male masturbation. Nicolas tells us that six women knock at his door over a period of several hours while he is reading Dom Bougre; realistically, what are the chances? Goulemot locates the potential humor in the text in the "hyperbole" through which Nicolas's reading "multiplies his sexual powers by ten and allows him to attain a level of sexual potency without parallel or precedence" (39), but the central point of nonrealism in this story is the substitution for the predictable and intended effect of the reading of pornographic literature—compulsive masturbation—the presentation of six "imaginary objects as if they were real" (ix), the successive arrival of six women at Nicolas's door.

Hiding the scene of Nicolas's repeated masturbation behind an allegory of sexual conquest preserves the pornographic contract as it keeps hidden the purpose of this passage, which is to enable the masturbation of the male reader. Rousseau's frankness about his own autoerotic habits thus challenges both of the major premises of libertine literature: its claim to speak the truth of sexuality with perfect candor and its materialist view of human psychology that enables sex and power to seem external to each other. Rousseau is no match for the hyperbolically virile Nicolas or Count ***, but neither is the reader of porn; the very possession of masturbation material betrays the gap between the masturbator and the sexual prodigy of pornography. Rousseau's initial paradox—his simultaneous uniqueness and exemplarity—is reflected in his autoeroticism and in his challenge to the reader at the outset of the Confessions: Can anyone be as frank as Rousseau and still say "I was better than that man"? Rousseau's behavior is ordinary, but his willingness to provide a written record of that behavior makes him unique. Libertine literature, though it prided itself on exploding the hypocrisy of the sexual norms of its period, is not as honest as Rousseau. Rousseau's substitution of details of his inner life for graphic physical description in incipiently erotic situations also subverts the materialist psychology of libertinism; as Rousseau describes sex, bodies are neither equal, interchangeable, nor wholly sufficient to explain the strange behaviors and affects that comprise human sexuality. The Confessions illustrates, in a personal case study in which Rousseau is both analyst and analysand, a disjunction between what Rousseau calls in the Second Discourse "physical love" and "moral love" in a way that precludes either term from serving as the "real" for which the other is a perversion or a mystification.

In the Second Discourse, Rousseau identifies "physical love" as a natural force, "the general desire which urges one sex to unite with the other." The "moral part of love," which "fixes this desire exclusively on a single object," is disparaged as "a factitious sentiment; born of social practice, and enhanced with much care and skill by women, to establish their rule and to make dominant the sex that should obey" (70). This disdain for the artificiality of romantic sentiment fits the argument of the Discourse, but the first treatment of sexuality in the *Confessions*, which describes the courtship and marriage of Rousseau's parents, embraces this sentimentality. Isaac Rousseau and Suzanne Bernard, Rousseau tells us, were inseparable from childhood and united by "fate"; they enjoyed a "harmony of souls," and Isaac died with Suzanne's "image at the bottom of his heart" (6–7). The proliferation of romantic cliches (*le sort, l'accord des ames, au fond du coeur*) suggests that the force binding this couple is something more than physical need, and Rousseau's narrative offers an empirical fact as the material proof that these two people were made for each other: the simultaneous marriage of two Rousseaus and two Bernards (Isaac and Suzanne and their siblings) brought about by "Love": "Love [*L'amour*] arranged everything, and the two marriages took place on the same day" (6).

The conjunction of sentimentality and empirical reality is unraveled by the fact that the two marriages did not in fact take place on the same day. They were five years apart, a fact that is easy enough to uncover, but as Rousseau explains in the coda to the *Confessions*, "If anyone knows some things contrary to what I have just set forth, even if they are proven a thousand times, he knows lies and impostures" (549–50). It is easy to read the factual inaccuracy as a deliberate pathetic fallacy; the idealized portrait of two people whose lives were united by the inevitability of fate is the view of the childish Jean-Jacques. But Rousseau also offers the terms for a different interpretation of the knowledge possessed by young Jean-Jacques of his parents. At the apex of sentimentality, material details intervene; after the death of Rousseau's mother at his birth, the union of inseparable souls is dissolved, and Rousseau writes of his father that "Forty years after having lost her, he died in the arms of a second wife, with the name of the first on his lips, and her image at the bottom of his heart" (7). This sentence is structured on a progression of three anatomical terms (arms, lips, heart) that moves from surface to depth, but the "arms of a second wife" are a good deal more verifiable than what was on the lips of Isaac Rousseau at his death, let alone what was *au fond du coeur*.

This passage conforms to Derrida's description of Rousseau's characteristic rhetorical strategy, whereby he declares one thing and describes another: "he *declares* what he wishes to say," and "*describes* that which he *does not wish to say*" (Derrida's emphases; OG 229). Rousseau declares the perfect concord of the souls of Isaac Rousseau and Suzanne Bernard, and he describes the material surfaces that tell another story—the repeated separations of the two, and the eventual rerouting of Isaac Rousseau's desire into "the arms of a second wife." The materialist error, according to Rousseau, is to take the second story as the entire truth and to believe that the bodies of Suzanne Bernard and Jeanne François really are interchangeable. Libertine materialism had two targets: the first was a Christian dualism that privileged the soul and called for a renunciation of the body, and the second was a romantic sentimentality that adapted this dualism to a concept of erotic love that could be raised above, and separated from, its material embodiment. As libertinism sought to free the body from these false oppositions, it conceived of any impediment to the sexual drive as an artificial force introduced from outside the realm of desire. Rousseau's treatment of this theme differs dramatically from his philosophical to his autobiographical works. In the *Second Discourse*, Rousseau views the spirit/body dualism from a materialist perspective; in the terms of the *Discourse*, the power exerted by Suzanne Bernard over Isaac Rousseau that keeps her always *au fond du coeur* is merely a "factitious force." But the opening chapter of the *Confessions* reverses the polarity of what is declared and what is described and presents a very different perspective on the material and moral nature of desire. In the brief account in the *Confessions* of the lives of Suzanne Bernard and Isaac Rousseau, Isaac takes up the role of the wanderer who is presented in the *Discourse* as the "natural man," while Suzanne acts as the curb on his nomadic tendencies, always bringing him back to his native city. In Rousseau's political works, he finds it easy to judge that the desire to travel is inimical to the stability of a state. In the "Letter to Bordes" defending the *First Discourse*, he declares that if he were the head of an insular state in Africa, he would execute any European who tried to enter it and any citizen who tried to leave (83). Such a rule would have disastrous consequences for the subject of the *Confessions*, who feels that "the wandering [*ambulant*] life is what I need" (144).

The contradictions between Rousseau's philosophical and his autobiographical works are generally resolved through a privileging of the normative values of the philosophical works; thus Kelly compares the *Confessions* and *Emile* by saying, "The Jean-Jacques of the *Confessions* could be considered the anti-Emile. He is the exemplar of precisely the civilized corruption avoided in the natural education" ("Introduction," xxii). But it is difficult to identify exactly what is "natural" in Rousseau's description in *Emile* of heterosexuality: "In the constitution of the two sexes . . . the stronger party seems to be master, but is as a matter of fact dependent on the weaker. . . . For nature has endowed woman with a power of stimulating men's passions in excess of man's power of satisfying those passions, and has thus made him dependent on her goodwill, and compelled him to endeavor to please her, in order to obtain her consent that he should be strongest" (*Emile*, 323). This passage suggests that the desire to "be strongest" is as powerful as genital need, and it shows how the satisfaction of that desire is always a fiction. A materialist view of pornography conceives of desire as a physical force and of pornography as the means of awakening and satiating that force; as Goulemot writes, the aim of pornography "is to give rise to the desire for physical pleasure in the reader, to place him or her in a position of tension and lack, the only escape from which can be provided by a recourse to the extra-literary" (115). The repetition-compulsion of reading and action then corresponds to the repeated reawakening of the material cause that resides within a subject. But the climax of Restif's scene of conquest is not the final sex act but the response of imaginary woman number five as she watches the ravishing of imaginary number six: "He has to be seen to be believed" (342). The reassuring fiction of extraordinary virility is as important to the masculine reader of porn as the description of the sexual act, and this guarantee has to be offered in the voice of a woman. Rousseau identifies the lack in desire not as material but as an interpersonal, imaginary effect; men's desires only become insatiable when women, or texts, "stimulate men's passion in excess of men's power of satisfying those passions." Desire becomes a compulsion when it becomes something more than physical need and is fixed on a particular object. To think that the courtship of Isaac Rousseau and Suzanne Bernard was entirely a matter of genitalia, arms, and lips, and not a preference of the "heart," mistakes the nature of desire.

Such contradictions between Rousseau's philosophical and his autobiographical texts are too precise and coherent to be anything but deliberate. Rousseau's political and pedagogical works operate from a prospective viewpoint that attempts to dictate future events through the application of principles; his autobiography, which adopts a retrospective position, registers an uncertain relation between events and narrative patterns. There is a conflict at the level of principle between the "natural" virtue of freedom exemplified in Isaac Rousseau's wandering and his idealized love for Suzanne Bernard, but it is not clear that this contradiction actually occurs at the level of events. We are told that Isaac Rousseau died with the image of his first wife *au fond du coeur*, but we are also given ample reason to doubt that this is true. As de Man puts it, when these two conflicts—the first between two principles, and the second between a principle symbolized by "the heart" and an empirical event symbolized by "arms"—do not meet at the same "level of explicitness," the result is that "the very possibility of assertion" is "put into question" (AR 103). The clarity of the mind/body duality that allows sex to be characterized either as sinful (in spiritual autobiography) or as both the object and the vehicle of our freedom (in libertine literature) is undone by the fundamental fissure that emerges in the retrospective structure of autobiography since it is never clear that the integration of a particular event into a causal narrative pattern is anything more than a retrospective imposition.

When the pivotal term ("lips") in the signifying chain arms/lips/heart remains indeterminable—since it is impossible to know what Isaac Rousseau said or thought on his deathbed—the resulting uncertainty throws a shadow over two of the most fundamental structures of coherence in autobiographical writing: psychological causality and ethical consequentiality. No one, certainly not Jean-Jacques, knows what sort of exchanges of power and ethical obligations passed between Isaac and Suzanne Rousseau, and the uncertainty in each of these areas deepens the problematic status of the other; the opacity of motive makes it difficult to judge how much guilt is to be assigned when one's actions harm someone else, and the inability to know the effects of each act leaves open the question of how closely motives need to be scrutinized and of whether there is any point to such scrutiny. When Rousseau turns to the record of his own, hypothetically exemplary sexuality he aspires to the clarity associated with the virtues of truth and justice, but he is only able to recount, at an anecdotal level of explicitness, the strange itineraries of the force that differentiates desire, a force that Rousseau describes not as a supervening third party but as something that emerges in the friction between subjects of desire.

Rousseau's identification of an immaterial realm of desire that rivals physical need in its force reintroduces the structure of the soul/body split that was the target of the materialist sexual polemic, but the affairs of the heart (despite the doctrine of "natural goodness") do not recover the purity of the soul that has overcome its body. Relations of interiorities, because of their ontological interdependence, are subject to vicissitudes of power and contingencies of ethics that are far more complex than the material relations between bodies. In Rousseau's sexual relations, neither the "is" of power nor the "ought" of ethics is placed outside a couple that is a pure locus of desire, standing in opposition to a socially repressive apparatus. Desire in the Confessions takes on a variability that defies the anthropological generalizations of Emile and the Discourses. As Rousseau's account of his own sex life shows, neither the roles of dominance and submission nor the desires to play those roles are filled naturally or inevitably by one sex or the other;

the roles are always subject to appropriation by either subject in the circulation of sexual power and pleasure. Social structures provide resources for the intimate struggle within the couple (e.g., Mme de Warens's money and worldly experience versus the young Jean-Jacques' naïveté, Rousseau's money and worldly experience versus Thérèse's economic dependence and youth, Rousseau's fame versus Sophie d'Houdetot's social status), but, in the story of the self that is the story of sex, power is always finally settled on a bilateral basis.

The primary markers of the ethical obligations entailed by sexuality in the *Confessions* are shame and guilt, yet neither of these affects is significantly connected to any useful moral principles. Shame acts as an impediment to the expression of the most natural (*veritable*) part of Rousseau's sexuality, and guilt serves only as a belated recognition of a lost moment of obligation. The first episode in the book that describes Rousseau's sexuality produces a parody of a connection between shame and morality when Rousseau introduces the anecdote of his spanking by Mlle Lambercier with the sententious claim that he can only overcome the "shame" that this story produces in him by thinking of "the great lesson that can be drawn" from it. He resolves to surmount his shame because of the potential benefit of bringing about a reform whereby the "methods with Young People would be changed" (13), but the story is far from fulfilling this moral claim. While the first irony here is self-indulgent—the telling of this story is itself an act of exhibitionism, with the degree of aggressiveness toward the reader that such an imposition entails—the second degree of irony involves the reader's pleasure in finding this amusing sexual confession when she had been advised to expect a moral tale. The apology called for by the act of exhibitionism is made unnecessary when the reader becomes complicit in the erotic scene. Rousseau serves the reader's pleasure, and he makes the reader serve his; pleasure and power circulate, and no one is clearly on top. The relation between Rousseau and the reader mimics that of young Jean-Jacques and Mlle Lambercier. She is in the dominant position, but the "sign" of Jean-Jacques' arousal gives him the "advantage" of embarrassing her while he hides behind childish ingenuousness; similarly, Rousseau metaphorically prostrates himself before the reader in the exposure of his childhood shame, but the evident glee with which he parades that shame and exaggerates the "precocious sexual instinct" manifested by the "sign" of his masculinity (Rousseau was eleven, not eight, as he claims, when he boarded with the Lamberciers) proclaims Rousseau's shamelessness and gives a perverse twist to his initial challenge to the reader to be as honest as he is.

The sadomasochistic structure of the scene of Jean-Jacques and Mlle Lambercier is mimicked in the exhibitionist/voyeurist relation between Rousseau and the reader: Rousseau is the exhibitionist and the reader the voyeur who monitors and judges Rousseau. But Rousseau's destabilizing of the dominant/submissive power structure of the voyeur/exhibitionist relation gives this scene its unsettling force. The positioning of the reader as a voyeur was a common theme in libertine pornography; both Darnton and Goulemot describe the narrative convention of placing an innocent narrator (usually a young woman, like Thérèse) in a position to receive her sexual education by spying on a couple. The reader is thus positioned to look "over her shoulder" (Darnton 104; Goulemot 127: "over the shoulder of the child narrator"), and the reader and the author share an understanding of the scene which exceeds that of the narrator. Pleasure is directed, as Goulemot says, through "that gaze which steals in secret from those bodies seized by desire" (35). Darnton, who is even more protective than Goulemot of the "secret" of the reader, suggests what is at stake in the reader's invisibility: "Because he alone cannot be seen, he need not avert his eyes" (104). Pornography conventionally protects the reader's secret, which is not just his voyeurism but his masturbation. The dominance of the voyeur depends on the preservation of his secret; if he were to be seen masturbating, he would become the object of shame.

While both conventional pornography and Freudian analysis stabilize the exhibitionist/voyeur relation at the surfaces of bodies, Rousseau constructs a Foucauldian spiral of power and pleasure. Rousseau plays a dual role in the Lambercier episode as both the ingenuous character and the knowing narrator, inveigling the reader into complicity with his own use of the scene. This solicitation asks for the reader's participation in the explicit standard of truth called for by the confession. As Foucault suggests, for the ritual of confession to produce the truth of sex, it must break through all of the barriers of repression: "the truth is corroborated by the obstacles and resistances it has had to surmount in order to be formulated" (HS 62). Those who are able to overcome their shame and fully exhibit themselves, as Rousseau has done, can claim to have discovered the truth of their sex, but as Rousseau produces this discovery he ridicules its moral seriousness. Rousseau pretends to feel shame and embarrassment only in order to legitimate his exhibitionism; he pretends that this is a difficult story to tell when clearly it gives him great pleasure to tell it. Rousseau solicits the complicity of the reader in a shared, repressed knowledge that remains hidden not only in respectable literature but even in a conventional pornographic narrative. His shameless exhibitionism invites the reader to overcome his own embarrassment and acknowledge his adolescent and submissive sexual tastes.

The Lambercier spanking produces a deflection of Rousseau's entire being—"my tastes, my desires, my passions, myself" (13)—from intercourse to masturbation. Shame stands at the hinge of this deflection; since Rousseau is unable to ask any of his sexual partners to indulge his fantasies, he turns from the path that he "ought to follow naturally" to a *bizarre* taste for which he finds only autoerotic satisfaction. This turn to masturbation is a Derridean turn; when Rousseau cannot ask anyone for the satisfactions of *veritable* sexuality but can only tell his readers of his *bizarre* tastes, ordinary communication is supplanted by textuality. The withdrawal from the material world of action into the virtual world of textuality structures both the opposition of need and desire and the separate ethical affects—guilt and shame—that depend on this opposition. Just as need arises as a series of discrete events, each capable of satisfaction in a single act, guilt is initially described by Rousseau as a similarly closed economy, in which a damaging act entails a single, materially commensurable debt to the person one has harmed. The imaginary world of *bizarre* sexuality is untroubled by guilt; Rousseau's ability to "enjoy many in my manner, that is to say, by imagination" is, he nonchalantly explains, "not extremely dangerous to the virtue of those who are its object" (15).

In Rousseau's account of his *bizarre* sexual tastes, shame, which in a normative text like *Emile* is described as an impediment to desire (322–23), serves to propel the stronger pole of his sexuality. His experience with Mlle Lambercier of "shame, [and] an admixture of sensuality" (13) informs the stronger of the "two sorts of love" he learns from the Mlles de Vulson and Goton, and which he divides into *bizarre* versus *veritable* sexuality.[5] Mlle de Vulson introduces Rousseau into *veritable* sexuality when she teaches him how to perform the social role of a lover, while from Mlle Goton he learns how to kindle a heightened, nearly intolerable sensuality: "I believe if I had stayed with her for too long I would not have been able to live; the palpitations would have suffocated me" (24). But it would be misleading to think, as the libertine tradition suggests, that the sexuality that Rousseau learns from Mlle Goton is more "natural" because it is more closely allied to the senses. Rousseau's masturbatory habits are exemplary in that they are common, but this does not mean that Rousseau presents masturbation as natural. The deviation "of my tastes, of my desires, of my passions, of myself" from the path "that ought to follow naturally" into the "bizarre taste" (13–14) for masturbatory fantasy is from the outset driven not by genital need but by the factitious force of object-preference. In Rousseau's first sexual experiences, Mlle Goton becomes the first iteration of his "so many Mlles Lambercier" (14). The inability to convert this desire into "that path that ought to follow naturally" results from the force of shame. Rousseau is paralyzed before the women who inflame his passion; the anxiety that results from the first artificial social affect, *amour-propre*, deflects Rousseau's sexual interests away from the *veritable* sexuality of intercourse and into the *bizarre* activity of masturbation.

Mlles de Vulson and Goton inherit from Mlle Lambercier the dominant role in the sexual relation with Rousseau, but the different lessons they teach lead to two distinct sexual histories. These "two sorts of love which are very distinct, very real, and which have almost nothing in common" (23) can easily be distinguished at the level of action: de Vulson puts Rousseau on the path that leads to conjugality, while Goton gives him a taste that will only be satisfied by masturbation. Mlle de Vulson's successors in Rousseau's *veritable* sex life are Mme de Warens and Thérèse le Vasseur, while his experiences with Mlle Goton lay the groundwork for Rousseau's imaginary "seraglio of Houris" (358) and for the emotional intensity of his unconsummated affair with Sophie d'Houdetot. Rousseau makes a clear connection between Mlle de Vulson and his first sexual partner, Mme de Warens, when he says that in Mme de Warens, "I found again all the fire that Mlle de Vulson had inspired in me" (Paris manuscript, 606). The odd episode in which Mme de Warens gives Thérèse her last remaining jewel, a ring which she places on Thérèse's finger and which Thérèse "instantly put back on hers" (328), identifies Thérèse as the successor to Mme de Warens and as the terminus of Rousseau's *veritable* sexuality. His rueful comment on Mlle Goton, that her face is one that he "still recalls, often too much for an old fool" (23) places Goton at the origin of the imaginary seraglio of "angelic loves" (360) that serves Rousseau as an alternative to his passionless marriage with Thérèse.

In the *bizarre* history that runs from Goton to Sophie d'Houdetot, Rousseau finds it relatively easy to find ethical redemption. Since Rousseau's *bizarre* sexual desires have no effect on the women who inhabit his fantasies, he only has to overcome the shame of being a masturbator in order to deliver a confession that liberates him through the completeness of its truth. *Veritable* sexuality takes a far greater toll on Rousseau's image of himself as a good person and forces him to become more evasive about the motives and the effects of sex. Intercourse produces children and guilt; its physical results and material obligations are not easily controlled by acts of representation. One of the earliest writers to suggest that Rousseau's abandonment of his children had a pervasive effect on his writing was Mary Shelley, who argued that Rousseau's emphasis on the independence of natural man was a rationalization, "a balm to the remorse that now and then stung him" for having "thrust his offspring from parental care to the niggard benevolence of a public charity" ("Rousseau," 337). Shelley's insight is a canny foreshadowing of Derrida's distinction between what Rousseau declares and what he describes; what is least susceptible to a summary declaration of rectitude, Rousseau's guilt over his children, is, Shelley suggests, subversively disseminated through the structures of belief that allowed Rousseau to imagine himself to be a good person. While shame lends itself to role reversal, a game Rousseau plays like a master, guilt has a stubborn basis in materiality that makes it far less susceptible to rhetorical manipulation.

Questions of candor exist, but only at a relatively trivial level, in Rousseau's *bizarre* narrative of shame and masturbation. Although the language Rousseau uses as early as the Mlle Lambercier episode certainly suggests masturbation ("in my erotic furies, in the extravagant acts to which they sometimes carried me, I imaginatively borrowed the help of the opposite sex" [15]), Rousseau insists that he did not figure out how to perform the act until he was nineteen years old (91). Up to that point, although he complains that "my inflamed blood continuously filled my brain with girls and women" and "in a bizarre way I made use of them," he declares that he simply did not know how to "relieve myself" without the help of "a Mlle Goton" (74). Rousseau acknowledges that he had finally figured out the technique by the time he returned to Mme de Warens from Italy at the age of nineteen, but he insists that returning to her caused an immediate suspension of the practice. Although he spent the period before the beginning of his sexual relation with de Warens "lodged in the home of a pretty woman, caressing her image at the bottom of my heart, ceaselessly seeing her during the day, at night surrounded by objects that recalled her to me, sleeping in a bed in which I know she has slept," the effects of this voluptuous setting were negated by the presence of Mme de Warens herself: "I always saw in her a tender mother, a dear sister, a delightful friend, and nothing more"; "I was chaste because I loved her" (91–92).

Derrida proposes a single, "exorbitant" rule for Rousseau's sexuality: Thérèse is a supplement to Mme de Warens, masturbation is a supplement to Thérèse, and these supplements appear because "Mama" de Warens is herself a supplement: "that which words like 'real mother' name, have always already escaped, have never existed"; all is supplementarity, "*il n'y a pas d'hors texte*" (*OG* 158–59). But Rousseau delineates two distinct economies of desire, and he places Warens outside the one that leads to masturbation. Rousseau admits no double entendre to "caressing her image at the bottom of my heart," and despite his fascination with Warens's appearance at their first meeting ("I see a face full of charms, beautiful blue eyes full of sweetness, a dazzling complexion, the outline of an enchanting breast. . . . I became hers at that moment, certain that a religion preached by such missionaries could not fail to lead to paradise" [41]) and his anticipation of their first liaison ("my heart was full, not only with her kindnesses, her lovable character, but also with her sex" [163]), he declares that she cannot serve his masturbatory fantasies: "I had a tender mother, a dear friend, but I needed a mistress. I imagined one in her place. . . . If I believed I held mamma in my arms when I was holding her there . . . I would not have enjoyed. Enjoyment! Is that a fate for man?" (183). *Je n'aurois pas joui*; Rousseau introduces, and immediately deflects into philosophical speculation, a pun on enjoying and coming, but he makes it clear that he cannot come autoerotically while thinking of Mme de Warens. The rule of the sexual economy that runs from de Vulson through Warens and Thérèse is the sublimation and circumscription of desire; Mlle de Vulson's "caresses were sweet to my heart, not to my senses" (24). The alternative, extravagant economy of sex reaches its zenith in the relation with Sophie d'Houdetot, and Rousseau advises the reader "not to imagine that my senses left me calm on this occasion, as they did with Thérèse and with Mamma" (374). Rousseau adopts another euphemism at key points to distinguish the "two sorts of love." Even "at an advanced age," he "could not make the short journey that separated me from [Sophie] *impunément*" (164). But the adolescent Rousseau was "familiar" with Mlle de Vulson "*impunément*" (24); as the forerunner to Mme de Warens, Mlle de Vulson did not, even for the young Rousseau, have the effect that Sophie d'Houdetot produced on a much older man.

In the fantastic economy of Rousseau's *bizarre* sexuality, it is impossible to distinguish fact from fiction. Although Rousseau's biographers generally report Rousseau's encounters with young women in the early books of the *Confessions* as matters of fact, several of these passages, particularly the Basile and the de Graffenried/Galley episodes, have all the plausibility of Restif's serial conquests. In the case of the Basile episode, the documentary record is mixed. There are three different versions of Rousseau's encounter with Mme Basile; some details from a conversation with Rousseau reported by Bernardin de Saint-Pierre and in a draft manuscript differ from the account published in the *Confessions* on the matters of how long Rousseau spent in the room with Mme Basile, whether they had ever spoken before that day, whether he touched her during the encounter, and whether they exchanged letters after their separation (*Confessions*, 61–63, 592). Starobinski is untroubled by these discrepancies; he acknowledges that Rousseau "was fond of 'poeticizing' his memories, starting with a few fixed details and adding embellishments," but he insists that these stories are nonetheless accurate representations of actual events: "the variations are constrained by the cantus firmus provided by memory" (153). Rousseau's biographers have proceeded with a similar confidence, treating Rousseau's accounts of his romantic adventures as essentially factual, but Rousseau's own retrospective account of these romantic affairs suggests the need for a higher level of skepticism. Rousseau tells us that at "the gateway of old age," he despairs over never having "tasted in their fullness almost any of the pleasures for which my heart was greedy"; driven to "withdraw into myself," he finds "all the objects that had given me emotion in my youth assembled around me, Mlle Galley, Mlle de Graffenried, Mlle de Breil, Mme Basile, Mme de Larnage, my pretty students, and all the way to the piquant Zuiletta" (358). These memories propel Rousseau into masturbatory fantasies which take place in "the country of chimeras . . . an ideal world which my creative imagination soon peopled with beings in accordance with my heart" (359). There is no way of knowing how much of the stories of Basile, Galley et al. included in the *Confessions* are the memories that form the basis of the fantasies with which Rousseau later "intoxicated myself" (359), or if these stories are themselves the autoerotic fantasies that construct Rousseau's imaginary interiority. The conventionality of the most elaborate of these stories suggests that the confidence of Rousseau's biographers that these encounters represent the *veritable* economy of mimesis rather than the *bizarre* economy of fantasy may be misplaced.

The Basile episode has its share of generic cliches; Rousseau takes a temporary position in a house where the mistress is "too pretty not to be a little coquettish" (61), her husband is much older than she is, he's very jealous, but he travels a lot—thus motive, opportunity, and a heightened expectation of conflict are quickly established, all within the transient setting of picaresque. In M. Basile's absence, Rousseau is immediately drawn to the wife, and he describes his feelings for her as entirely different from his devotion to Mme de Warens: "I did not feel for her that respect as true as it was tender that I had for Mme de Warens, I felt more fear and much less familiarity. I was bothered, trembling. I did not dare look at her. I did not dare breathe near her; nevertheless, I feared leaving her more than death" (62). This overwhelming physical response revives the *bizarre* feelings Rousseau had experienced with Mlle Goton: "By merely seeing Mlle Goton, I no longer saw anything; all my senses were disrupted. I was familiar with the former [de Vulson] . . . I was trembling and agitated before the latter. . . . If Mlle Goton had ordered me to throw myself into the flames, I believe I would have obeyed her instantly" (23). While Rousseau enjoys a "familiarity" with Mlle de Vulson and Mme de Warens, the stakes are clearly higher in the desires awakened by Goton and Basile; he is unable to control his physical being in their presence, and he can only describe the terror of the desire they cause by saying that it surpasses the terror of death.

The attraction that would, in a conventional libertine text, lead to a sex scene plays out very differently in the interior focus of Rousseau's *Confessions*. While his physical feelings for Mme Basile recall those he had for Mlle Goton, Rousseau is now a little older and a little less timid. He was capable only of obedience with Mlle Goton, but the power relation between the young Jean-Jacques and Mme Basile is more equivocal. Rousseau emphasizes his youth in this encounter and complains that it was really up to Mme Basile to take the initiative, but as the episode begins he occupies the conventionally male, voyeurist position: "With an avid eye I devoured everything I could see without being perceived: the flowers of her dress, the tip of her pretty foot, the interval of a firm white arm that appeared between her glove and her cuff, and the one that was sometimes made between her throat and her handkerchief" (62). The extended description of a woman's body presumes a complicity with a heterosexual male reader, and the entry into the climax of this episode takes up the salient detail of this description, "allow[ing] the whiteness of her neck to be seen" as Rousseau enters her room. Trusting to the invisibility of the voyeurist position, "certain that she could not hear me, and not thinking that she could see me," Rousseau behaves extravagantly, throwing himself on his knees and stretching out his arms to the silent, embroidering Mme Basile. But then the power of the gaze is reversed: "There was a mirror on the mantle that betrayed me" (63). While the mirror appears in every written account of the scene, in de Saint-Pierre's report of his conversation with Rousseau and in the draft manuscript Mme Basile is very much in control of the situation and of herself; she finds Rousseau already kneeling, points to "show me a better place at her feet," and then ignores him: "attentive to her embroidery, she did not speak to me or look at me" (592). The final draft in the *Confessions* gives a much fuller account of her feelings, which are less austere than her actions in the draft: "She did not appear either more tranquil or less timid than I was. Troubled at seeing me, bewildered at having attracted me . . . I judged that she shared my confusion, perhaps my desires, and that she was held back by a shame similar to mine" (63). As Rousseau imagines an interiority for Mme Basile, he constructs a symmetry of their desires; finding Rousseau on his knees, she is rendered speechless by the intoxicating effect of the power that has put him at her feet.

When Mme Basile's mirror reverses the power of the gaze, Rousseau's narrative reverses the implicit gender of the reader of the erotic scene. As the scene changes from constructing a passive tableau for male voyeurism to producing a woman who is able to look back, it invites the woman reader of the *Confessions* to identify with a woman who is in a position of power in an intimate situation with Rousseau. Regressing from the standard porno-graphic tableau, Rousseau undoes the oedipal contract that underlies ho-mosocial pornography. In Restif's account of his serial rapes, he presumes the willingness of the male reader to bond with him in the imaginary enjoy-ment of women's bodies. As Rousseau clings to his immature, submissive sexual tastes, he refuses the deflection of his desires into the oedipal path of male identification. Rousseau's preference for the immediate proximity of women rather than the deferred values of the paternal order is stated repeatedly in the *Confessions.* When Rousseau is offered a position by the Comte de Gouvon, he laments that "not seeing any women in it, this man-ner of succeeding seemed slow, painful and sad to me" (82); he prefers the job of a music teacher because the students are women (158). When his op-era *Le Devin du Village* is performed before the king, Rousseau finds a great advantage in the fact that "one does not clap in front of the King"; this con-vention allows him to hear the praise "whispered by women who seemed as beautiful as angels," an experience that moves him to tears. In Rousseau's analysis, "I am sure that the pleasure of sex entered into it much more than an author's vanity, and surely if there had been only men there, I would not have been devoured, as I was ceaselessly, with the desire to collect with my lips the delicious tears I was causing to flow" (318). Rousseau is far more interested in the responses of women than in the approval of the king.

Starobinski sees in both the Basile and *Devin du Village* stories Rousseau's fascination with the "magic of signs" (156), whereby perfect signs are able to transcend "common language" and allow "pure communication" to oc-cur (154). Mme Basile's pointing finger is one such "magic sign," and the music of *Devin du Village* is another that creates "an immediate pleasure that negates the cumbrous opacity of the flesh; soul touches soul" (176). But for all Rousseau's rhapsodizing over such perfectly romantic nonconsummations as that offered by Mme Basile ("Nothing of the feelings caused in me by the possession of women is worth the two minutes I spent at her feet not even daring to touch her dress" [64]), the Basile anecdote contains a number of expressions of regret about the failure of ordinary communication and the resulting frustration of desire. Rousseau introduces the scene with the lament that "I would have found pleasures a thousand times more delightful if I had brought it to a conclusion" (60), and he blames the lack of a "conclusion" on Mme Basile, implicitly contrasting her with Mme de Warens: "If only she had had experience, she would have set about animating a little boy differently" (64). Even in retrospect, Rousseau expresses some annoyance that Mme Basile did not live up to the responsibility her age placed on her: "Even today I find that I thought accurately, and certainly she had too much intelligence not to see that a novice like me needed, not only to be encouraged, but to be taught" (63). As Rousseau imagines a *veritable* conclusion to this stylized erotic encounter, his rhetoric alternates between romantic hyperbole and libertine pragmatism. Similarly, when the success of *Julie* resembles that of *Devin du Village* in kind and exceeds it in scope, Rousseau gloats that "women were intoxicated by both the book and its author, and there were hardly any, even in the highest ranks, whose conquest I might not have made if I had undertaken it" (456). The sign of perfect communication, this pragmatic analysis suggests, is that it leads to flesh touching flesh.

Rousseau's immediate intellectual context provides him with more sophisticated terms for the analysis of sexuality than a simple opposition of body and soul. The critique of the body/soul antithesis was advanced in two ways by different genres of libertine pornography. As Goulemot outlines the difference between the genres he calls the *roman libertin* and the pornographic novel, the first operates in terms of persuasion and seduction, while the second imagines a world of natural spontaneity in which the need for a "common language" is eclipsed by the physical desires of bodies and pleasures. In the more complex world of the *roman libertin*, the "soul" is replaced by reason, as the seducer must demonstrate that "the law of pleasure is right and that one must yield to that law" (49). Mme de Warens's instruction at the hands of M. de Tavel follows this regime of rational persuasion, but Rousseau finds the application of "her systematic spirit" a very "unskillful" teaching method when she comes to set conditions on her relation with Rousseau (163). In the truly pornographic novel, according to Goulemot, there is no resistance to be overcome because there is nothing but body;

pure pornography depicts a world of "spontaneous desires and immediate pleasures," where "all men and all women, of whatever age and condition, are ready to respond to the first overtures they receive" (50). Rousseau's frankness about sexuality always contains the reminder that such pornotopias exist only as fantasies. His own sexual history shows that sexuality is learned and that the most efficient scene of instruction involves an experienced teacher and a willing student. As Rousseau initially plays the submissive role of student to Mlles Lambercier, de Vulson, and Goton, and to Mmes de Warens and de Larnage, he acquires a taste for passive, even masochistic, pleasures. But the development of Rousseau's sexual imaginary does not end there. Despite the routine acceptance of the idea of Rousseau's "fundamental masochism" (Grimsley 112), his encounters with Mme Basile and with Sophie d'Houdetot show Rousseau creating scenarios in which rules and roles are suspended, sexuality is played as a scene of power, and the object of the game is to indulge one's own submissive fantasy while producing a similar loss of control in the other player. Rousseau's pleasure in his recollection of the encounter with Mme Basile depends on her "confusion" and "shame" that he elaborates (or imagines) in his final account of the scene since they indicate to Rousseau that she had "involuntarily surrendered to the feeling that swept her away" (64). What Rousseau cannot decide, and what he finally assigns to "two sorts of love," is whether this imaginary satisfaction is to be preferred to ordinary, conjugal sexuality.

The Mme Basile episode is no less artful than the Mlle Lambercier story in constructing a relation to the reader, and it is far more decisive about what sort of reader interests Rousseau. Rousseau's declarations of his romantic character ("Never have passions been at the same time more lively and more pure than mine; never has love been more tender, more true, more disinterested" [64]) and his lament at the persistent disappointment of those passions ("My lack of success with women has always come from loving them too much" [65]) are not directed to a male reader. Maintaining his persona as the naïve, hopeless romantic and bringing the scene with Mme Basile to a delicate consummation with the woman character in control, Rousseau offers the woman reader the opportunity to imagine herself in a position of power and intimacy with an author of an exquisite romantic sensibility. The payoff for Rousseau is one to which he alludes repeatedly in the *Confessions*; confessing his own inadequacy at the role of the seducer allows him to manipulate the libidinal investment of the woman reader, and it is that imaginary production of desire that propels Rousseau into the "country of chimeras."

The story of Rousseau's encounter with the Mlles de Graffenried and Galley is even more formulaic than the Mme Basile episode. Rousseau helps two young women ford a stream with their horses, he gets his pants wet in the process and he finds, to his surprise, that they declare it a matter of "conscience" to get those wet pants dried off. They invite Rousseau home, he wonders how he can appear at their house in this condition without previously having been properly introduced to the mother—guess what, she's away for the weekend, and they're alone. The episode is marked from the outset by signs of fictionality and opens with a notably clichéd piece of pastoralism: "The earth in its greatest finery was covered with grass and flowers; the nightingales near the end of their warbling seemed to take pleasure in increasing it; all the birds joined in concert their adieus to the spring, singing the birth of a beautiful summer day" (113). It quickly becomes clear that this is a representation of the imaginary world of the speaker, and not of an actual day, when Rousseau remarks that this "beautiful summer day" is "one of those beautiful days that one no longer sees at my age." Rousseau later tells us that such rural scenes are his preferred setting for his meetings with his "angelic loves": "my imagination, which is enlivened in the country and under the trees, languishes and dies in a room and under the beams of a ceiling" (360). The sudden appearance of two beautiful girls, in distress, "as if they were real" (Goulemot ix) gently nudges the scene from pure pastoral to potential eroticism. The reader is drawn into the eroticism of the scene through a rhetoric of innuendo; Rousseau plays dumb, but he provides hints that guide the reader to a more suggestive reading of the scene than the explicit action provides.

The episode maintains a façade of saccharine innocence over a subtext of erotic possibility. Jean-Jacques once again plays the role of ingenu; having gotten the horses across the stream, he is such a "simpleton" [benêt] that he tries to leave the young women, but they insist that "you must come with us; we are taking you prisoner" (114). The dominant/submissive roles are firmly established, and the image of Rousseau as "prisoner" contains the startling hint, that must be completed by the imaginative reader, of full-fledged bondage. The discrepancy between proclaimed innocence and implied eroticism becomes most pointed when Rousseau addresses the math of the scene: "What could they have done with me between the two of them?" (115). The question, along with the boldness of the two women, teases the male reader to imagine his superior virility to the bumbling Jean-Jacques in this potential pornotopia, but it is Rousseau who is in control. While the libertine reader has been given every reason to hope for a sex scene involving at least one of these women, Rousseau frustrates that desire as the episode ends with the same anticlimax as the Basile scene: Rousseau kisses Mlle Galley's hand. In Rousseau's reflections on the scene, he restates the principle he had announced at the end of the Basile episode that these romantic memories are more desirable than ordinary sexual fulfillment: "The remembrance of such a beautiful day touches me more, charms me more, returns more to my heart than that of any pleasures I have tasted in my life" (116). In this case, there are no contradictory statements of regret about the lack of a conventional sexual "conclusion," but only an emphatic challenge, directly addressed to the male reader whom Rousseau imagines laughing at him, that "perhaps I have had more pleasure in my loves which ended with that kissed hand, than you will have in yours, which begin with that at the very least" (116).

Having dismissed the male reader, the de Graffenried/Galley episode offers the woman reader ample opportunity to sympathize with poor Rousseau, but the duplicitous rhetoric of the scene resets the balance of power in terms that serve Rousseau's erotic interests. The realism of the end of the scene is as dubious as that of the opening: "I left them almost in the same spot where they had met me." In other words, Rousseau sets out at dawn on a solitary walk, slips into a reverie on the beauty of the day, and, twelve hours later, finds himself alone at the same spot where the reverie began. No wonder "the sweet remembrance of the day cost nothing to those wonderful girls" (116). As Rousseau describes his characteristic timidity that leads to the result that "I have possessed extremely few, but I have not failed to enjoy many in my manner, that is to say, by imagination," he reassures his reader that this sensibility "is not extremely dangerous to the virtue of those who are its object" (15). Rousseau's motive for "falling upon the pleasant moments of my youth from time to time" (113) is elaborated later in the *Confessions* where de Graffenried and Galley claim first mention in Rousseau's "seraglio of houris" (358). The narrative logic of the scene brings the erotically imaginative reader to a scene of masturbation, but it is not the reader's masturbation. An episode that begins with the unlikely scene of a young man being forced by two young women to take off his pants so that they can repay their obligation to him as if this is real ends with a discreet display of textual exhibitionism offered to the reader who shares Rousseau's talent for sexual imagination.

When Rousseau constructs the textual implication that he has displaced the reader as the one driven to masturbation by his quasi-pornographic set pieces, his account of his autoerotic sexuality operates as a benign form of libertinism. Rousseau adopts the libertine ethos that shame is so inconsequential that it can serve as a target of parody and that an eccentric sexual taste is essentially a source of amusement. But there is also a serious difference between the implausibility of Rousseau's autoerotic fantasies and Restif's equally unlikely adventures. *Monsieur Nicolas* creates a fictional scenario that makes a joke of rape, while Rousseau exposes both the fictionality of such scenes and their purpose: the Graffenreid/Galley episode clearly shows that these fictions are created precisely because such events do not occur in real life. As Rousseau declares his satisfaction with the imaginary substitutes for spectacular sexual exploits, he retreats into the harmless world advocated by the Abbé T. of *Thérèse Philosophe*, where enjoyment occurs without physical consequences.

Rousseau goes far beyond the studied sophistication of libertinism in the first instance of ethical trauma in the *Confessions*, the episode of Marion and the ribbon at the end of Book Two. This story originates in the natural spontaneity of desire, but it quickly becomes entangled in uncontrollable ethical forces. Rousseau says of Marion, "One had only to see her to love her" (70), but his attempt to act on this feeling of love produces a troubled moral economy in which the negligible force of shame generates the serious consequentiality of guilt. Shame indirectly causes Rousseau's first crime in this scene, the theft, and directly causes the second, the lie. Rousseau says that he stole the ribbon in order to give it to Marion, suggesting that his characteristic shyness led him to try to find an indirect way of attracting her. But the attempt to overcome shame in the *veritable* world of action proves impossible. Shame acquires an overwhelming force as Rousseau tells us in a string of dramatic hyperboles that it caused him to blame the theft on Marion: "I feared only the shame, but I feared it more than death, more than crime, more than everything in the world. . . . Invincible shame outweighed everything, shame alone caused my impudence, and the more criminal I became, the more intrepid I was made by the fear ["shame" in the Paris manuscript] of acknowledging it" (72). Rousseau's euphemistic concerns that "poverty and abandonment" might not be "the greatest danger" facing a female servant dismissed without a reference, and that it is hard to speculate "where the discouragement of dishonored innocence might have carried her," suggest that Marion's subsequent life may have fallen entirely within the power of shame, as both a social and a psychological force, to drive her into prostitution.

This episode ends with Rousseau's request to be "permitted never to speak of" this event again (73), but the story reappears as the instigating event of Rousseau's reflections in the "Fourth Walk" of the *Reveries* on the moral economy of intentions and consequences. If it can be stipulated that the "Fourth Walk" is no more successful than the *Confessions* in resolving Rousseau's sense of guilt, this repeated return to a scene of ethical anxiety (lived once, told twice) can be seen as a form of repetition-compulsion in its inability to work through the harrowing experience. While the classic Freudian understanding of trauma and its repetition involves an event that is experienced as a sudden threat to life (Freud's example is a railroad accident [SE 18:12]), Rousseau shows how trauma can be produced not only at the material level of a physical threat but through the guilt that emerges from the effects of one's actions on another person. The theory of power that produces shame is the repressive hypothesis, in which power is unfairly imposed on us from the outside. But guilt occurs only through our own collaboration; it arises, as Foucault puts it, "from below" (94), from the intimate contacts of bodies and subjects.

Paul de Man's reading of this passage from the *Confessions* suggests that its opacity depends on a rhetorical conflict manifested in Rousseau's two very different excuses for his behavior. On the one hand, Rousseau claims that "she was present to my thought, I excused myself on the first object that offered itself," a sort of accident that, as de Man contends, belongs to the realm of metonymy. But within a moment, Rousseau offers a second excuse: "I accused her of having done what I wanted to do and of having given me the ribbon because my intention was to give it to her" (72). This elaborate parallelism introduces the structure of substitution, or metaphor: the ribbon stands for Rousseau's desire for Marion, and he wishes that it had stood for her desire for him. This bifurcation between metaphoric and metonymic forms replicates the division between the sentimental and materialist versions of the story of Isaac Rousseau and Suzanne Bernard: On the one hand, metaphoricity produces a sentimental possibility of a perfect reciprocity and exclusivity of desire, whereas metonymy displays only a material realm of bodies and accidents. The split between the two stories is, once again, determined by what issues from someone's lips, in this case Rousseau's: the lie against Marion.

Marion's single comment on the economy of substitution between Rousseau and herself challenges the most fundamental premise of the *Confessions*, Rousseau's claim that he is a good person. Marion says to him, "Ah Rousseau! I believed you had a good character. You are making me very unhappy, but I would not like to be in your place" (71). Rousseau attempts to incorporate Marion's unwillingness to trade places with him into the most elaborate excuse for his lie: not that it was an accident, nor that it issued from weakness rather than malice, but that he has suffered terribly for having committed it. Rousseau's description of the suffering caused by his guilt is even more hyperbolic than that of the shame that occasioned the lie:

> If the remorse for having made her unhappy is unbearable, judge of my grief for having been capable of making her worse than myself.
> This cruel memory troubles me at times and upsets me so much that during my sleepless nights I see that poor girl come to reproach me for my crime as if it had been committed only yesterday. (71)

While this hyperbole functions mimetically as a representation of the traumatic effect of this incident on Rousseau, its performative impact is to integrate Marion's accusation into Rousseau's own defense. Rousseau's sleepless nights testify to the depth of his suffering, and his sententious interpretation of the cause of his grief invites the reader to judge that his misery really did exceed Marion's: "In the midst of a stormy life it deprives me of the sweetest consolation of persecuted people who are innocent; it makes me feel very much what I believe I have said in some work, that remorse sleeps when fate is kind and grows sour in adversity" (71). The innocent Marion can at least believe that she is a good person who does not deserve her misfortune, but Rousseau is deprived even of that consolation.

While de Man suspects that this scene functions as just another example of Rousseau's exhibitionism, in which the "obvious satisfaction in the tone and eloquence of . . . the easy flow of hyperboles" demonstrates "the obvious delight with which the desire to hide is being revealed" (AR 285), there is none of the lush masochism and sophisticated irony of the Lambercier episode in Rousseau's attempts to absolve himself for the material harm done to Marion. Instead, the desperate accumulation of contradictory excuses begins to sever the bond of intimacy between Rousseau and his reader. Even the sentimental rhetoric of feeling becomes self-defeating. If the depth of Rousseau's suffering is intended to demonstrate a sensibility capable of remorse, the very claim that Rousseau's torment surpasses Marion's betrays another, contrary cause: If Rousseau's suffering is greater, it is because he cannot, like Marion, take refuge in the belief that he is a good person who deserves any better. When the rhetoric of confession fails to produce absolution, Rousseau concludes that Marion's pains can only be requited by a similar amount of suffering visited upon him, in the "so many misfortunes that overwhelm the end of my life." The expiation of material harm requires not only a confession but a material penance.

The failure of the sentimental rhetoric of interiority, where "feelings are what count," to absolve Rousseau's guilt reintroduces the competing narrative of bodies and actions, which has a devastating effect on Rousseau's story of his benign intentions and terrible remorse. Rousseau's declarations that he never desired to harm Marion, coupled with his account of his panicked response to a terrifying situation, suggest that culpability can be weighed entirely as a matter of intentions and mitigating circumstances. But Rousseau's claim that he had no wish to harm Marion overlooks the obvious facts in the competing narrative centered on his actions and their consequences. Once the ribbon was found among Rousseau's property, someone was going to be punished, and Rousseau chose that to be Marion rather than himself. As de Man points out, neither the eloquence nor the persuasiveness of Rousseau's excuses is of any use to Marion. The collapse of the florid hyperbole of this passage into the terse, formal request with which the chapter ends, "May I be permitted never to speak of it again," does not suggest much confidence on Rousseau's part in his own excuses. And despite his flat declaration that he is "not very afraid of carrying off the guilt" of this affair into the next world, when this event is recalled in the "Fourth Walk," the hyperbole returns, and the requisite degree of suffering surpasses any possibility of expiation: "I can swear to Heaven that at the very moment when invincible shame dragged this lie from me, I would joyfully have given my life's blood to deflect the blow onto myself alone" (64). After long reflection, Rousseau decides that a commensurate response for the harm done to Marion would require Rousseau's own death at the moment of the lie.

The rhetorical deflation of this scene in its conclusion foreshadows Rousseau's eventual withdrawal into a haunted and solitary paranoia. The paranoia that pervades the second half of the *Confessions* is the active manifestation of an overwhelming sense of guilt, and this pathology ultimately destroys any plausible contract between Rousseau and his reader. When Rousseau asks the reader at the beginning of Book Twelve to be "generous enough" to "reread the three preceding books with care" in order to discover the "impelling hand" (493) behind the plots against him, this is not a request that an author can realistically make of his reader. No reader will believe that there is any real hope that a second reading of Books Nine through Eleven of the *Confessions* would yield the key to the mysteries that baffle Rousseau. No such answer exists, because Rousseau's sense of persecution is not the result of the trials inflicted on him by his enemies, which the request for a rereading presumes. His paranoia is the traumatic effect of his guilt for his own actions.

The *Confessions* constructs a bifurcated story, through declaration and description, of the causes of Rousseau's sufferings. On the one hand, Rousseau persistently states that his life is disfigured by "fatal accidents." In the first two books of the *Confessions*, the list includes his mother's death, his father's exile, the spanking by Mlle Lambercier, Captain Minutoli's early closing of the gates of Geneva, and the insensitivity of the Comte de la Roque. Locating himself as the victim of these malign forces, Rousseau implies that the essential goodness of his own nature would have emerged if it were not for these external obstacles. But the *Confessions* also constructs a parallel story, in a less explicit rhetoric, which contests this "anthropological optimism" and weighs the ethical responsibilities incurred by Rousseau and others in their exchanges of power through sexuality. Starobinski's optimism recovers, in a deeroticized form, the libertine confidence that the free exercise of our inner being could serve as a liberating force, if only the artificiality of social conventions could be exposed as an unnecessary constraint on our freedom. It is a mistake to attribute such optimism to Rousseau. The reappearance in the "Fourth Walk" of the lie against Marion and the continuing lies that Rousseau tells about his abandonment of his children construct the overarching structure of guilt that frames Rousseau's personal life. Encompassing the inner narrative of *bizarre* behavior in which Rousseau mocks the libertine fascination with sexuality as the core of both liberty and identity, the narrative of Rousseau's actions and the consequent guilt they provoke give his life story a tragic seriousness that refutes the libertine equation of sex and liberation by rendering such claims trivial.

Rousseau's *veritable* affairs with Mme de Warens and Sophie d'Houdetot take place on the borders of libertinism, but in each case Rousseau carefully weighs the ethical debts incurred by the participants in these affairs. De Warens is the more complete libertine; introduced to sexuality by her philosophy teacher, she has learned that the sex act has no inherent moral significance, and she regularly arranges her household so that she has two men available to her at all times. D'Houdetot follows the more conventional path of supplementing her elderly husband with a single lover. Since both of Rousseau's significant affairs involve triangular structures, the presence of these triangles in his life (Rousseau/Sophie/St. Lambert, Rousseau/Warens/Anet) and in his work (St. Preux/Julie/Wolmar, Emile/Sophie/Emile's tutor), and the congruence of these triangles with the standard oedipal formation of one woman with two men, one with some authority over the other, have led many of Rousseau's commentators to suggest that Rousseau found these triangles a gratifying structure of desire or even an idealized pattern of social organization.[6] But contrary to the psychoanalytic model, Rousseau represents triangularity as an ethical effect rather than as a generative structure of desire; triangularity represents the possibility that either member of a couple can be substituted for at any time.

In making his judgments of his affairs with Mme de Warens and Sophie d'Houdetot, Rousseau adopts the vocabulary of sentimentality in order to register what he calls in the "Fourth Walk" "moral truth, which is infinitely superior to factual truth" (71). In the terms of the "Fourth Walk," Rousseau's accounts of his affairs with de Warens and d'Houdetot are fictions but not lies. Empirical facts may be misstated, but Rousseau endeavors to capture the essential moral balance of these affairs. Placing de Warens entirely within a *veritable* history that begins with Mlle de Vulson, Rousseau takes pains to specify that the word *amour* does not apply to his relations with her (*Confessions*, 348). Rousseau searches for the terms that can capture the depth of his connection with de Warens, but he knows that it is not "love": it is "not at all that of love; but of a more essential possession which—without depending on the senses, on sex, on age, on looks—depends on everything by which one is oneself, and which one cannot lose without ceasing to be" (186). At another point, while continuing to distinguish this emotion from love, he suggests that it might be something more than love: "Whoever feels only love does not feel what is sweetest in life," he insists; there is "another feeling," which is "not friendship alone; it is more voluptuous, more tender," and can only be felt for someone of the opposite sex (87–88). The heterosexist assumption in Rousseau's attempt to anatomize this emotion can be filtered out, and what is left behind is the assertion that the feeling that unites Rousseau to de Warens gains its voluptuousness from a libidinal cathexis, but not the sort of cathexis that causes trembling knees, blurred vision, and a paralyzing shame.

For Sophie, though, Rousseau declares that "this time it was love (*amour*)" for "the first and only time in my whole life" (369). Though Rousseau had previously used the word *amour* in describing his feelings for Mme de Basile and Mme de Larnage, he is not simply inconsistent on this point. His claims that "Never has love been more tender, more true" (65) than in his encounter with Mme Basile, and that with Mme de Larnage, "at very little cost I was falling totally in love" [*à bon compte je me prenois d'amour tout de bon*] (210) mark a continuity between the affective experiences of the Basile and de Larnage affairs and Rousseau's grand passion with Sophie, but Rousseau also insists on a uniqueness to the liaison with Sophie. Even in the course of recounting his affair with Mme de Larnage, he remarks that "I have felt true love [l'amour vrai] only a single time in my life, and it was not with her" (212). The Basile and de Larnage affairs are based in amour but they do not qualify as l'amour vrai because they were too easy, too much of a bon compte. The vocabulary of love is not only psychological but ethical; the right to use the word demands a certain degree of investment of the self. If Rousseau could so easily walk away from Basile and de Larnage, then those affairs are to be distinguished from his passion for Sophie not only in degree but in kind.

Although Rousseau indulges in the rhetoric of sentimentality in his account of his affair with Sophie, he cuts this rhetoric with both a graphic physicality and a rhetoric of calculation. His admission that he was never able to make the journey to Eaubonne to meet Sophie "with impunity," but that he always arrived "weak, exhausted, dead tired, holding myself up with difficulty" until the sight of Sophie caused "the importunity of an inexhaustible and always useless vigor," barely euphemizes his compulsive masturbation and his reawakened erection in her presence. The mock solemnity of his description of the hernia that resulted from the months of "continuous irritation and privation" provoked by Sophie reestablishes Rousseau's oblique affiliation to the libertine tradition, where both masturbation and sexual frustration are occasions for laughter. Rousseau's claim that the hernia will follow him "to the tomb" (375) recalls the mock gravity of his allegation that he only told of his spanking by Mlle Lambercier in order "to improve the methods with young people"; in each case, Rousseau's scandalous stories mock those who would look on the bizarre economy of spanking and masturbation with moral seriousness.

But the veritable world presents other, more serious ethical challenges, which Rousseau describes through a paradoxical conjunction of sentimental and financial rhetorics. He returns to the economic metaphor of the de Larnage affair to suggest that Sophie made out well in her dealings with him: "It is perhaps unique," he observes, "that a woman could come to the point of bargaining [marchander] and extricate herself at such little cost [à si bon compte]" (372). This rhetoric of calculation sits oddly alongside the florid romanticism of "it was love this time, love in all its energy and in all its furies" (374), and Rousseau himself comments on the discrepancy: "as if genuine love leaves one reasonable enough to pursue deliberations" [comme si l'amour véritable laissoit assez de raison pour suivre des délibérations] (370). The various explanations that have been offered of Rousseau's motives in his affair with Sophie—that he preferred women who were unattainable, that having imagined his ideal woman while composing Julie he fell in love with the first woman who vaguely resembled this imaginary figure, that he was compelled to enter romantic triangles in order to play either the role of the son who sacrifices the woman to the father, or that of the paternal counselor to the childlike lovers—cobble together, from psychoanalysis and the rhetoric of virtue, deterministic models of the forces that drove Rousseau through this affair. But if Sophie was bargaining, so was Rousseau; at the point that a psychological model of love succeeds to an ethical model that constructs a hierarchy between "true love" and lesser varieties, subjects acquire obligations as they claim responsibility for the affective content of their lives. The juxtaposition of the florid rhetoric of "falling in love" for "the first and only time in my whole life" with the pragmatic "bargaining" for a *bon compte* suggests that "love" is the deliberate construction of a reflective subject. The hyperbole of sentiment takes on a proleptic quality; "love" acquires a transcendent value not because it emerges from some mystical depth but because subjects consciously affix their future destinies to it.

Foucault argues that in the modern era, sex has claimed the ethical ground once held by love; now it is sex that creates an equivalence to death. In Foucault's hyperbole, "sex is worth dying for" (HS 156). In this situation of the "first and only love in all my life," it is clearly sex, in the plainest sense of the word, that Rousseau is bargaining for with Sophie. When he claims that "if I attempted to make her unfaithful sometimes when I was led astray by my senses, I never genuinely desired it," he launches into a rhapsody in the rhetoric of virtue to explain his voluntary sacrifice: "The duty of privations had exalted my soul. In my eyes the gleam of all the virtues adorned the idol of my heart; to soil its divine image would have annihilated it . . . to debase my Sophie? Ah that could never be! No no I told her directly a hundred times; had I been the master of satisfying myself, had her own will put itself at my discretion, aside from several short moments of delirium, I would have refused to be happy at this price. I loved her too much to want to possess her" (373). But a letter that he wrote to Sophie during the affair suggests that Rousseau's lapses did not consist only of a few "short moments of delirium" while sexually aroused. In the letter, the rhetoric of virtue is carefully interwoven into his seductive strategy, even as Rousseau had to take into account that an accomplished seduction would belie that rhetoric: "No, Sophie, I may die of my frenzies, but I shall never defile you. If you were to betray any sign of weakness, I would succumb that very instant. . . . A hundred times have I willed the crime. If you have willed it too I shall consummate it, and become the most treacherous and the most joyful of men, but I cannot corrupt the woman I idolize. Let her stay faithful and I will die—or let me read in her eyes that she is guilty, and nothing will hold me back" (Cranston 63).

This is a remarkable offer; Rousseau refuses to have sex with Sophie on the grounds that it would be a desecration of her virtue ("I cannot corrupt the woman I idolize")—unless she is willing to have sex with him, in which case she is no better than he is, and there is no virtue to be lost. This is a daring strategy but an unavoidable one. In La Nouvelle Heloise, Rousseau showed how effectively the rhetoric of virtue could be used from the defensive position. In Julie's response to St. Preux's first overture, she confesses her love for him but warns that if he were to try to take advantage of those feelings, her desire would disappear: "Contempt and indignation would restore the reason I have lost." Julie effectively blocks St. Preux's advances with this choice: "You will be virtuous or despised" (33). Rousseau faces the challenge of appropriating this rhetoric and of leading Sophie to imagine not an invidious choice between sex and virtue but a complementarity through which the difficulty of overcoming the demands of virtue raises the value of sex to the point where it becomes ethically legitimate—to where it becomes "love." Based on Sophie's willingness to prolong the liaison with Rousseau and on the popular reaction to La Nouvelle Heloise, Rousseau seems to have correctly calculated that he could transform the rhetoric of virtue into an anguished struggle with the demands of duty rather than a strategy of "attack and defense," which Julie describes as "natural" to "the moral difference between the sexes" (104).

At the level of declaration, Rousseau attributes to Sophie perfectly virtuous motives for continuing their liaisons; he explains that she did not want to produce a rupture between Rousseau and St. Lambert, and, pitying Rousseau's folly, "she was sorry for it and tried to cure me of it" (371). Years later, Sophie took an even more high-minded stance, telling Maria Edgeworth of Rousseau that "he had a thousand bad qualities, but I turned my attention from them to his genius, and the good he had done to mankind" (Cranston 61). Cranston does not believe that Sophie's interest in Rousseau was entirely altruistic; Rousseau was a "literary celebrity," and Sophie, Cranston judges, "clearly enjoyed the admiration of a celebrated writer" (59). Rousseau suggests that, in addition to Sophie's benevolence, there was a genuine self-interest on her part; he reports an "involuntary outburst" in their climactic tête-à-tête in which she exclaims "never has a man been so lovable, and never has a lover loved as you have!" (374). While it is easy to suspect Rousseau of self-serving exaggeration on this point, he claims to have proof both of his talents as a lover and of their effect on Sophie. When she asks for her letters back, he asks for his, and she claims to have burned them. Rousseau demurs; he insists that "one does not put such letters in the fire . . . the one who can inspire such a passion will never have the heart [courage] to burn the proofs of it" (389). "As if genuine love leaves one reasonable enough to pursue deliberations," Rousseau calculates the importance to Sophie of these "proofs" of the passion she inspired, and he concludes (probably correctly) that she did not burn those letters.[7] What mattered more than anything to Sophie, he suggests, is the amount and the quality of the desire she was able to bring about in Rousseau. He could offer written proof of his "exquisite faculties" (358), and in jeopardizing both his marriage and his patronage by Mme d'Epinay for her sake, he could make a persuasive case that he was offering more than empty rhetoric. His demands for sex from Sophie were about both physical satisfaction and something more; the sex act was the only possible proof of how much she was willing to risk for him.

When Foucault argues that the belief that "sex is worth dying for" is a "Faustian pact, whose temptation has been instilled in us by the deployment of sexuality" (HS 156), the image of a "deployment" departs from Foucault's own insight that "power comes from below" (94), from local, unstable intersections of lack, need, and demand. The dyad that Rousseau describes as the generative nexus of "spirals of power and pleasure" is the couple, any two subjects who enter into a scene of desire, when there is no guarantee what role one will be called on to play. Rousseau could only describe his adolescent passions for Mlle Goton and Mme Basile by saying that they inspired terrors greater than death; with Sophie d'Houdetot, he enters into the Faustian pact with eyes wide open. The affair begins when Rousseau fears that he will die without ever having loved (358), and he identifies a deficiency in his marriage with Thérèse that plays a part in producing his "empty heart" [coeur vide]: "the mere idea that I was not everything to her made it so that she was almost nothing to me" (356–57). To find an equivalence to death, Rousseau wants to be everything to Sophie d'Houdetot and to find in her the vehicle for the expression of his unique talents, for "what good was it to have been born with exquisite faculties only to leave them unused until the end?" (358). Sophie's ability to cathect Rousseau's libidinal and rhetorical faculties creates an inextricable bond between sex and love. As Sophie replaces the other figures in Rousseau's imaginary seraglio, the factitious force of a preference stimulates Rousseau's passions to the point of a compulsive masturbation that still cannot quench desire. Having produced this exorbitant passion, Sophie was the only one who could requite its exorbitant significance.

Despite Rousseau's polemics against Parisian sensibilities, he realized that his talents could only be admired by overeducated, cosmopolitan souls. Commenting on the reception of *La Nouvelle Heloise*, Rousseau judged that "one must have a delicacy of tact, which one acquires only in the education of high society in order to feel—if I dare speak this way—the subtleties of the heart with which this work is full" (456–57). The simple Thérèse could not possibly see any difference between *La Nouvelle Heloise* and any other book, and she would probably be relatively unafflicted by the need to find in a sexual partner an equivalence to death. Rousseau's novel enjoyed its greatest success in Paris, where its way was prepared by Sophie herself (456), who was evidently more gratified to be known as the model for the sublime passions in the novel than she was concerned over the continual reminders to St. Lambert of the liaisons that had caused him such anxiety. If Rousseau was not everything to Sophie, neither was St. Lambert. In a letter written to Rousseau after the dissolution of their affair, Sophie wrote that "the most delightful of my occupations is giving myself up to the feelings of my heart, meditating on them, nourishing them, and expressing them to those that inspire them" (Cranston 100). What Sophie offered Rousseau was the possibility of a *narcissisme à deux*, a forum perfectly suited to the endless expression and cultivation of his talents, and he decided, like St. Preux and Julie, to take the wager: However long or short it would last, he would make love to this person and risk an aftermath as unpromising as death.

For all of Rousseau's attempts to impose an operatic conclusion on this affair as one more fatal accident in which "a love as unfortunate as it was senseless had been the instrument of my ruin" (407), the consequences of the end of the d'Houdetot affair were actually less than apocalyptic. Rousseau's rupture with the d'Epinay circle was pretty much *de rigueur* for him in his dealings with patrons and friends. His erotic life returned to what it was before he met Sophie; he remained with Thérèse, he had the pleasure of general acclaim among women in Parisian society, and he enjoyed the particular affection of his new patron Mme de Luxembourg, who was "crazy about Julie and its Author," "kissed me ten times a day," and "always wanted me to have my place at table beside her" (438). His romantic encounters dwindle down to a few final flirtations initiated by younger women, but he realizes that "I am neither foolish enough nor vain enough to believe I could have inspired them with an infatuation at my age" (455). He returns to the state he occupied before Sophie's arrival at the Hermitage, when he was driven into the "country of chimeras" by the knowledge that he could not "forget my age and my situation, or flatter myself at still being able to inspire love" (359). Throughout the *Confessions*, the ability to inspire love is the most fundamental measure of Rousseau's emotional well-being, and it is a power that diminishes with age. The affair with Sophie d'Houdetot was a disaster not because of its effect on the circumstances of Rousseau's life but because his greatest ambition was to join the "two sorts of love," the *bizarre* and the *veritable*, in a grand passion that unites "that [which] ought to follow naturally" with the inexplicable force of a preference, and his greatest disappointment is to have come so close.

When in the rhetoric of romance Rousseau exaggerates his power to inspire love, he comes up against the rhetoric of ethics, which looks at the effect of this power on other subjects. Rousseau's assessment of the ethical charges that could be lodged against him in his affair with Sophie produces the characteristic series of displacements of guilt and shame. Despite all of Rousseau's professions of esteem and concern for St. Lambert, he is ultimately pleased to find out that St. Lambert's antipathy for him is based not on disdain but on jealousy over whether Sophie was going to leave him; Rousseau reports that this discovery "consoled me and calmed me" (419). The guilt of making St. Lambert anxious matters less than the shame of being an inconsequential rival. But since guilt operates in the material realm of actual effects on other people, Rousseau must acquit himself here, too, and he cites the material facts of the case: "Was it I who had sought out his mistress, was not he the one who had sent her to me? . . . could I have avoided receiving her? . . . They alone had done the harm, and it was I who had suffered it" (388). To avoid guilt, Rousseau is willing to take on the shame of being hopelessly inferior to St. Lambert as a lover; he imagines that, if the roles were reversed, St. Lambert, "a more enterprising man," would have accomplished far more than Rousseau did with Sophie. Despite the emotional raptures of Rousseau's climactic encounter under the acacia with Sophie, he assures us that "she left this grove and the arms of her friend in the middle of the night as unsullied [*intacte*], as pure in body and heart as she had entered it" (374). The implications of *intacte* are clear; where guilt is concerned, it is only material facts that matter, and where a woman's virtue is concerned, there is only one material fact.

Although one could quarrel with the justice of a number of representations Rousseau makes of his affair with Sophie, Rousseau judges that, in the end, he treated others no worse than they treated him. His narrative preserves this balance; therefore, he has not actually lied against "moral truth." This distinction between fictions and lies serves Rousseau well in his assessment of his affair with Mme de Warens. Rousseau's insistence on her essential benevolence is based on the difference between "errors" and "vices"; apostrophizing Mme de Warens, he assures her that "your conduct was reprehensible, but your heart was always pure" (219). This purity of heart, manifested in her "sensitivity toward the unfortunate" (42), has the effect of spreading benevolence all around her: "One of the proofs of the excellent character of this lovable woman is that all those who loved her loved each other. Jealousy, rivalry even, gave way to the dominant feeling she inspired, and I have never seen any of the people around her wish for the harm of another" (150). Warens's generosity thus joins her with Anet and Rousseau in a perfect society of three: "All our wishes, our cares, our hearts were in common" (169). If this description could be taken at face value, it would seem to present a triangular structure of desire without rivalry.

The relentlessly cheerful description of Rousseau's relationship with Mme de Warens in the First Part of the *Confessions* does not always accord with Rousseau's later accounts of de Warens's life. Initially, he describes the "loving and gentle character" he found in their first encounter and he promises that her inner goodness always transcended her circumstances: "Even at the drawing near of old age, in the bosom of indigence, ills, and diverse calamities, the serenity of her beautiful soul preserved all the gaiety of her finest days until the end of her life" (42–43). But when he meets her after a twenty-year separation, he exclaims, "My God! what degradation! what was left of her first virtue? Was this the same Mme de Warens, formerly so brilliant?" (328). And Rousseau's defense of her moral lapses as mere "errors" does not stand up well against the moral principles that he declares in *La Nouvelle Heloise* and in his affair with Sophie d'Houdetot. While Mme de Warens adopts Tavel's sophisms that make "nothing" of "unknown infidelities," since they "acquire existence only from the scandal" (166), Rousseau refers to Julie's virtue in the *Confessions* in terms that offer an implicit reproach to Mme de Warens's behavior: "What is more revolting than the pride of an unfaithful woman who openly tramples all her duties underfoot and demands that her husband be penetrated with gratitude for the favor she grants him of trying very hard not to be caught in the act?" (366). Rousseau's indignant response to Mme d'Epinay's suspicions about Sophie and himself, that it is an insult to suggest that "the woman I esteem most would, with my knowledge, divide her heart and her person between two lovers, and I would have the infamy of being one of these two craven men" (379) casts an odd shadow over de Warens's *ménage* with Anet and Rousseau.

Rousseau's final judgments of both Sophie and Mme de Warens are mixed, but he judges them neither by the world's standards nor by a single principle of his own. Instead, he assesses each woman by her own principles, and in each case he reaches an equivocal conclusion that registers different degrees of culpability that ensue from different levels of conscious and unconscious motive. For Sophie, who believes in the holiness of the heart, Rousseau notes her declaration that "my heart cannot love twice" (374) and her adherence to that principle in her actions. At the same time, he suggests a less than fully conscious arena in which her pleasure in having stimulated the passions of a famous author and of finding herself admired as the model for a literary character who was seen as a paragon of both passion and virtue mattered more to her than the effects of that celebrity on her lover. Mme de Warens, Rousseau realizes, is a materialist, and in those terms her only fault is to be too generous with her purse and her person. For her sexual partners, "she hardly favored anyone but unfortunates; brilliant people wasted their time with her" (166), and when Wintzenreid arrives at Les Charmettes, she believes that she has deprived Rousseau of nothing once he understands that "my rights remained the same" (220).

Rousseau's insistence that Mme de Warens was never motivated by the "pleasure of the senses" (166) but that "she knew only one true pleasure in the world, and that was to give it to those she loved" (167), is a "moral truth" about her inner nature and not necessarily a material fact. While de Warens's sexual experience has led her to believe that "nothing attaches a man to a woman so much as possession" (166), she does not perceive her lavishing of sexual favors as an exercise of power. Her preference for a household in which she has two available sexual partners seems to her a free exchange of bodies and pleasures. She is unabashed in telling Rousseau and Anet that "we were both necessary for the happiness of her life," and Rousseau chastises the reader who will "smile maliciously" at this confession (169). But for all of Rousseau's professions of Warens's altruism and of a complete lack of jealousy between Anet and himself, he provides clues to much that is contradictory in this story. Rousseau's repeated references to Anet as a "gardener," a "peasant," a "lackey," and a "servant" (107, 148, 149, 171) display the same disdain he shows toward Wintzenreid when he calls him "a wig-maker's boy" (219). It is hard to distinguish the casual sexuality of Mme de Warens, who flirts with priests and sometimes lets one "lace her up" (98), who could "have slept with twenty men everyday with an easy conscience" (193), and whose woman friends consider the defloration of young boys a "point of honor" (161), from that of any other libertine. When she defies the world's censure and declares that "they will say what they want" (87) as she takes in the sixteen-year-old Rousseau, it is not clear how the world is wrong in its suspicion of why "a woman of her age" is "keeping a young man near her" (45). Rousseau's first assessment of Mme de Warens's Roman Catholicism, that "a religion preached by such missionaries could not fail to lead to paradise" (41) adopts the blasphemous rhetoric of libertinism, in which "paradise" is a euphemism for orgasm.[8] Even in Rousseau's praise of de Warens's "excellent character," he allows the casual slur that, despite her generosity, "she is in other respects the worst of Whores [Catins]" (150).

Rousseau describes his own callous reaction to Anet's death without much introspection about what his designs on Anet's coat might mean about his feelings toward Anet, and he provides a record of events in both the Anet and Wintzenreid triangles in which the displaced first lover becomes dangerously ill at about the same time as the arrival of the second, but no causal connection is drawn between the arrivals and the subsequent accidents. The first set of events provides the closest links; Anet takes poison soon after Rousseau's arrival at Chambéry, and Rousseau attributes this to Mme de Warens having "said something to him that he could not stomach" (149). Rousseau's sexual relation with Mme de Warens begins about a year later, and a year after that Anet falls ill and dies, supposedly from an accidental poisoning from mushrooms. Although Rousseau claims that "nothing that happened" during the "cherished epoch" of Les Charmettes "has escaped my memory" (189), the account of Les Charmettes in the *Confessions* defers Rousseau's recognition of the significance of Wintzenreid's appearance until long after that recognition must have occurred. This fiction makes it impossible to say which came first, the arrival of Wintzenreid or the series of illnesses, the first of which followed an "accidental" explosion of chemicals that caused Rousseau to swallow arsenic (183), and the second which led him to "look at myself as a dead man" (191).

The cynical assessment of Mme de Warens as a sexual predator who made young men suicidally jealous would be the simplest explanation of her behavior, but Rousseau insists that this is not the entire "moral truth." Rousseau gains some understanding during his time with de Warens of the link between sex and power. He says he knew nothing at their first meeting of the advantage his appearance gave him (40), but by the time de Warens makes her sexual offer to him he realizes that he cannot turn it down (163). Rousseau sees that de Warens's vanity is on the line, and when he refuses to take up his old "rights" he knows why she becomes cold to him: "Take even the most sensible woman in the world," he says, and "the most irremisible crime that the man she desires can commit, is to be able to possess her and not to do it" (223). Nevertheless, he knows that Mme de Warens believes her offer to him is not a demand; she is guilty of an error but not a vice, and Rousseau is as forgiving of her errors as he is of his own. Perhaps the most serious effect de Warens has on Rousseau is the result of her greatest generosity. He believed that he was everything to her in the three years between Anet's death and Wintzenreid's appearance, and his inability to "be a supernumerary before her for whom I had been everything" (226) foreshadows his disappointment with Thérèse, with whom "the mere idea that I was not everything to her made her almost nothing to me" (357). But de Warens can be blamed only for enhancing, and not for creating, Rousseau's romantic temperament, his "bizarre and romantic notions about human life, from which experience and reflection have never been able to cure me completely" (8). The relation between Rousseau and de Warens is both sexual and pedagogic; the scene of sexual instruction carries within it the edge of power that informs every student/teacher relation, and it is in de Warens' lack of understanding of her responsibility in handling that power that Rousseau finds some degree of fault. Rousseau's eulogy to de Warens, "the best of women and mothers," a "sweet and beneficent soul" who deserves to "pass into the abode of the good" (519), contains a hint that perhaps she should have been a little more aware of the effects of the attachments she created. Among the great souls Rousseau imagines her joining is "Catinat," a respectable figure, but one whose name contains the term Rousseau had used earlier to censure Mme de Warens' sexuality: "*Catin*"—whore. The culpability for actions that occurred without conscious intention is punished by a seeming linguistic accident—a surreptitious pun.

The distinction between fictions and lies allows Rousseau to minimize whatever is ethically dubious in his affairs with Sophie d'Houdetot and Mme de Warens, because moral truth, as Rousseau describes it in the "Fourth Walk," is a matter of representations and not of facts, and it is only in the malleable, factitious world of representation that any damage is done in these affairs. St. Lambert's feelings are hurt by Sophie, Rousseau is wounded by de Warens, she is disappointed by him, but, as de Warens teaches him, "one does not die from such things" (220). But in Rousseau's attempts to address the most ineradicable material effects of his sexuality, the distinction between fictions and lies proves useless. The "Fourth Walk" begins with Rousseau receiving a book from the Abbé Rozier whose title page contains a version of Rousseau's motto, "*vitam impendere vero*" [to live for truth]. Rousseau understands "this apparent compliment" as a "cruel piece of irony," and he wonders, "on what grounds? Why the sarcasm? How could I have deserved it?" (63). The essay takes up Rousseau's relationship to truth and lies, and it describes the lie about Marion and the ribbon as one in which, although Rousseau intended no malice, he lied because of his inability to overcome shame. As a further example of the debilitating effect of shame on his best intentions, he gives another, more recent example: Asked by a young woman at a dinner party if he has any children, he replies that "I had not had that happiness" (75). Since everyone at the party knows the truth, Rousseau describes his response as a useless fiction rather than an actual lie. Far from exonerating himself, he suffers the double shame of being caught in a lie and of being publicly reminded of a shameful truth.

Rousseau declares that this encounter shows how the power of shame compels him to lie because it deprives him of the ability to think clearly. He later realizes what he should have said: "'That is an indiscreet question from a young woman to a man who has remained a bachelor until his old age.'" Rousseau judges that that answer would have been literally true, not even a fiction, and that it would also meet the criteria for "moral truth" because it would not deny the young woman anything that she was owed. Rousseau would "have the laugh on my side," and she would have deserved the humiliation due to her own impertinence. But Rousseau's assessment of the dinner party scene seems oddly to miss the point in a story about his abandoned children. Rousseau's ostensible purpose in telling the story of the dinner party is to reinforce his previous declarations about the moral sufficiency of his previous textual confessions; a story that happens to be about his parental status is supposed to illustrate the larger point of Rousseau's difficulty in properly defending himself. But Rousseau's lack of candor about his children was the source of the most serious doubts about his self-representation as an exemplar of natural goodness.

Rousseau addressed the question of his children obliquely in *Emile* and then returned to it in the *Confessions*, where he marveled at those who continued to reproach him after the "almost public admission of my fault at the beginning of *Emile*" (497). But the recurrence of this topic in the essay that begins with Rousseau's admission that "the 'know thyself' of the temple of Delphi was not such an easy precept to observe as I had thought in my *Confessions*" (63) registers the insufficiency of all of the excuses Rousseau had ever given about the fate of his children. The "Fourth Walk" is a more tightly unified essay than it appears. In its conclusion, it answers an inexplicable question—Why does Rousseau deserve to be mocked?—with a seemingly accidental allusion to an inexplicable fact: Rousseau, the supposed paragon of virtue, abandoned his children. The reminder of this fact in an episode in which, once again, Rousseau is unable to find an explanation that would both reflect the moral truth of the act and prove that he is a good person, exemplifies the stubbornness of the moral economy of guilt. It only becomes necessary for Rousseau to concoct a fiction—that he had no children—because he is covering up a lie. Rousseau's reiteration of the story of the dinner party in a written form, far from expiating the shame of the conversation, further disseminates it to a wider audience. The resigned tone of the essay's conclusion, in which Rousseau decides that he should never have adopted such a presumptuous motto as "to live for truth," suggests that even this act of self-punishment is incapable of eradicating Rousseau's guilt. In the "Fourth Walk," the Abbé Rozier personifies the "impelling hand" of the conspiracies against Rousseau in the *Confessions*, but Rousseau now admits that he deserves no better than mockery at the hands of his enemies. He is "deprived of the sweetest consolation of persecuted people who are innocent," the comforting belief that he does not deserve such sarcasm. Rozier's actual intention remains as unclear as the identity of the "impelling hand" in the *Confessions*, but whether Rozier intended to compliment or to insult Rousseau does not matter. Rousseau's drama of guilt and paranoia is entirely a matter of self-judgment.

In Rousseau's assessment of the people he knew best, Mme de Warens and Sophie d'Houdetot, he absolved them of most of their faults because he believed he could see the fictitious self-representations they had created, and he understood how they could be beguiled by those fictions. But when it came to his own behavior involving his children, Rousseau never found a story, even a fiction, that fit. Like anything else involving sex, Rousseau's abandonment of his children is subject to both a psychological and an ethical vocabulary. But nothing that Rousseau could tell himself on this point—that he himself was an orphan, that he was poor, that he was an imaginary member of Plato's Republic—enabled him to understand and justify his own behavior. The *Confessions* thus ends with a resounding anticlimax. Rousseau's vehement assertion that "If anyone knows things contrary to what I have just set forth, even if they are proven a thousand times, he knows lies and impostures," depends upon the bifurcation of empirical facts and moral truths. The *Confessions* allows itself a great deal of latitude with facts while it claims a scrupulous fidelity to moral truth, but it finally founders on Rousseau's inability to reconcile his actions with what he believes to be the truth of himself—"my natural disposition, my character, my morals, my inclinations, my pleasures, my habits" (550)—and he angrily disputes the virtual authority of the reader to resolve this paradox.

Rousseau's critique of the "repressive hypothesis"—the belief that power is external to sex—is ultimately denser than Foucault's. In the disjunction between Rousseau's rhetoric of interiority and his descriptions of the acts and consequences of his most intimate relationships, Rousseau shows that the rhetoric of interiority, which produces the domain of love, shame, intentions, remorse, and excuses—all that Foucault would bring within the regulation of "the care of the self"—consists of fictions that satisfy the requirements of "books, where the most austere morals cost the author nothing," and allow for the continuity of the optimistic fiction that we are all, *au fond du coeur*, good people. But these stories have no explanatory or evaluative value "in life, where the morals of books are seen as idle and impracticable chatter" ("Fourth Walk" 65), and where power flows through every personal transaction. There is some irony in the fact that the figure who has entered the canon of modern philosophy as the exponent of "natural goodness" used his own autobiography to contest the most optimistic theory of sexuality of his own day, one that imagined that the pleasure of sex could occupy the center of an ideology that would purge the world through its truth, by displaying his own sexuality as a document in which it could be read that there is nothing, and certainly not the truth of sex, that is outside the most intimate exchanges of power.

2

What Is a Poet?

A Man Who Is More

⋮

WHEN Wordsworth begins to answer his own question "What is a Poet?" with the assertion that "He is a man speaking to men," his colloquial vocabulary establishes the Poet's connection to the "essential passions of the heart" that flourish in "humble and rustic life" and that can be expressed in "the very language of men" (LB 156, 161). At the same time, the masculine pronouns that appear three times in these seven words reflect a central theme of Wordsworth's meditations on himself in the years between the *Lyrical Ballads* and the completion of the 1805 *Prelude*. For Wordsworth, a Poet is a Man, and *The Prelude* works out just how central the achievement of masculinity is to Wordsworth's success, and to Coleridge's failure, to become a Poet.

As Wordsworth elaborates his definition of a Poet as both natural and masculine, he produces another, even more crucial distinction that certifies Poetic identity: The Poet has more interiority than other men. The 1800 "Preface" to *Lyrical Ballads* asserts an affinity between the Poet and the denizens of "humble and rustic life," but the 1802 revisions emphasize the Poet's exorbitant difference. He is now "more" than ordinary men, more "soul," more "sensibility." The Poet is "a man . . . endued with *more* lively sensibility, *more* enthusiasm and tenderness, who has a *greater* knowledge of human nature, and a *more* comprehensive soul, than are supposed to be common among mankind; a man . . . who rejoices *more* than other men in the spirit of life that is in him. . . . affected *more* than other men by absent things as if they were present . . . he has acquired a *greater* readiness and power in expressing what he thinks and feels" (LB 165; my emphases). In the modern era, the true name of this "fictitious point" of interiority, Foucault argues in *The History of Sexuality*, is "sex" (HS 156). At a glance, it might seem that Wordsworth offers a test case of resistance to Foucault's thesis. *The Prelude*, taken at face value as the story of the first thirty years of Wordsworth's life, looks like the story of a young man who is nearly oblivious to the existence of sex.

From another angle, *The Prelude* offers a case study of the range of Foucault's thesis that "sex" names an interior agency that has little to do with bodies and pleasures, but which is itself constructed in an act of agonistic revelation. The working title of *The Prelude* as the "poem to Coleridge" (D. Wordsworth, *Journals* 53) is generally taken simply to reflect the circumstances of the Wordsworth-Coleridge friendship at the time of the poem's composition, but *The History of Sexuality* suggests that the apostrophic form of *The Prelude* is in fact the generic form in which the self is produced. In Foucault's words, "The truth does not reside solely in the subject who, by confessing, would reveal it wholly formed. . . . blind to itself, in the one who spoke, it could only reach completion in the one who assimilated and recorded it" (HS 66). As Wordsworth's poetic identity evolves from "a man speaking to men" to a Poet speaking to Coleridge, "Coleridge" becomes the imaginary standard against which Wordsworth measures his Poetic supersession of other men.

While studies of Wordsworth's relationship to Coleridge have focused on the philosophical differences between the two poets, the oblique account in *The Prelude* of the personal and ethical relation between the two friends is both compelling in its own terms and central to Wordsworth's troubled understanding of his identity as a Poet. Wordsworth discovers the "Genius" that resides at "the Point . . . within our souls, / Where all stand single" (3.171, 186–87) at the end of an arc that stretches from his collaboration with Coleridge on the initial production of *Lyrical Ballads* to his adoption of the myth of autogenesis in *The Prelude*, where this "Genius," Wordsworth emphasizes, comes "Not of outward things" but "of my own heart" (3.174, 176).[1] This assertion corresponds to the argument in the 1802 "Preface" that the Poet's greater "power in expressing what he thinks and feels" manifests itself especially in "those thoughts and feelings which, by his own choice, or from the structure of his own mind, arise in him without immediate external excitement" (LB 165). This Romantic conception of innate genius plays a central role in the analytical vocabularies of Wordsworth and Coleridge, where genius stands to talent as imagination does to fancy.[2] Talent, like fancy, is an indiscriminate quality; one person may have more of it than another, but it has no personally distinctive character. Genius, like imagination, is of a different, higher order, and its presence marks the unique identity of its possessor; thus Coleridge speaks of Wordsworth's "uniqueness of Poetic genius" (CL 2.1065). But when Wordsworth's conception of his own genius is framed in strictly epistemological terms in which "the mind / Is lord and master and that outward sense / Is but the obedient servant of / Her will" (11.271–73), an elision occurs of a crucial dimension of the Wordsworth/Coleridge conception of genius: the belief that the exercise of genius is of intrinsic moral benefit to humanity. Wordsworth's expressions of this belief span the period from the "Preface to Lyrical Ballads" to the conclusion of The Prelude. In the 1800 "Preface," Wordsworth claims that the "permanent" value of his poetry lies "in the multiplicity, and in the quality of its moral relations" (LB 154); The Prelude closes with the claim that "what we have loved / Others will love; and we may teach them how" (13.444–45).

The glowing, self-congratulatory identification of Coleridge and himself as the "we" who can serve as moral guides for future generations seems like a welcome release from Wordsworth's anxiety during the composition of The Prelude, when he wondered whether such a long, self-referential work could be justified by anything less than the completion of The Recluse (Letters1 470). This concern is assuaged, at least rhetorically, when Wordsworth asserts that Coleridge will understand that "the history of a Poet's mind" is a "work [that] shall justify itself" (Prelude 13.408, 410). But the evasions, suppressions, and overly emphatic assertions that pervade The Prelude—the enigmatic texture that leads W.J.T. Mitchell to conclude that "Wordsworth confesses nothing and yet seems to feel excessive, unmotivated guilt for some unnamed crime" (647)—indicate a lack of certainty on Wordsworth's part that is more fundamentally ethical in nature than it is epistemological or aesthetic. The greatest anxiety that pervades The Prelude is not whether Wordsworth lacks Milton's talent as a Poet. The ability to produce over seven thousand lines of The Prelude in seventeen months was a pretty good sign of Wordsworth's technical proficiency, but this did not address the question of whether his moral nature was such that he would ever be capable of producing a work that would "benefit my countrymen" (Preface to The Excursion; PW 589).

The ostensible story of The Prelude involves Wordsworth's achievement of a spiritual rejuvenation through his imaginative relation to nature ("How Impaired and Restored"), a story that is easily formalized as a secular version of the spiritual autobiography of fall and redemption. Alan Liu has thoroughly elucidated the argument that Wordsworth's relation to nature is mostly a cover story for a more difficult engagement with history, but the most troubled and poetically complex parts of *The Prelude* involve neither Wordsworth's relation to nature nor to politics; they describe his intimate ties to Coleridge, Dorothy, Mary Hutchinson, and Annette and Caroline Vallon. While the story of Wordsworth's imaginative relation to nature can be told in an uplifting narrative of impairment and restoration, the project of nostalgic recovery in which "invigorating thoughts" can gladly be fetched "from former years" is shadowed by a darker story in which guilt serves as an impetus to poetry, where recollection might "haply meet reproaches, too, whose power / May spur me on" (1.650–53).

Wordsworth's treatment of his culpability for his sexual past operates not through a straightforward referentiality but through a parabolic rhetoric that resembles Freudian "primary process." As Freud describes "primary process," "unbound charges . . . may easily be completely transferred, displaced or condensed" (SE 18.34); in the terms of the "Preface to Lyrical Ballads," "outward things" lose their identities and are reimagined as the "thoughts and feelings" of the Poet's "own mind" (LB 165). The stakes of such transformations are raised considerably when this imaginative power is applied to people rather than to thorn trees or mountains. Wordsworth's ability to unbind identities and trace the emerging pattern of his own life while seeming to write of others makes a coherent, though vexed, unit of three sequential passages in Book Seven that focus on illicit sexuality as they move from the story of Mary Robinson, the "Maid of Buttermere," to the tableau of the London prostitute and her child at Sadler's Wells, and then to the description of a prostitute who swears in public on the road to Cambridge and thus seems to Wordsworth to "split[] the race of Man / In twain" (*Prelude*, 7.426–27).³ In this sequence, the teleological progress of the poem is repeatedly interrupted by reproachful figures and diegetic asides. As Wordsworth attempts to turn from his account of Mary Robinson back into the "argument" of the poem, he finds that "in the way which I must tread / . . . thy image rose again, / Mary of Buttermere!" (7.348–51). The twinned image of Mary Robinson and her dead child provokes the recollection of yet another mother and child, the Sadler's Wells prostitute and her "rosy babe," which produces a second instance of Wordsworth being thwarted in his desire to move the poem along: "I am cross'd / Here by remembrance of two figures" (7.366–67). At the end of the story of the Cambridge road prostitute, the forward motion of the narrative can only be recovered through the self-conscious declaration that "I quit this painful theme; enough is said" (7.436).

These three passages present three women who are, in conventional terms, fallen, and two children, one peacefully dead, one unfortunately alive. The episodes move backward in time; the first episode tells the story of the seduction of Mary Robinson, which occurred in 1802 and was theatricalized at Sadler's Wells in 1803; the second depicts a prostitute's child in the tavern at Sadler's Wells, whom Wordsworth saw in 1791; and the third section describes Wordsworth's encounter with a prostitute on the road from Hawkshead to Cambridge in 1787. The first story insists that a woman who has borne a child out of wedlock and has lost it is not really fallen; the second woman is fallen, but is relatively unimportant in herself, and is remembered only as the vehicle of her child's double misfortune as an urban bastard; the third woman is decidedly fallen, and her moral status is of apocalyptic importance. As a unit, these three stories construct a thematic opposition between rural purity and urban decadence, and they secure that opposition through the figure of a lost child. The entire sequence functions as an allegory of Wordsworth's myth of his own sexual fall and redemption.

The story of the "Maid of Buttermere" in The Prelude initially seems to suggest that Wordsworth saw the play Edward and Susan, or the Beauty of Buttermere performed at Sadler's Wells during his residence in London in 1791. In fact, the play was not produced until 1802. By then, Wordsworth had met Mary Robinson in 1799, and he later found out about the play from a letter written to Dorothy by Mary Lamb in the spring of 1803 (de Selincourt 608G). The fictional narrative of The Prelude thus displaces what Wordsworth actually saw at Sadler's Wells in 1791—the tableau of the prostitute's beautiful child—to the second part of the sequence, after a report of a fictionalized account of the seduction of the "artless Daughter of the hills" by "'a bold bad man'" (Prelude, 7.323, 325). Wordsworth strengthens the comparative relation between the two parts of the narrative by giving Mary Robinson a child (which is neither biographically true nor a feature of the play),[4] and he then heightens the pathos of Mary's plight by killing off her child, thus producing the imaginary fear that the prostitute's child "may now have liv'd till he could look / With envy on thy nameless Babe, that sleeps / Beside the mountain Chapel, undisturb'd" (7.410–12). The stories that take place on- and offstage at Sadler's Wells are superficially connected through a thematic contrast between Mary's rural innocence and the urban corruption of the prostitute whose "tints were false" (7.373). Wordsworth is at some pains to maintain this opposition and to protect Mary Robinson from the identity of a fallen woman; he emphasizes to Coleridge, his interlocutory foil, that she is "Unsoil'd" and "Without contamination" (7.339, 353). But the strain on the moral contrast does not come only from the potential social stigma incurred by Mary Robinson. The role of the "bold bad man" had been played by Wordsworth himself in his affair with Annette Vallon, and the description of the bigamous marriage in which Mary Robinson's seducer "wedded her, in cruel mockery / Of love and marriage bonds" (7.327) resonates oddly when it comes from someone who left behind a woman who calls herself "la veuve Williams," and whose natural daughter is christened "Wordswodst" and signs her wedding certificate twenty years later as "Caroline Wordsworth."

While Mary Robinson plays the role of Annette Vallon in one analogue to Wordsworth's life, the pastoral imagery dedicated to her also links her to both Mary Hutchinson and Dorothy Wordsworth. Wordsworth describes this sympathetic "memorial verse" as Mary Robinson's "due" because they were geographically proximate in childhood:

> For we were nursed, as almost might be said,
> On the same mountains; Children at one time
> Must haply often on the self-same day
> Have from our several dwellings gone abroad
> To gather daffodils on Coker's Stream.
> (7.342–46)

As Wordsworth recalls in Books Six and Eleven of The Prelude, the girls who actually gathered daffodils with him on those mountains were his sister Dorothy and Mary Hutchinson. Only a slight geographic accident, Book Seven suggests, placed Mary Hutchinson, rather than Mary Robinson, at Wordsworth's side in his youth. As Freud would suggest, such an association must have a motivation, and Wordsworth supplies the motivation. He reminds Coleridge that when they saw Mary Robinson in 1799, they were "Both stricken with one feeling of delight, / An admiration of her modest mien, / And carriage, mark'd by unexampled grace" (7.332–34). Wordsworth clearly found Mary Robinson attractive in 1799, so much so that he had no trouble in 1803 recalling their first meeting, and no doubt that Coleridge would also remember that encounter.

The similarity of the pastoral roles played by Mary Robinson and Mary Hutchinson suggests that Wordsworth's marital destiny was fixed by nothing but an accident of proximity, yet it is only the consequences of that accident that allow for the maintenance of the distinction between corrupted urban sexuality and the rural purity, embodied in Mary Hutchinson, that restores Wordsworth's moral nature. The significance of the fact that Wordsworth and Mary Hutchinson knew each other in their teenaged years is emphasized by the iteration, in Books Six and Eleven, of the scene in which William and Mary enjoyed "A spirit of pleasure and youth's golden gleam" (6.245) during their 1787 sojourns near Penrith. When this scene is recalled in Book Eleven, this line is virtually repeated when Wordsworth declares that an even earlier childhood adventure in 1779, when he had lost sight of his guide "Upon the naked pool and dreary crags" (11.321), had enhanced "The spirit of pleasure, and youth's golden gleam" in 1787 (11.323). The ability of one experience to inform a later one with a transcendent significance is celebrated in Book Eleven in the famous declaration about the importance of "spots of time": "So feeling comes in aid / Of feeling, and diversity of strength / Attends us, if once we have been strong" (11.326–28). The repetition of "feeling" here purports to refer to a phenomenological relation between Wordsworth and a landscape; Wordsworth's boyhood feeling of 1779 is said to enhance his feeling for this scene in 1787. But this repeatedly visited spot which grounds a relationship based in repetition also enshrines a second repetition of feeling. The reunion and marriage of Wordsworth and Mary Hutchinson in 1802 recovers their romantic experience of a "spirit of pleasure and youth's golden gleam" in 1787. The repetition confers a mythic importance on Wordsworth's marriage with a woman who had been a part of his innocent youth; this seemingly fated union suggests that Mary Hutchinson's role as Wordsworth's life partner is as inviolable as Wordsworth's role as a "chosen Son" (3.82). The iteration that links the two scenes involving Mary Hutchinson, one which occurs before and one after the Vaudracour and Julia story in Book Nine, constructs the myth of sexual fall and redemption in *The Prelude*. The implicit story is that Wordsworth fell into corrupted French sexuality but was saved by his return to the bosom of "Nature's inmate," a woman who epitomized rural English virtue. Mary Hutchinson's "appetites" are, Wordsworth claims, "wholly free" from the corrupt urbanity of "the turns and counter-turns, the strife / And various trials of our complex being / As we grow up" (11.196–203).

While the schematic opposition between Mary Robinson and the Sadler's Wells prostitute illustrates the stakes of sexuality in *The Prelude*, the clarity of that moral opposition is undermined by the ability of Mary Robinson to play the role of either Annette Vallon or Mary Hutchinson in the narrative of Wordsworth's life. As a liminal figure, Mary Robinson illustrates how easily Mary Hutchinson and Annette Vallon could have changed places: Annette could have become Mrs. Wordsworth, and Mary Hutchinson an "artless daughter of the hills" seduced and abandoned with an illegitimate child by a "bold bad man"—e.g., the seventeen-year-old William Wordsworth. Mary Hutchinson's role in Wordsworth's story of having been "singled out . . . For holy services" (1.62–63) is less secure than it seems; the myth of uniqueness comes to rest on the precariousness of circumstance.

Wordsworth's rhetorical protection of Mary Robinson's reputation against the stigma of fallenness suggests that moral narratives, such as those that stigmatize unmarried mothers, can oversimplify sexual circumstances, while the concatenation of the three stories of sexuality in Book Seven indicates how Wordsworth's own sexual myth of fall and redemption has a few loose ends. As the figure of the child grows in both vivacity and pathos in the progress from the lost infant of Mary Robinson to the babe in the tavern, these unfortunate children raise the specter of the awkward place of Caroline Vallon in the teleological story of the "Growth of a Poet's mind." This three-part sequence enables Wordsworth to raise that question in a parabolic form that displays more guilt than it dispels.

The first story in this sequence, dedicated to the purity of Mary Robinson, has its own internal enigma. Why does Wordsworth fabricate the existence of a child only to kill it off and then imagine it as happily dead? This may seem a long way to go just to get back to zero, but the construction of this pathetic melodrama both creates heightened sympathy for Mary Robinson and obscures the role of her seducer. The mother's loss of "her new-born Infant" makes her a pathetic figure, while the image of the child who "sleeps in earth . . . / fearless as a lamb . . . / beneath the little rock-like Pile / When storms are blowing" (7.355–59) locates both mother and child in a pastoral world of pitiful incidents governed by natural forces. The crimes of the "bold, bad man" are deflected by the protective imagery of the "rock-like Pile," so that his crimes seem to have had no greater consequences than the fictions of the urban, theatrical world of Sadler's Wells. If this story is properly reported, "uncontaminated" by urban irreverence, it becomes not a scandalous account of corruption by urbanity but a proof of the durability of pastoral purity. But, as in the case of "The Thorn," even if sympathy for the mother requires a forgetting of both the seducer and the dead child, "some remember well" ("The Thorn," line 163); no matter how deeply buried, this child does not entirely disappear. He rises again in the second part of this sequence, where his vibrancy revives the ethical question that had been too easily elided by the death of Mary Robinson's infant. The immemorability of the painted prostitute and the vividness of her child force a recognition that the stigma attached to the mother cannot fairly be transferred to the child, but it does not answer the question it provokes: What is due to bastards? This is not an easy question for Wordsworth. The pragmatic excuse that he provides elsewhere in The Prelude for his abandonment of Annette and Caroline Vallon ("absolute want / Of funds" [10.190–91]) is supplanted here by a clash of two discourses that transcend the empirical level of the narrative. The first is the mythology of Wordsworth's sexual fall and recovery, and the second is his ethical self-examination of his actions.

The sudden scene shift from the Sadler's Wells prostitute and child to the swearing prostitute on the Cambridge road provides the answer, however inadequate, to the ethical question raised by the second story: Who is responsible for inconvenient, illegitimate children? The encounter with the swearing prostitute is not sequentially mimetic—it takes place three years before the visit to London being narrated in Book Seven—but is a syncretic scene that distills the story of Wordsworth's fall into sexuality. As many commentators have noted, this scene seems distinctly undermotivated, and one mark of this lack is that Wordsworth is cast simply as an observer; he "saw" this woman in the street, he "heard" her swear. Even if we presume a high degree of sexual naivete for the seventeen-year-old Wordsworth, the cataclysmic effect that this event supposedly had on his imagination—"from humanity divorced / The human Form, splitting the race of Man / In twain, yet leaving the same outward shape" (7.425–27)—is pretty dramatic. The disproportion between cause and effect makes this scene a classic example of Mitchell's thesis that Wordsworth repeatedly suggests some "excessive, unmotivated guilt for some unnamed crime" (647). The crime here seems to be unnamed because of the opacity and the range of its representation. Whatever the facts involving Wordsworth's introduction to sexual intercourse, whether it involved Cambridge or London prostitutes or Annette Vallon,[5] this passage represents Wordsworth's introduction to sexuality, and the hyperbole in this scene synthesizes his recoil from everything, from sights in the streets to actual intercourse, that upset his conception of female purity. At the end of this passage, Wordsworth becomes the rural youth who stands amazed that the "voice of Woman" could express anything other than "her soul's beauty" (7.418, 433). The scene depicts what the sexual mythology of The Prelude requires: that Wordsworth should stand entirely apart from a sexuality that is incomprehensible to pure, rural Englishness.

Each section of this opaque melodrama depends on another part of the sequence for its explication. The moral opposition between the young Wordsworth and the swearing prostitute is compromised by his shadow from the first story, the "bold, bad man" who participated in an affair that became "a cruel mockery / Of love and marriage bonds" (7.325–26) and left a woman and her illegitimate child "to open shame / Abandon'd, and the pride of public vice" (419–20). The unfairness to the child in this story is underlined by the imaginary fate of the blessed bastard, who may have lived long enough to envy those who died in childhood. The enigma of the first story in the sequence—Why create a fictional child only to kill it off?— is answered by the evasiveness of the third story in the face of the ethical burden of the second, which implicitly asks what is due to bastards. For Wordsworth to secure his identity as an innocent northern youth, a bastard child has to be abandoned as if she (represented as "he") were dead, and the irrelevant moral status of its mother must be elevated to apocalyptic dimensions. In this three-part sequence, the sexualized woman becomes an increasingly corrupt figure, and her child vanishes. In the final tableau, the image that twice rises up against Wordsworth and blocks the narrative of personal growth—the image of a woman with an illegitimate child—is finally divested of the reproachful figure of the child. What stands between Wordsworth and the swearing prostitute on the Cambridge road is a missing child, and her absence accounts for the unspeakable, apocalyptic significance of the scene.

The obsessive quality of this erotic sequence, in which Wordsworth's attempts to proceed with his story of "the Growth of a Poet's Mind" are repeatedly interrupted by images that rise up and interrupt the forward motion of the narrative, is produced not out of Wordsworth's sympathy for victims in general but by his guilt over the sufferings of those whose lives were intertwined with his own. The last level of Rousseauean defense—"my actions may have been mistaken, but my heart was pure"—does not survive Wordsworth's self-examination in this erotic sequence. As Wordsworth composes this passage in 1804, he connects the 1803 production of The Beauty of Buttermere with his own recollection of Mary Robinson from 1799, and he now sees her in a new light: not as the "modest" virgin who had waited on Coleridge and himself but as the young woman who was on the brink of an affair that would be "treated with irreverence" on the stage at Sadler's Wells. The prurient edge of the "delight" he had felt in her physical "grace" had also been felt, and acted upon, by Edward Hatfield, her seducer. As Mary Robinson stands, like Annette Vallon, in a liminal position, with prostitution (a common fate for unwed mothers) on one side and domesticity on the other, Wordsworth is faced with the ambiguity of his own emotions in his encounters with women. For someone who maintained a clear categorical opposition, before the age of seventeen and after the age of thirty, between sexual purity and corruption, any reminder of his own sexual activity in those intervening years is bound to dim the brightness of the line between domestic and erotic affections. The uneven texture of this passage—its disruptions of temporal sequence, its portentous and enigmatic referentiality, and its peremptory termination—"I quit this painful theme, enough is said"—indicate that, however much Wordsworth can be faulted for his actions, it would be difficult to doubt his rationalizations any more deeply than he did himself.

The closest Wordsworth comes in *The Prelude* to acknowledging the existence of Annette and Caroline Vallon is the story of Vaudracour and Julia, which is entirely cut from the final version of the poem, an excision that helps to confirm the preeminent place claimed by Mary Hutchinson in the story of the "Growth of a Poet's Mind." Mary Hutchinson's status is further cemented by a double excision, in the final *Prelude*, of Dorothy. In 1805, Wordsworth takes his teenaged walks in Penrith "With those two dear Ones" (11.317); by 1850, there is only "the loved one [Mary] by my side" (1850; 12.262). As Wordsworth begins to wrap up the poem in 1805, he worries that Dorothy has been too little featured, and he acknowledges "that Sister of my heart / Who ought by rights the dearest to have been / Conspicuous through this biographic Verse" (13.339–41); in 1850, those lines are cut. As *The Prelude* evolves from a private to a public poem, it withholds from the public details that, Wordsworth seems to believe, do not belong to them.

If we were to ask, in Rousseau's terms, whether Wordsworth's falsification of his past constitutes a fiction or a lie, we would come to the contradiction at the heart of the "Fourth Walk." One can be accused of lying, Rousseau argues at some length in that essay, only if one withholds information that is owed to others because it could be of some use to them, but later in the essay he briefly suggests that it is also a lie, and not simply a fiction, if one describes oneself as better than one really is. After the first distinction is so exhaustively defended on utilitarian grounds, it is not immediately obvious why an autobiographer should be accused of lying, and not a lesser offense, if he cleans up his own past in a way that does no harm to the reader. It is only at the end of Rousseau's meditation that it becomes clear that seemingly harmless fictions operate as indicators of bad faith and as evasions of deeper untruths. In its final, public form, *The Prelude* takes the liberties that Rousseau disallows. Even the excision of Annette Vallon from the poem does not remove all of Wordsworth's excuses for his behavior toward her. His claim that he had no choice but to leave France—"Reluctantly to England I return'd, / Compell'd by nothing less than absolute want / Of funds for my support" (10.189–91)—suggests the parallel between Wordsworth and Vaudracour as it echoes the 1805 description of Vaudracour's attempt to "hie / Back to his Father's house, and there employ / Means aptest to obtain a sum of gold, /A final portion, even, if that might be" (9.647–50). But the litany of excuses offered for Vaudracour is so extravagant that we might doubt that we are meant to take any of them seriously. The Vaudracour and Julia story is told by a sympathetic narrator who only "reluctantly" admits that there is a pregnancy (9.609) and whose disclosure of facts is selective; he is uncertain of the lovers' motives and reticent about their actions ("I pass the raptures of the pair" [9.635]), but he claims to be fully privy to Vaudracour's thoughts about his father: "thought / Unfilial or unkind had never once / Found harbour in his breast" (9.715–17). The narrator offers the insanity defense twice, first to describe the temporary state of the "delirious hour" in which the sexual affair begins and then in the permanent "imbecile mind" that is Vaudracour's final lot, and he characterizes the two deaths that occur as a result of Vaudracour's actions as either a matter of negligence rather than malice or as self-defense.

The diegetic protection afforded by this sympathetic narrator fails when he is compelled to protest of this "tragic Tale" that supposedly happened long ago and far away that "Theirs be the blame that caused the woe, not mine" (9.911). The morally restorative function of the dead infant in Book Seven becomes less convincing when the parent must make his own excuses; Vaudracour veers into Rousseauean narcissism when he prays that his child "might never be / As wretched as his Father" (9.790–91). Like the Blessed Babe, this baby is indeed saved from such a fate in a passage that is so bizarre that it risks provoking inappropriate laughter. The baby is consigned to his father's care, but "after a short time by some mistake / Or indiscretion of the Father died" (9.908–09). As the tale makes no further mention of the infant but instead dwells on the suffering of Vaudracour, the deflection from the dead infant to the remorseful parent forces the reader to choose between these two figures as objects of a sympathy, and it dictates that the proper choice is the suffering father.

The most unbalanced feature of the Vaudracour and Julia episode is the persistent representation of Vaudracour as a victim, first of his father's malice, then of Julia's beauty ("He would exclaim, 'Julia, how much thine eyes / Have cost me!'" [9.819–20]), and finally of his child's need for a caretaker. This last force becomes the most powerful in determining Vaudracour's fate, and the difference between Vaudracour's paternal care and Wordsworth's neglect produces the most elaborate structure of self-accusation and exoneration in *The Prelude*. The painstaking care that Vaudracour takes with his infant recalls a London street scene that Wordsworth describes with admiration:

> Sate this one man, and with a sickly Babe
> Upon his knee, whom he had thither brought
> For sunshine, and to breathe the fresher air.
> Of those who pass'd, and me who looked at him
> He took no note; but in his brawny Arms
> (The Artificer was to the elbow bare,
> And from his work this moment had been stolen)
> He held the Child, and, bending over it
> As if he were afraid both of the sun
> And of the air which he had come to seek,
> He eyed it with unutterable love.
> (8.849–59)

In 1850, this passage is moved to Book Seven (607–18) and placed soon after the stories of the children of Mary Robinson and the Sadler's Wells prostitute. As the comparison between the children in those stories shows, the fate of this urban child is precarious, a danger registered in the description of the baby as "sickly" and of the father's fear "of the sun / And of the air." When Wordsworth moves toward the final peroration of *The Prelude*, he finds it necessary to add "one word more of personal circumstance" concerning the years "Since I withdrew unwillingly from France": "I led an undomestic wanderer's life, / In London chiefly was my home" (13.332–34, 343–44). The passing reference to his "personal circumstance" in 1792 shows how little he could have offered a child at that time; he was confined mostly to London, and his could not have been, like Mary Robinson's child and like Wordsworth himself, a "cottage child" (7.380). Caroline Wordsworth would have been doomed to the urban life that, the Sadler's Wells passage suggests, might be worse than death.

The speciousness of this reasoning is refuted by Wordsworth himself in a devastating Shakespearean allusion at the end of the Vaudracour and Julia episode. When the narrator recounts of Vaudracour that after his child's death, "From that time forth he never utter'd word" (9.912), the line echoes Iago: "From this time forth I never will speak word" (*Othello* 5.2.300). The abandonment of his children was Rousseau's most notorious crime, and

Edmund Burke described it as the ultimate proof of the unnaturalness of Rousseau's character. Burke also denounced the flimsiness of Rousseau's excuses: poverty and political necessity. Second in venality only to the act itself, according to Burke, was the telling of it; it was a sign of Rousseau's "deranged, eccentric vanity," Burke wrote, that he "was impelled to publish a mad confession of his mad faults" (Mitchell 654). The passage that is interpolated between the Sadler's Wells/swearing prostitute sequence and the scene of the solicitous father in Book Seven of the 1850 *Prelude* is the tribute to Burke; as Mitchell suggests, Wordsworth never confronts Rousseau directly but has Burke do it for him.

If it is under Burke's guidance that Wordsworth is persuaded to remove nearly all of the traces of "a mad confession of his mad faults" in the final version of *The Prelude*, then much of the perceived superiority of the 1805 text depends on its greater richness as a personal poem in which Wordsworth offers both the structure of excuses that he created to explain his selfish behavior to himself and his demolition of those excuses. A clever enough man can produce a plausible justification of just about any behavior, but as Wordsworth learned from Burke, the justification itself only compounds the initial crime. The only alternatives are to say nothing, which is to emulate Iago and accept the verdict implicit in one's actions, or to falsify one's past. In the "Fourth Walk," Rousseau suggests that the latter choice, lying to make oneself look better, is a forfeiture of "self-respect"; it purchases the "respect of others at the expense of one's own" (72). As Wordsworth explores the nuances of *amour-propre*, walking the line between vanity and self-respect in the composition of *The Prelude* in 1804–5, his first completed effort asserts the right of self-judgment, and it exercises that right with a scathing rigor and candor. In its indifference to the availability of public meaning of its gnomic allusions, the poem is also, Iago-like, beyond caring how a reader might "judge, punish, forgive, console, [or] reconcile" (HS 61–62) its hermetic, Olympian author.

The critiques of associationist psychology that appear in Wordsworth's prose and poetry have led to a critical focus on the theme of self-authorship as an epistemological issue; autogenesis is generally presumed to involve a quest to find an interior faculty that is creative rather than reflective of an exterior reality. But the ability to become what Wordsworth calls a Poet is even more tellingly involved in a struggle with "the agency of domination . . . in the one who listens and says nothing" (HS 62). It has become widely recognized in Wordsworth studies that this "agency of domination" was personified for Wordsworth, during the initial stages of composition of *The*

Prelude, in Coleridge. Since Thomas McFarland's essay "The Symbiosis of Wordsworth and Coleridge" was expanded into *Romanticism and the Forms of Ruin* in 1981, there have been at least four books entirely devoted to aspects of the Wordsworth-Coleridge collaboration in the years between the composition of the *Lyrical Ballads* and *The Prelude*.[6] Each of these studies recounts Coleridge's response to the news that Wordsworth has returned to the "poem on my own earlier Life" (*Letters1* 436) in the latter part of 1799 in order to reframe it as a "poem to Coleridge":

> I long to see what you have been doing. O let it be the tail-piece of "The Recluse!" for of nothing but "The Recluse" can I hear patiently. That it is to be addressed to me makes me more desirous that it should not be a poem of itself. To be addressed, as a beloved man, by a thinker, at the close of such a poem as "The Recluse," a poem *non unis populi*, is the only event, I believe, capable of inciting in me an hour's vanity. (CL 1.538)

Beneath the extravagant rhetoric of praise, Coleridge gently imposes a demand on Wordsworth; work on the self-referential "poem on my own earlier Life," which only existed in the preliminary two-book form at this time, is acceptable only if it is part of the great "philosophical poem" to which he was urging Wordsworth to devote his energies. The innocent pronoun "it" ("that it is to be addressed to me"), which conflates the two works, pushes Wordsworth toward the larger and more demanding task.

This blend of genuine affection and admiration mixed with some degree of rivalry flowed in both directions between Coleridge and Wordsworth in the years 1797 to 1805. Studies of the two poets during this period have focused on their poetic dialogue, and particularly on the extended conversation that begins with Wordsworth's composition of the stanzas "There was a time" in 1802, which leads to Coleridge's verse "Letter to Sara," Wordsworth's "Leech-Gatherer" and "Resolution and Independence," Coleridge's revision of the "Letter to Sara" into "Dejection: An Ode," and culminates, two years after it began, with Wordsworth's completion of the "Ode: Intimations of Immortality." Gene Ruoff's *Wordsworth and Coleridge: The Making of the Major Lyrics, 1802–1804* is devoted entirely to this sequence, and Ruoff masterfully shows how each of the poets mobilizes the conventions of various genres in order to better articulate his position in a highly personal debate. While these studies generally make some mention of the perception within the Wordsworth circle that, at their initial meeting, Coleridge's erudition and flamboyance had somewhat overshadowed the quieter Wordsworth, each study arrives at the same conclusion: Wordsworth becomes a Poet, and Coleridge becomes a story of wasted potential.

The ascendancy of Wordsworth over Coleridge had a personal dimension, and Coleridge described this disparity in gendered terms. He wrote to Cottle in 1797 that "I feel myself a little man by his side . . . He is the greatest Man, [I] ever knew" (CL 1.325). In 1798, he praised "The Giant Wordsworth" (1.391) and, later in life said that "Of all the men I ever knew, Wordsworth has the least femineity in his mind. He is all man" (Coburn 296). As Wordsworth becomes the greater Man and Poet than Coleridge, women become counters in their rivalry; a subtext of envy is easy to discern in Coleridge's complaint that "WW liv[es] wholly among Devotees—having every the minutest Thing, almost his very Eating and Drinking, done for him by his Sister, or Wife" (CL 2.1013). Wordsworth's acquisition of a household of "Devotees" stands in stark contrast to Coleridge's unhappy marriage. But the Wordsworth regime always had both its internal fault lines and its foreign entanglements, and the persistent academic focus on the professional relationship between the two poets suppresses some highly suggestive details about the genesis of Wordsworth's poetry in this period. Ruoff cites Wordsworth's reading of Jonson's poetry in early 1802 to propose that Wordsworth looked to Jonson for lessons in style ("epitaphic terseness") and versification ("intricately varied rhymes that would have furnished a respite from the tediousness of . . . blank verse"), and for "a source for the topological, locodescriptive tradition in English poetry" (47–48). The one Jonson poem named in Dorothy's journal as part of their reading in February 1802 is "On My First Daughter." Annette's letters begin to arrive, after the war embargo, in January 1802; Wordsworth goes to France and sees Annette and Caroline in March.

Ruoff is the most emphatic of the commentators on this period in his denunciation of psychobiographical readings of Wordsworth's poetry, but he is only the most explicit defender of a generally observed critical rule. The attempt to discover "a direct emotional occasion" for Wordsworth's work, Ruoff warns, runs the risk of diminishing the poetic accomplishment; "the affective force" of the work "could shrivel pathetically into [a] kind of mawkish self-pity" (56). Other commentators seem, silently, to acquiesce in this view. The first draft of the opening stanzas of what will become the "Immortality" ode is written on 27 March 1802, and it concludes with the lament "Whither is fled the visionary gleam / Where is it gone the glory and the dream." Dorothy's journal of 22 March contains the following entry: "we resolved to see Annette, and that Wm should go to Mary" (Journals 82). The connection is generally unremarked in studies of the "Ode"; any mention of Wordsworth's relation to Annette Vallon in this period is quickly subordinated to the narrative of his crisis of creativity (his "struggle with his writing in 1802 and the unfulfilled promise of 1800" [Magnuson 275]).

What is at stake in this difference of emphasis is a dispute about the nature of Wordsworth's genius. If Wordsworth is the most important English poet since Milton, his formal proficiency is an important part of his greatness, but it is far from comprising the whole of his value. The presumption that Wordsworth's canonical stature depends either on his place on the public stage of history or in his continuity with a national literary history is largely dictated by the fear that the recovery of biographical context can decline so quickly into gossip. Ruoff's analysis of Wordsworth's desexualization of the conventions of erotic pastoral in "There was a time" and the "Immortality Ode" and Coleridge's reactivation of those conventions in the "Letter to Sara" may well seem a more promising way of valuing these poets than following the content of the dialogue in these poems. Taken in its bare bones, the exchange has a depressingly soap-opera quality to it. After Coleridge hears Wordsworth's lament of a vanished "visionary gleam," within a month he visits the Wordsworths and trumps Wordsworth's complaint with a florid account of his hopeless love for Sara Hutchinson. Coleridge's first performance of the "Letter to Sara" asks, in effect, what Wordsworth, with an engagement to one Hutchinson sister and the devotion of Dorothy and the other Hutchinson sister, has to complain about. Wordsworth's response in "The Leech-Gatherer" upbraids Coleridge by insisting that his state of dejection is a matter of character, not circumstance: "But how can He expect that others should / Build for him, sow for him, and at his call / Love him, who for himself will take no heed at all?" (40–42). The Coleridge of whom Wordsworth would later say that he was "too much in love with his own dejection" (Ruoff 221) is clearly the target of this barb. For literary history, this dispute between Wordsworth and Coleridge becomes a matter of serendipity. The "Ode" that holds such a central place in English literary history is produced as a continuation of Wordsworth's refutation of Coleridge; there was no other reason for Wordsworth to return to "There was a time" and construct a dialectical response to his own lament. Evaluating the justice of Wordsworth's judgment of Coleridge can be consigned to the dustbin of literary gossip, or it can spice up the critical biography.

What gets lost in the marginalizing of domestic biography in the study of Wordsworth's poetry is an understanding of why there is so much that is counterfactual in his work and of how Wordsworth constructs determinative, reciprocal relations between fact and fiction. The controversy over the grounds of Wordsworth's importance is an argument over a self-created myth named "Wordsworth," in which it is too easily presumed that Wordsworth's autogenic myth acquires its greatest value in its terminal form. The finished product of Wordsworth's identity as a Poet can be identified and defended in a variety of ways; while Jonathan Bate celebrates the sentimental Wordsworth as an exemplar of natural affection, Helen Vendler's Wordsworth is the representative of higher literacy. Charles Altieri has constructed the most thorough and forceful argument for the ethical value of the sublime Wordsworth. It is in Wordsworth's "direct passionate personal utterance" (133), Altieri contends, that he achieves the "writerly sublime" and acquires a moral status as an exemplar for others, demonstrating newly imagined responses to the world beyond the text. But Wordsworth did not always share such confidence that the Poet is naturally more ethical than other men. He wrote of being "dejected" at the completion of *The Prelude*: "when I looked back upon the performance it seemed to have a dead weight about it, the reality so far short of the expectation" (*Letters*1 594). This factual disappointment stands in distinct contrast to the glorious fictional conclusion of the poem itself, which depicts Wordsworth and Coleridge as "Prophets of Nature," who "will speak / A lasting inspiration, sanctified / By reason and by truth" to generations "yet to come" (13.441–44). The gap between the poetic peroration and the epistolary confession marks the distance between what Wordsworth believed the poem should accomplish and his sense of falling short of that goal. The peroration is driven by the desire to have a moral effect on the public audience of *The Prelude*, which might be accomplished if the revelation of the inner nature of a singularly blessed "mind of man" could instruct by force of example: "what we have loved / Others will love; and we may teach them how" (13.444–45). But the "dead weight" to which Wordsworth admits in retrospect betrays a lack of faith that the Poet depicted in *The Prelude* can actually serve that exemplary function.

Marjorie Levinson's identification of a palimpsestic structure in "Tintern Abbey" offers an alternative to locating Wordsworth's poetic value in directly representational rhetoric that depicts the Poet as the epitome of either the sentimental or the sublime. Levinson locates the affective force of "Tintern Abbey" not in its representation of the permanence of nature but in Wordsworth's awareness of historical mutability; as Wordsworth constructs a pastoral scene "with an eye that compares, interprets, and predicts" what the present prospect has been and what it will be, Levinson argues, he knows of "those little farms" so precious to him that "such spots are doomed" (37). The conclusion of *The Prelude* is similarly fragmented between present realities and imaginary alternatives, and it finally presents a composite fiction of the Poet made up of imaginary versions of Wordsworth and Coleridge.

The Poetic "we" that is finally entrusted with the moral education of the future offers not just Wordsworth but Coleridge as a moral exemplar. As Lucy Newlyn has argued, in this claim for Coleridge's "redemptive status," the "myth-making process is being asked to do too much." Newlyn details a series of images in *The Prelude* in which Coleridge is "a solipsistic figure, shut out from the light of knowledge, his imagination feeding solely on itself," and she concludes that he can hardly now stand as "an emblem of outgoing love" (Newlyn 190–91). So why does Wordsworth suddenly reintroduce the discredited Coleridge as his own equal in imaginative power? Newlyn's answer is that this passage is a propitiation of Coleridge: "Wordsworth's mood, in May 1805, as he writes these lines, is one of acute anxiety. With Coleridge expected back from Malta at any time, he is asking himself whether *The Prelude* will be well received, whether his neglect of *The Recluse* will count against him, whether—in any terms—the work can 'justify itself'" (191). Newlyn's explanation of this passage as an expression of Wordsworth's subordination to Coleridge elides the way it sutures the public function of autobiography with the private demands of the confession. For a poetic autobiography of over 7,000 lines to justify its "alarming length" in a public forum, it must demonstrate some point to this "thing unprecedented in Literary history, that a man should talk so much about himself" (*Letters1* 586). But the confession, in its strongest form, is uninterested in public ratification; its goal is to discover the "fragile treasure, a secret that must be discovered at all costs" (HS 121). This process, Foucault warns, is less straightforward than it looks: "We demand that it tell us our truth, or rather, the deeply buried truth of that truth about ourselves that we think we possess in our immediate consciousness" (HS 69). In the course of the composition of *The Prelude*, Wordsworth discovers the elusiveness of this "truth about ourselves that we think we possess." He had imagined that "a Poem on my own earlier life" should serve as a manageable "preparatory Poem" for *The Recluse* (PW 589): "as I had nothing to do but describe what I had felt and thought, therefore could not easily be bewildered" (*Letters1* 586–87). His letters detailing his progress on the poem tell a different story. In February 1804, the work "will take five parts or books to complete, three of which are nearly finished" (*Letters1* 436). A month later, four books are finished, but the end seems, if anything, further off; the work is now "better [than] half complete" (*Letters1* 454). By late April, seven books are written, but there is no end in sight; Wordsworth now only knows that it "will turn out far longer than I ever dreamt of" (*Letters1* 470). A year later, in May of 1805, eleven books are written, and the end seems as far off as it was the previous February: "Two books more will conclude it" (*Letters1* 586). The confessional journey of *The Prelude* produces no guarantee of closure, let alone of moral efficacy. The extravagant outpouring of moral love in the poem's conclusion is the effect of the generic formula of autobiography: The story of my life will serve as a lesson for how you can live yours. The incredibility of this moral to Wordsworth himself produces a weird supplement; a fictional "Coleridge" is drafted to fill in the gap between "Wordsworth" and what a morally exemplary Poet should look like.

An understanding of the unsatisfactory resolution of *The Prelude* in generic terms can help to suggest both why the poem is so difficult to see in a unified form but is at the same time so central to Wordsworth's importance as an English poet. The sublime style of the public poem, which becomes increasingly prevalent in the 1850 text, is a derivative Miltonism, while the originality and greatness of the 1805 *Prelude* lies in the depth and the subtlety of Wordsworth's private self-examination. As Levinson has so brilliantly shown, Wordsworth's poetic fantasies are conscious formations, held up for comparison to the seeming irrefragability of facts. The affective force of *The Prelude* resides in its feeling for what is precious and mutable in the past; its fictions register the Poet's investments in what, it seems even in retrospect, could so easily have become true. Wordsworth's addresses to Coleridge in *The Prelude* illustrate how the most blatant fictions in the poem stand for unrealized possibilities that were once no less plausible than present realities; its sense of loss registers the gap between those lost possibilities and an impoverished present. The final inclusion of "Coleridge" in the exemplary "we" at the conclusion of *The Prelude* is so false that it betrays the deliberate manipulation of facts. Wordsworth's praise for Coleridge's creation of "The bright-eyed Mariner" and "Lady Christabel" (13.397–98) inappropriately raises the specter of the crucial moment in the severing of the Wordsworth/Coleridge partnership when Wordsworth took control of the preparation of the second edition of *Lyrical Ballads.* When Wordsworth published the second edition of the *Ballads* solely under his own name, he removed the "Mariner" from its original place as the first poem in the collection and accompanied the poem with a long note describing its "defects." In the summer of 1800, when the second edition was being completed, Coleridge was desperately trying to hold up his part in their collaboration by producing a new, long poem that would help to fill out the second volume. On 4 October, he finally completed "Christabel" and read it to the Wordsworths; Dorothy's journal for that date records, "Exceedingly delighted with the 2nd part of Christabel." The journal entry for the next day reads, "Coleridge read a 2nd time Christabel—we had increasing pleasure." The next day, things change: "Determined not to print Christabel with the LB" (*Journals* 24). The missing subject of that sentence is, obviously, William.

The effect on Coleridge of this rejection by Wordsworth was devastating. He wrote to Godwin in March 1801 that "The Poet is dead in me—my imagination (or rather the Somewhat that had been imaginative) lies, like a Cold Snuff, on the circular Rim of a Brass Candle-stick" (CL 2.714). The decline of the nominative ("my imagination") into the adjectival ("the Somewhat that had been imaginative") reflects Coleridge's belief in the essential quality of "Imagination"; it is not only something one has, more or less, but what one is, or, in this case, is not. Coleridge's judgment of Wordsworth's genius was that Wordsworth was exactly what he himself was not; Wordsworth was "a man of true poetic genius" who possessed "the gift of imagination in the highest and strictest sense of the word" (*Coleridge: Oxford Authors* 347, 410). As the dialogue of reciprocal offerings of truth and judgment between Wordsworth and Coleridge terminates with a clear winner, Wordsworth emerges with a full identity—he is a Poet—and Coleridge disappears.

He does not go quietly. His reading of the "Letter to Sara" at Grasmere in April of 1802 greatly depressed Dorothy: "Coleridge came to us, and repeated the verses he wrote to Sara. I was affected with them, and was on the whole, not being well, in miserable spirits" (*Journals* 89). Wordsworth was more taciturn than Dorothy, but Coleridge had a public forum in which he could continue to challenge the magisterial edifice that "Wordsworth" was becoming. The revised version of the "Letter to Sara," "Dejection: An Ode" was published in the *Morning Post* on 4 October 1802, Wordsworth's wedding day, and within a week of the wedding the *Post* published an anonymous parody of an announcement of the Wordsworth nuptial:

Monday last, W. Wordsworth, Esq. was married to Miss Hutchinson, of Wykeham, near Scarborough, and proceeded immediately, with his wife and his sister, for his charming cottage in the little Paradise Vale of Grasmere. His neighbour, Mr. Coleridge, resides in the Vale of Keswick, 13 miles from Grasmere. His house (situated on a low hill

at the foot of Skiddaw, with the Derwent Lake in front, and the romantic River Greta winding round the hill) commands, perhaps, the
most various and interesting prospects of any house in the island. It
is a perfect *panorama* of that wonderful vale, with its two lakes, and its
complete circle, or rather ellipse, of mountains. (Johnston 788–89)

Johnston reports a more serious attack by Coleridge on Wordsworth's suppression of his own checkered past. A few weeks later, the *Post* published
Coleridge's satire of a self-righteous confessor who could often be found
"At Annette's door, the lovely courtesan!" (Johnston 789). This private allusion would only be available, as Johnston suggests, to about six people in
England, but it apparently still mattered to Coleridge to continue to challenge the myth of the austere rectitude of "Wordsworth" within the inner
circle.

Wordsworth's and Coleridge's comments on each other for the rest of
their lives were marked by intellectual respect and personal ambivalence.
Coleridge's remarks on Wordsworth in the *Biographia* are the most public
and decorous statement of their differences; his paranoid speculations on
the sexual arrangements of the Wordsworth household, which he seems
to have disclosed to Wordsworth, the least so. His effusive response to
The Prelude, "To William Wordsworth," which addresses Wordsworth as
a "Friend of the Wise! and teacher of the good," and "Great Bard," and a
member of a timeless "truly great," seems to hover somewhere between an
address to his friend and an offering to the icon "Wordsworth." His private
comments could be less reverent; he worried to Poole that Wordsworth's life
among "Devotees" was causing a "Film [to] rise, and thicken on his Moral
eye" (CL 2.1013). Wordsworth's personal ambivalence toward Coleridge can
be summarized in a comment to Poole regarding Coleridge's attempt to
start a self-published newspaper, *The Friend:*

> It is in fact *impossible* utterly impossible—that he should carry it on;
> and, therefore, better never begin it; far better, and if begun, the sooner
> it stop, also the better—the less will be the loss. . . . he neither will nor
> can execute any thing of important benefit either to himself his family
> or mankind. Neither his talents nor his genius mighty as they are nor
> his vast information will avail him anything; they are all frustrated by a
> derangement in his intellectual and moral constitution—In fact he has
> no voluntary power of mind whatsoever, nor is he capable of acting
> under any *constraint* of duty or moral obligation. (Letters2 352)

Coleridge's unreliability was largely due to his opium habit by this time, but after Wordsworth's rejection of "Christabel" had done so much to destroy Coleridge's sense of his own ability to complete a difficult project, this assessment of his constitutional intellectual paralysis, offered to someone whom Coleridge was soliciting as a financial backer for The Friend, takes on the quality of a self-fulfilling prophecy. Wordsworth's acknowledgment of Coleridge's "talents," "genius," and "vast information" is overshadowed by his perception of an innate moral flaw. As Wordsworth sees it, Coleridge is incapable of producing any benefit to others because of his own self-inflicted sufferings. Coleridge's greatest doubt about Wordsworth is that he is suffering from a similar defect but from the opposite cause; Wordsworth's moral vision, Coleridge surmises, is being obscured by a life of excessive comfort.

The Prelude does not tell both sides of this story but only of the occlusion of "Coleridge" by "Wordsworth." In Wordsworth's acquisition of the identity of the Poet, he takes on both of the roles described by Foucault in the confessional structure; finally, he is both the speaking subject who compulsively discloses "the truth we think we possess" in the depths of ourselves and the "virtual authority" who "judges, punishes, forgives, consoles and reconciles" (HS 61–62). As the fabricated union of these roles becomes the "Wordsworth" so beloved of cultural conservatives from Arnold to Vendler and Bate, "Coleridge" becomes an imaginary entity, and the addresses to him in The Prelude become increasingly divorced from material facts. The extended address to Coleridge at the end of Book Two of the 1805 Prelude is virtually identical to the one attached to the conclusion of the two-book Prelude of 1799, but the differences that arise between the two poets in those years give these words a far different contextual range of personal reference in 1805 than they had possessed in 1799. The passage addresses Coleridge as "my Friend" and "my Brother" and describes the two poets as equals: "we by different roads at length have gain'd / The self-same bourne" (2.468–69). It closes with a "Fare Thee well" and a hope that "Health, and the quiet of a healthful mind / Attend thee!" (2.479–81).

The wish for Coleridge's health is, in 1799, simply part of the conventional "Fare thee well." While Coleridge's health later became a crux of Wordsworth's doubts about his moral character, in 1799 it was Wordsworth who was the hypochondriac. He wrote in December of 1798 to Coleridge from Goslar of "an uneasiness at my stomach and side, with a dull pain about my heart" which "renders writing unpleasant" (Letters1 236). Similar complaints in the fall of 1799, relayed through intermediaries (Letters1 270; Johnston 682), were enough to bring Coleridge from London to Sockburn for a visit, where Coleridge found Wordsworth well enough to embark on a month-long walking tour of the district. Immediately after Coleridge's departure, Wordsworth quickly completed the two-book *Prelude*. Some combination of the walking tour and Coleridge's meeting with Sara Hutchinson at Sockburn led Coleridge to decide to move to the North to be near the Wordsworths and Hutchinsons. The "Fare thee well" of 1799 addresses Coleridge's temporary return to the "haunts of men" in London before he moves to Keswick, to be near Grasmere, in the spring of 1800.

The farewell wish for "Health and the quiet of a healthful mind" resonates very differently in 1804, when Wordsworth sends Coleridge a copy of the first five books of *The Prelude* to take with him on his journey to Malta. By that time, Coleridge's health had so declined that the Wordsworths thought that they might be seeing the last of him, a prospect that Wordsworth found potentially calamitous for his poetic future. He wrote desperately to Coleridge begging for his "notes for the Recluse": "I cannot say how much importance I attach to this, if it should please God that I survive you, I should reproach myself for ever in writing the work if I had neglected to procure this help" (*Letters1* 452). Even after the rejection of "Christabel" and the criticism of the "defects" of the "Ancient Mariner" in the second *Lyrical Ballads*, and all of the vexations surrounding Coleridge's "Letter to Sara," Wordsworth's respect for Coleridge's "talents," "genius," and "vast information" remained undiminished. When this plea resulted not in Coleridge's notes for *The Recluse* but with a report of another attack of illness, Wordsworth's response made his fears over Coleridge's survival, and the effect this might have on the completion of *The Recluse*, more explicit:

> [I] had a most affecting return home in thinking of you and your narrow escape. . . . I cannot help saying that I would gladly have given 3 fourths of my possessions for your letter on The Recluse at that time. I cannot say what a load it would be to me, should I survive you and you die without this memorial left behind. Do for heaven's sake, put this out of the reach of accident immediately. We are most happy that you have gotten the Poems, and that they have already given you so much pleasure. Heaven bless you for ever and ever. No words can express what I feel at this moment. Farewell farewell farewell. (*Letters1* 464)

Among the poems Coleridge had received were the first five books of *The Prelude*, but the first extended address to him in the poem had to strike with a good deal more irony, and less pleasure, in 1804 than it had in 1799. Not only is the wish for Coleridge's health far less likely to be realized in 1804, but the passage speaks glowingly of a time when the partnership between the two poets was characterized by perfect equality and transparency. Coleridge, it says, had overcome the disadvantage of his urban upbringing to become identical to Wordsworth in his love of nature:

> Thou, my Friend! wert rear'd
> In the great City, 'mid far other scenes;
> But we by different roads at length have gain'd
> The self-same bourne.
> (2.466–69)

Coleridge's achievement as "one, / The most intense of Nature's worshippers" (476–77) promises a perfect openness between the two poets; they speak a language "Of beauty and of love" uncontaminated by "The insinuated scoff of coward tongues" (475, 471). During the years 1801–4, Coleridge's unhappy marriage led him to spend a good deal of his time back "In the great City" writing for the *Post*, and during that period both Wordsworth and Coleridge became quite adept at speaking a language of veiled criticism of each other's perceived faults.

The particular target that Coleridge chose for his "insinuated scoffs," Wordsworth's wedding day, shows that the competition between Wordsworth and Coleridge was as much erotic as professional. Coleridge's "Letter to Sara" breaks the decorum of the Wordsworth household not only because of Coleridge's complaints about his "coarse domestic Life" where "two unequal Minds / Meet in one House, and two discordant Wills" (*Coleridge's Dejection* 257, 243–44), or even his flamboyant declarations of love for Wordsworth's wife's sister. His description of an evening spent with the Hutchinson sisters in August of 1801, without Wordsworth, exceeds the bounds of sensual representation in the Wordsworth circle. Addressing Sara, he writes

> It was as calm as this,—the happy Night
> When Mary, Thou and I, together were,
> The low-decaying Fire our only Light,
> And listen'd to the stillness of the Air!
> O that affectionate & blameless Maid,
> Dear Mary!—on her Lap my Head she lay'd—
> Her hand was on my Brow,
>   Even as my own is now;
> And on my Cheek I felt thy Eye-lash play.
> (99–107)

This particularly vivid moment from a week that Coleridge spent at the seaside with the Hutchinson sisters is the kind of intimate scene one does not find in *The Prelude*. Coleridge's notebook account of an earlier week with the Hutchinsons, in 1799, is equally erotically indiscriminate. After taking the month-long walking tour of the Lakes with Wordsworth in October, Coleridge detoured back to London through Sockburn—again, without Wordsworth—and a heavily blotted passage in his Notebook preserves the account of his departure: "I was just about to take Leave of Mary—& having just before taken leave of Sara—. I did not then know Mary's and William's attachment: The lingering Bliss, / the long entrancement of a True-love Kiss" (*Notebooks* 1:1575). The "Letter to Sara" repeatedly disavows any erotic self-interest on Coleridge's part and reassures Sara that it is only her happiness that matters: "Be happy, and I need thee not in sight!" (144). But as the reassurances multiply, and eventually involve not only Sara but "Mary, William and dear Dorothy" in their address, they take on a self-martyring quality: "While ye are well and happy, 'twould but wrong you / If I should fondly yearn to be among you— / Wherefore, O! wherefore, should I wish to be / A wither'd Branch upon a blossoming Tree?" (165–68). As hyperbolically as the poem proclaims a renunciation of the "Delights" it names, it conveys a desire to be "nested with the Darlings of thy Love" (325) in the eroticized bosom of the Wordsworth/Hutchinson household.

Wordsworth's final response in this dialogue with Coleridge occurs in the first extended passage in *The Prelude* that is addressed to Coleridge after his departure for Malta, a passage that revisits the central themes of the most personal exchanges between the two poets—Coleridge's health, the comparative effects of his urban upbringing and Wordsworth's country childhood, and the domestic destinies of the two poets—and, between the lines, settles the matter of their erotic competition. When this passage returns to the 1799 premise that "we by different roads at length have gained / The self-same bourne," it makes a more equivocal statement on the equality of the two men: "I, too, have been a Wanderer: but alas! / How different is the fate of different men / Though Twins almost in genius and in mind!" (6.261–63). When the causes are sought that turned identity "in genius and in mind" into such a difference in "fate," Wordsworth cites the rural/urban theme that, the Sadler's Wells passage suggests, makes some children's lives worth living and others not: Wordsworth grew up among "Rivers, Fields, / And Groves" (274–75), while Coleridge's youthful "mind" was "Debarr'd from Nature's living images, / Compell'd to be a life unto itself" (313–15). The rest of the passage reads as a lament for Coleridge's bad luck. If only the two of them had been at Cambridge at the same time, Wordsworth's "calmer habits, and more steady voice" might have saved Coleridge from the "airy wretchedness" of his youth (323–26); if only Coleridge were healthy, he would be more productive: "health suffers in thee; else / Such grief for thee" would be unnecessary (329–30).

The litany of "if only" is what the Wordsworths were used to from Coleridge by this time; if only the man from Porlock had stopped at the next house, "Kubla Khan" would be a much longer poem. The loss of Coleridge's notes for *The Recluse* may be the most spectacular example of this syndrome. Coleridge claimed to have sent two copies from Malta of his advisory notes on the poem; one was burned when the carrier died of the plague in Gibraltar, and the other was lost when the ship on which it was carried was attacked by pirates (Johnston [819] is skeptical; Holmes [34] is not). Wordsworth eventually decided that the predictability of failure on Coleridge's part was a matter of character rather than circumstance. When he warned Poole of Coleridge's "derangement of intellectual and moral constitution," he had determined that Coleridge was flawed at the core and that no improvement in his circumstances would lead to better results.

It was not always so, and the address to Coleridge in Book Six looks for the origin of Coleridge's "derangement." His urban upbringing had not seemed to be an insuperable problem in 1799, when his childhood in "the great city" had not prevented him from reaching "the self-same bourne" as Wordsworth as "one / The most intense of Nature's worshippers." But the contextual range of the urban reference changes by 1804; the first reference to "the great City" in the 1799 two-book "Prelude" alludes to Coleridge's "Frost at Midnight," where Coleridge speaks of how he was "reared / In the great city" (51–52). The reference in Book Six of the 1805 *Prelude* refers not only to "Frost at Midnight" but to the "Letter to Sara." Wordsworth's description of Coleridge lying "on the leaded Roof / Of that wide Edifice, thy home and School" (6.277–78) echoes Coleridge's lines in the "Letter to Sara" where he speaks of having "often on the leaded School-roof lay" (66). The extended address to Coleridge in Book Six, taken as a whole, locates his fall from genius and equality of mind with Wordsworth not in his ill health, his urban upbringing, or in his innate character, but in his erotic competition with Wordsworth.

The direct address to Coleridge in Book Six begins with a reference to Dorothy as a joint possession of the two poets: "that sole Sister, she who hath been long / Thy Treasure also, thy true friend and mine" (6.214–15). The initial attraction between Coleridge and Dorothy is clear in the letters each wrote immediately after their first meeting in 1797. She wrote to Mary Hutchinson, "You had great loss in not seeing Coleridge. He is a wonderful man. . . . At first I thought him very plain, that is, for about three minutes . . . But if you hear him speak for five minutes you think no more of [it]" (*Letters1* 188–89). Coleridge wrote to Cottle of Dorothy that "She is a woman indeed!—in mind, I mean, & heart—for her person is such, that if you expected to see a pretty woman, you would find her ordinary—if you expected to find an ordinary woman, you would think her pretty!—But her manners are simple, ardent, impressive . . . Her eye watchful in minutest observations of nature—and her taste a perfect electrometer" (CL 1.330–31). The similarities between the two notes are striking. From both sides, it takes only a brief conversation before intellectual affinities bring about a reevaluation of the other's physical appeal. From Dorothy's side, Coleridge is William without the incest taboo, and she makes the comparison between the two; Coleridge, "like William, interests himself so much about every little trifle," and "his animated mind" has "more of 'the poet's eye in a fine frenzy rolling' than I ever witnessed." Coleridge's position is more complicated; he is married, and his letter to Cottle about "Wordsworth & his exquisite sister" is at great pains to deeroticize his description of Dorothy. He describes her qualities of intellect, her "mind," "heart," "manners," "information," "eye," and "taste," but it is clear that he sees her as a better match for himself than the present Mrs. Coleridge.

By the time Coleridge could possibly read the 1804 address to him, Dorothy was no longer a shared possession, "Thy treasure also"; she was securely niched in the Wordsworth/Hutchinson household. As the address to Coleridge leaves the diegetic present of 1804, it signals its return to the mimetic present of 1787 with a temporal shifter—"Now"—that establishes Wordsworth's singular possession of Dorothy: "Now, after separation desolate / Restor'd to me" (6.216–17). The "now" of line 216 is not the "now" of 1804; this "now" refers to the summer of 1787, when William and Dorothy were reunited after their nine-year separation. When Wordsworth speaks of the landscape that may have "seen us sit in many a summer hour" (227), the 1787 setting means that this "us" includes William and Dorothy but not Coleridge. A third figure is soon introduced into the scene, "Another Maid there was, who also breath'd / A gladness o'er that season" (233–34), Mary Hutchinson, who is, like Dorothy, initially marked as a common property: "That other Spirit, Coleridge, who is now / So near to us, that meek confiding heart / So reverenced by us both" (237–39). But even though this "now" returns to the diegetic present of 1804, Mary Hutchinson is not "now

/ So near to . . . us both"—Coleridge is on his way to Malta—unless "us both" once again refers to Dorothy and William but not to Coleridge. The ambiguous pronominal and temporal shifters create a second instance in this address where Coleridge comes tantalizingly close to becoming a joint proprietor with Wordsworth of the Wordsworth/Hutchinson *ménage* but is then excluded.

The passage goes on to reassure Coleridge that his geographic separation from the Wordsworth household is superseded by an imaginative and affective bond that joins him to its members. Although Coleridge was not present on the nature walks of 1787–88, Wordsworth imagines that he was: "O Friend! we had not seen thee at that time; / And yet a power is on me and a strong / Confusion, and I seem to plant Thee there" (246–48). This "Confusion" is brought about, Wordsworth pledges to Coleridge, by the power and the quality of the "love" that binds him to "us":

> But Thou art with us, with us in the past,
> The present, with us in the times to come:
> There is no grief, no sorrow, no despair,
> No languor, no dejection, no dismay,
> No absence scarcely can there be for those
> Who love as we do. Speed thee well!
> (6.251–56)

Since this passage is not only about but addressed to Coleridge, it is worth pondering how he would have read all that is counterfactual in it. Without even putting too much emphasis on the word "dejection," the catalog of "grief," "sorrow," and "despair" would accurately describe Coleridge's state of mind at his departure from England in 1804. He was not, as this passage is at pains to point out, with the Wordsworths and Hutchinsons during those blessed moments "in the past," he is not with them in the present, and, if the consensus on his health were accurate, he would not be with them "in the times to come." Everything in this passage would only underline the differences that had emerged between the equality Wordsworth and Coleridge had shared at the last "Fare thee well" (2.279) in 1799 and the "more" that had fallen to Wordsworth's lot as the greater Man, and the truer Poet, by the time of this "Speed thee well" in 1804.

The premise that an imaginative union is more important than a physical separation recalls the most transparently manipulative moments of the "Letter to Sara," when Coleridge maintains that it is only the happiness of the Wordsworths and Hutchinsons, and not his own affective or erotic interests, that matters to him: "While ye are well and happy, 'twould but wrong you— / If I should fondly yearn to be among you." If this were true, then a reminder that he was not, is not, and will not be "with us" in our happiest moments of the past, present, or future should carry no sting for the magnanimous Coleridge. Wordsworth's promise that an imaginative "love" transcends geographic distance is no truer than Coleridge's claims of disinterestedness in the "Letter to Sara." All that is false in this pledge to Coleridge is false because such a degree of disinterestedness is inhuman. In the real world, as Wordsworth reproached Coleridge for the weakness of character he showed in the "Letter to Sara," "how can He expect that others should / Build for him, sow for him, and at his call / Love him who for himself will take no heed at all"? Wordsworth seems to have predicted Foucault's turn from the technique of the confession to the ethic of the "Care for the Self," but Wordsworth is less sanguine than Foucault about the ethical effects of this practice. Wordsworth agrees with Foucault that "Care for others should not be put before the care of oneself" (EST 287), but The Prelude offers only an equivocal endorsement of Foucault's guarantee that "If you take proper care of yourself correctly, that is, if you know onto-logically what you are . . . you cannot abuse your power over others. Thus, there is no danger" (EST 288). The danger to Coleridge of Wordsworth's practice of taking care of himself is registered in the difference between the wish for Coleridge's health that had been a formality of the farewell in Book Two and the revised version of the formula in Book Six. In the latter instance, Wordsworth describes Coleridge and himself as "Predestin'd, if two beings ever were, / To seek the same delights, and have one health, / One happiness" (6.267–69). "One health" and "one happiness" could mean two very different things: Either these "two beings" will enjoy the same degree of health and happiness, or else there will only be "one health" and "one happiness" to be divided between them. That they are destined to "seek the same delights" is equally ambiguous; are these "delights" the natural beauty of the Lake District or the Hutchinson sisters?

As Wordsworth's "I seem to plant thee there" reminds Coleridge, it could have turned out differently. "Twins almost in genius and in mind," we could have become great Poets and married the Hutchinson sisters—but we didn't. This can be taken as Wordsworth at his most glacial, offering a taunting rejoinder for Coleridge's barbs at Wordsworth's marriage and for his suggestion in the "Letter to Sara" that he thought he could com-pete with Wordsworth for both Sara and Mary Hutchinson. It could also be Wordsworth at his most disillusioned. William, Dorothy, and Coleridge were still close enough in August of 1803 to set out on a tour of Scotland as the old threesome, leaving behind Mary and a two-month-old baby. After two weeks, Coleridge separated from the Wordsworths and made his way back alone. The "strong Confusion" that causes Wordsworth to mix his nature walks with Dorothy and Mary in 1787 and his walking tour of the district with Coleridge in 1799 conflates two moments in Wordsworth's life when "A spirit of pleasure and youth's golden gleam" (6.245) persuaded him that one "spontaneous overflow of powerful feelings" need never conflict with another, but that all could be subsumed within the "beautiful and permanent forms of nature" (LB 157, 156). It did not work out that way, and the worse for Coleridge.

"Coleridge" is a fragmented figure at the conclusion of The Prelude; his greatest accomplishments, the "bright-eyed Mariner" and "Lady Christabel," pale before Wordsworth's epic achievement and finally signify little more than wasted potential while he simultaneously becomes a necessary supplement in a "we" that embodies the moral power of genius to impel a universal spiritual redemption. But as Book Six shows, Coleridge, however close he comes, is never really one of "us." The paradox of Coleridge epitomizes the paradoxical conclusion of The Prelude: the superficial blame cast on others for a failure of moral sublimity does not entirely mask a more intractable problem within the speaker. The poem ends with a gesture toward the generic promise of spiritual autobiography; it wants to believe that its readers, however impaired by circumstance, can be restored to their better natures through the narrator's example. But this formulaic desire is riven by Rousseauean doubts, which produce a Rousseauean decision: Wordsworth only publishes his autobiography posthumously. The easily predictable failure of the publication of The Prelude to produce a general moral renovation in England is rationalized by a misanthropy toward the present. Wordsworth envisions his contemporaries slipping into "idolatry," "servitude," "ignominy," and "shame," and he imagines that it will only be future generations who might be capable of grasping the lessons of his work. If Coleridge was a failure, what hope was there for anyone else? The investment of Poetic identity in posthumous reception reflects Rousseau's choice of writing over speech. As Rousseau complained that since none of his contemporaries ever recognized his real value in his presence, it would be up to the readers of the future to recognize his value and to vindicate him, so Wordsworth imagines that his own work will only truly be appreciated in a more enlightened future. But that hope only occupies the most overt and declarative level of Rousseau's and Wordsworth's texts. Rousseau's terse request at the end of the Marion episode to be "permitted never to speak of this again" and Wordsworth's peremptory declaration on the Cambridge road that "I quit this painful theme—enough is said" (7.436) locate the absence of moral exemplarity in the autobiographer, and they confess the inability of words to repair that lack.

3
"Nothing More Unnatural"

Frankenstein and the Legacy of Rousseau

⋮

FOR all the popularity of *Frankenstein*, the intellectual heft of this book has been persistently underestimated. The usual scapegoating of Victor Frankenstein as the villain of the story for his violations of both natural law and family values flattens the knotty ethical paradoxes Shelley places at the disturbing core of the novel. In her depiction of a creature who is both a universal victim and an indiscriminate terror, Shelley conflates two modes of trauma: victim trauma and guilt trauma. In her portrait of this being's creator, she adds another dimension to this ethical overdetermination. Through the multiple roles she confers on the single parent of this aberrant being—he is the last survivor of his decimated family, the creator of the agent of their destruction, and the betrayer of his own creation—Shelley divides guilt trauma into structural or survivor guilt and perpetrator guilt, and she blocks any straightforward ethical judgment of her main characters even as she makes it impossible to avoid the choices they confront.

These paradoxes have been ironed out in readings of *Frankenstein* that describe the novel as a relatively unconscious reflection of Shelley's personal anxieties or of the immediate cultural forces of her historical moment. Earlier generations of critics stressed the book's singular status in Shelley's *oeuvre*, her age at the time of its composition, her gender, and her companionship with Percy and Lord Byron in order to classify it as something of a "lucky accident" (Joseph v). More recent work that has placed *Frankenstein* in the context of women's literary history has often depicted the novel as a relatively weak assimilation of the cultural forces that impinged on Shelley during its composition. Sandra Gilbert and Susan Gubar's characterization of Shelley's revision of Milton's creation myth as one of her "anxious fantasies" (227) places the work within a specifically literary history, a thesis that was soon supplemented by Mary Poovey's description of Mary Shelley as an exemplary case of a woman writer who succumbed to the cultural demand that she become a "proper lady." The beliefs that Shelley was particularly anxious about her relation to the literary tradition because of her gender, and that she became increasingly concerned to demonstrate her respectability in her later years, have had a significant impact on both scholarly work and wider reading practices. Anne Mellor (1990), Marilyn Butler (1996), and Susan Wolfson (1990) have successfully led the argument that the 1818 first edition of *Frankenstein* is the more authentic version of the novel in its reflection of both Mary Shelley's own convictions and the historical moment of the novel's production. As a result, the 1818 text has become the standard for classroom use; there have been at least six paperback editions of the 1818 *Frankenstein* introduced since 1990, and the three major anthologies of Romantic period literature that include the novel all adopt the 1818 text.[1]

I am going use a series of linked arguments to contest both of the major premises that have informed the recent study of *Frankenstein:* First, that the significance of the novel lies in its immediate reflection of a set of personal anxieties and literary and cultural forces; and, second, that the 1818 edition of *Frankenstein* is therefore the better text of the novel. I will argue (1) that the most significant literary precursor of *Frankenstein* is not Milton but Rousseau; (2) that Mary Shelley did not become increasingly conservative in her later years but that the 1831 revised edition of the novel, far from being a recantation of Shelley's iconoclasm in 1818, extends and elaborates her critique of the erotic hierarchies that simultaneously bind together the social order and turn Victor Frankenstein's creature into a monster; (3) that Shelley's ambivalence about the value of authorship is not a symptom of the problems faced by women authors but is the expression of a powerfully reasoned skepticism about the gap between knowledge and ethics; (4) that Shelley's identification of that gap emerges from the conflation of victim trauma and guilt trauma; (5) that *Frankenstein* becomes a highly autobiographical text as Shelley takes her own traumatic state as exemplary of an ethically responsible subjectivity, one that is able to recognize ethical dilemmas that are ordinarily repressed; (6) that the creature who embodies the conflation of victim trauma and guilt trauma becomes a privileged point of access to the perception of social processes ordinarily veiled by cultural mystifications; and (7) that it is impossible to say whether Victor Frankenstein's actions are right or wrong.

While Rousseau's name is never mentioned in *Frankenstein*, the depth of Shelley's interest in his life and ideas is displayed in her 1838 essay on his life and works, written for Dionysus Lardner's *Cabinet Cyclopedia*. In this essay, Shelley discusses Rousseau's concept of the "natural man" and, in an image that has as much relevance to *Frankenstein* as it does to Rousseau, offers her judgment that "nothing could be more unnatural than his natural man" ("Rousseau" 337). The production of Rousseau's "unnatural man," Shelley contends, emerges from the gap between Rousseau's ideals and their inefficacy in his life. In Shelley's account of Rousseau, she reprises Victor Frankenstein's lament that "I had begun life with benevolent intentions" yet "I had committed deeds of mischief beyond description horrible."[2] As Shelley describes Rousseau, he is "full of genius and aspiration after virtue," but ultimately he "failed in the plainest dictates of nature and conscience" (334). Shelley's judgment thus distills the thesis that launched Rousseau's career when he composed the *First Discourse* in response to the question posed by the Dijon Academy in 1750 of "Whether restoration of the Sciences and Arts has contributed to the purification of morals." Shelley brings this contradiction between pure and practical knowledge to bear on Rousseau himself, "a man so richly gifted with talent." When she writes of the rows that occurred among Rousseau, Diderot, Grimm and Madame d'Epinay, she concludes that these "People of refinement, of education, and genius" had, in their petty jealousies, only succeeded in presenting "to all the world, and to posterity, so humbling a proof of the worthlessness of talent in directing the common concerns of life" (346). Her cool disregard for the social status of Rousseau's circle contradicts the picture drawn of Shelley in her own time by Trelawny and revived by Poovey, who depict her as someone who fawns over social status and is timid in her own judgments.

The confident, judgmental tone of the Rousseau essay also appears in an important journal entry written by Shelley in the same year. This entry, in which Shelley defends herself against Trelawny's accusations that her political inaction was a betrayal of Percy's legacy, has been quoted selectively by Poovey to make the case for Shelley's "stereotypical feminine reticence" (115). In a phrase cited by Poovey that has a particular resonance for *Frankenstein* because it echoes the claim in the 1831 "Introduction" that "I am very averse to bringing myself forward in print" (360), Shelley laments that one reason for her political inaction is that she is incapable of "putting myself forward" (*MWSJournals* 559). But the entire 1838 journal entry is not similarly constrained. After a passage in which Shelley observes that "some have a passion for reforming the world: others do not cling to particular opinions," and "that my Parents & Shelley were of the former class makes me respect it," she goes on to say (in a passage elided by Poovey) that "my accusers—after such as these—appear to me mere drivellers" (553). In the rest of the diary entry, Shelley makes it clear that she believes she has maintained her allegiance not only to her parents and Percy but to the principles of the "good Cause" in her own way: "If I have never written to vindicate the Rights of women, I have ever befriended women when oppressed—at every risk I have defended & supported victims to the social system" (557). In contrast to Poovey's assertion that by the time of the 1831 edition of *Frankenstein* Shelley is "eager to disavow . . . the audacity" of "the defiant, self-assertive girl" (137) of 1818, Shelley herself writes in 1838 that "as I grow older I grow more fearless for myself—I become firmer in my opinions" (557).

In this journal entry, Shelley first classes herself among those who "do not cling to particular opinions," and yet she goes on to assert that she has "become firmer in my opinions." This seeming paradox is based in her explanation of why she has not become a more polemical writer: "I feel the counter arguments too strongly" (554). Shelley attributes her characteristic ambivalence not to a fear of social pressures but to an unwillingness to relinquish her own doubts. Near the end of this entry, she brings this relentless skepticism to bear on herself when she writes, "Thus have I put down my thoughts—I may have deceived myself—I may be vain—I may be in the wrong. I try to examine myself—& such as I have written appears to me the exact truth" (557). Written in the same year as her essay on Rousseau, this summary statement is Shelley's revision of Rousseau's conclusion to the *Confessions:* "I have told the truth. If anyone knows some things contrary to what I have said, even if they are proven a thousand times, he knows lies and impostures. . . . Anyone who . . . is capable of believing that I am a dishonest man, is himself a man fit to be stifled" (550). Shelley takes from her reading of Rousseau the imperative for scrupulous self-examination, but she also sees in Rousseau's failings the difficulty of this enterprise and the necessity of being less certain than Rousseau about the reliability of ethical self-evaluation.

Shelley is withering in her judgments of Rousseau's greatest offenses, particularly his abandonment of his children. Of this, she writes,

> Even in his Confessions, where Rousseau discloses his secret errors, he by no means appreciates the real extent of his misconduct on this occasion. . . . Five of his children were thus sent to a receptacle where few survive; and those who do go through life are brutified by their

situation, or depressed by the burden, ever weighing at the heart, that they have not inherited the commonest right of humanity, a parent's care. (334)

Never mitigating Rousseau's guilt, Shelley nevertheless takes his conduct not as a sign of his aberrance but as a cautionary tale: "It is insulting the reader to dwell on the flagrancy of this act. But it is a lesson that ought to teach us humility. That a man as full of genius and aspiration after virtue as Rousseau, should have failed in the plainest dictates of nature and conscience . . . shows us how little we can rely on our own judgment" (334). In her journal entry and in her essay on "Rousseau," Shelley's ambivalence does not manifest itself in a reticence or in a constricted range of judgment; it produces the emphatic expression of both poles of "counter arguments." Writing on Rousseau, she speaks of the "flagrancy of this act," yet she calls Rousseau himself a man "full of genius and aspiration after virtue." Shelley brings the lesson of humility that she derives from her reading of Rousseau to bear on her self-analysis when she admits that "I may have deceived myself—I may be vain—I may be in the wrong," but she nevertheless asserts her confidence that she is more honest than her accusers, who are "mere drivellers."

The seeming contradictions in Shelley's account of Rousseau are brought into focus in her portrait of a figure who is himself divided by guilt. As Shelley brings her essay on Rousseau to a close, she reiterates her charge that Rousseau "neglected the first duty of man by abandoning his children," and she speculates that "this crime, rankling at his heart, engendered much of the misery that he charged upon his fellow-creatures" (365). But the essay concludes in a very different key, as Shelley compares Rousseau, to his advantage, with Voltaire, who had been the subject of the preceding essay:

No author knows better than Rousseau how to spread a charm over the internal movements of the mind, over the struggles of passion, over romantic reveries that absorb the soul, abstracting it from real life and our fellow-creatures, and causing it to find its joys in itself. No author is more eloquent in paradox, and no man more sublime in inculcating virtue. While Voltaire taints and degrades all that is sacred and lovely by the grossness of his imagination, Rousseau embellishes even the impure, by painting it in colours that hide its real nature; and imparts to the emotions of sense all the elevation and intensity of delicate and exalted passion. (366)

Shelley's own eloquence in paradox is manifestly on display in this passage. After Rousseau is condemned for having "neglected the first duty of man by abandoning his children," what is the value of "romantic reveries that absorb the soul, abstracting it from real life and our fellow-creatures"? Can it be said of the same man that he "neglected the first duty of man" and that "no man [is] more sublime in inculcating virtue"? Does Shelley approve of Rousseau's ability to "embellish even the impure"? When this is described as "painting it in colours that hide its real nature" this would seem to be pure deception, but the final clause seems to valorize, through its stylistic choices, the "elevation and intensity of delicate and exalted passion."

In Shelley's reading of Rousseau, the guilt produced by the gap between his ideals and his actions not only informs Rousseau's autobiographical writings and accounts for his persecution complexes; this guilt disfigures even his broadest and most influential philosophical theses. In the most stunning critical insight of the essay, Shelley argues that Rousseau's adoption of the primitivist thesis of the solitary "natural man" is simply a rationalization of his abandonment of his children: "Poor Rousseau, who had thrust his offspring from parental care to the niggard benevolence of a public charity, found some balm to the remorse that now and then stung him, by rejecting the affections out of his scheme of the state of natural man" (337). Here Shelley extends Wollstonecraft's objection to Rousseau's claim that man is solitary in the state of nature. Where Wollstonecraft challenges Rousseau's anthropological speculations with one of her own, arguing that "he disputes whether man be a gregarious animal, though the long and helpless state of infancy seems to point him out as particularly impelled to pair, the first step towards herding" (*Vindication* 75), Shelley goes beyond this superficial objection when she locates the appeal of the idea of the natural man for Rousseau in his sense of guilt. When Rousseau asserts that it is simply natural to be a lone individual, he finds a justification for his paternal neglect, but his "natural man" becomes, Shelley argues, quintessentially unnatural. It is precisely because Rousseau's scrupulousness in principle was powerful enough to drive him mad that his writing takes on its deformed shape.

Shelley's warning that the *Confessions* is "an invaluable book, that discloses the secrets of many hearts to those who have courage to penetrate into the recesses of their own" (330) identifies a formative principle in the production of *Frankenstein*. Just as Rousseau's work, for all his talent and "aspiration after virtue," is twisted by guilt, making the natural unnatural, so Shelley's own "hideous" production is shaped by a double trauma: the ambiguous victim and guilt trauma manifested in her 1815 dream of her dead baby, and the guilt trauma occasioned by the suicide of Harriet Shelley. The 1831 identification of *Frankenstein* as "my hideous progeny" (365) answers the question posed by Shelley's publishers, "How I, then a young girl, came to dilate upon so hideous an idea" (360) with an echoing image of "hideous" deformity. The inflation of the pathetic infant into a monstrous avenger depends on the force of guilt, a process articulated in Rousseau's principle that "remorse sleeps while fate is kind but grows sharp in adversity." Shelley adopts Rousseau's use of the figure of personification to describe how misfortunes become torments; as Rousseau's sense of guilt "deprives me of that sweet consolation which the innocent feel under persecution" his sufferings become Marion's avengers: "Poor Marion finds so many avengers in this world" in the "many misfortunes that have overwhelmed the end of my life" (*Confessions* 71). Shelley concludes her encyclopedia account of the Marion story with an image that hauntingly echoes the doppelganger imagery of *Frankenstein*. Victor laments, "The fiend followed me," and he attributes this to his own sense of guilt: "I felt I had committed some great crime" (189). In Shelley's summary of the Marion episode, she pronounces, "This is one of the laws of life. The shadows of our past actions stalk beside us during our existence, and never cease to torment or to soothe, according as they are ill or good, that mysterious portion of mind termed conscience" ("Rousseau" 326). In Mary Shelley's life, Harriet Shelley became her Marion. Shelley writes of Marion and Rousseau in 1838 that "the thought of his victim driven to want and infamy by his lie made him often look on his after sufferings as but the just retribution of his crime" (326). A year later, in the midst of a row with Trelawny over the excision of a passage dedicated to Harriet Shelley in Mary Shelley's edition of Percy's poems, she writes in her journal of "Poor Harriet to whose sad fate I attribute so many of my own heavy sorrows as the atonement claimed by fate for her death" (560). The ability of a young girl to imagine the hideous forms of *Frankenstein* derives from Mary Shelley's awareness that, like Rousseau, and despite her best intentions, she had become a deadly presence in the lives of others.

The 1831 Introduction to the third edition of *Frankenstein* is often produced as the primary evidence of Shelley's self-deprecating character in her later years. Her assertion that "I am very averse to bringing myself forward in print" and the hyperbolic praise of Byron and Percy have led to a perception that the Introduction is not only an apology for the novel written thirteen years earlier but an admission of Shelley's "deep-seated conviction of literary inadequacy" and her acquiescence in Percy's "opinion of her inferior literary abilities" (Mellor, *Shelley*, 69). The famous description of the "waking dream" (365), in which Shelley describes her first vision of the creature coming to life, has encouraged a view of the novel as a brilliant but only semiconscious fantasy and of its creator as a momentarily inspired but not particularly thoughtful transmitter of mythic material. But the rhetorical diffidence of the entire Introduction has been consistently misread as deferential when it is often ironic. It has been assumed too easily that this Introduction honors the distinction between the fictional text of *Frankenstein* and its own presumptive status as a nonfictional comment on that text. Despite the agreeable tone of the opening in which Shelley asserts that she is "the more willing to comply" with her publishers' "wish that I should furnish them with some account of the origin of the story," because "I shall thus give a general answer to the question, so very frequently asked me" (360), it should be considered how little the 1831 Introduction ever actually complies with this request. The diverting tale of the ghost story competition and the waking dream obscure the fact that for this highly allusive novel, which is woven out of a wide network of literary, political, and personal concerns, there are virtually no references in this Introduction to the vast amount of source material so assiduously recovered by modern scholarship. There are glancing references to German ghost stories, *Don Quixote*, and Hindu myth, but there is no mention of Milton or of Rousseau. Despite the novel's dedication to Godwin, there is no acknowledgment of the convention, common from the 1790s, of using the image of a monster who has escaped the control of his creator as a caricature of the effect of Godwin's political writings; the political significance of Shelley's use of this image remains unexplained.[3] And despite the transformation of Shelley's 1815 dream of reviving her dead infant into Victor Frankenstein's dream of the creature's vivification, the Introduction presents the novel as a product of "happy days, when death and grief were but words, which found no true echo in my heart" (365), thus seeming to foreclose any connection between the horror story of *Frankenstein* and the death of Shelley's infant daughter or with the suicides of Fanny Imlay and Harriet Shelley.

The reason for this reticence is easy to find in the overly compliant tone with which the Introduction begins. The seeming tractability of an author who is "the more willing" to answer a question because it has been "so very frequently asked me" over a period of thirteen years can hardly be taken at face value. The thirteen-year history suggests both the persistence of the questioners and the resistance of the figure "so very frequently asked." The lurid form in which Shelley phrases the question, "How I, then a young girl, came to think of, and to dilate upon, so very hideous an idea?" signals her understanding of who is really being sought through this insistent question: not the Mary Shelley of 1831, the author whose work is being reprinted as part of the Standard Novels, but the Mary Shelley of 1818, the "young girl" who, according to the rumor mill of the time, had been sold by her atheist father to an atheist poet whom she had estranged from his lawful wife. The "young girl" from whom Mary Shelley distances herself is not a more audacious self, but the fictive figure constructed in the public imagination out of young Mary Godwin's role in a scandal involving adultery, atheism, an abandoned wife, illegitimate children, and suicide among radical intellectuals.

The commercial value of a retrospective personal statement from the intimate companion of Percy Shelley and Lord Byron, and the author of the most sensational literary work to emerge from the notorious Diodati *ménage*, would be undeniable, but the fulsome terms in which Shelley describes "the illustrious poets" offers her readers only the best of what they already know of these figures. Byron's work is "clothed in all the light and harmony of poetry," and "seemed to stamp as divine the glories of heaven and earth"; Percy is "apt to embody ideas and sentiments in the radiance of brilliant imagery, and in the music of the most melodious verse that adorns our language" (361–62). This hyperbolic praise has convinced some readers of Shelley's sense of inferiority in the face of "her models, almost all masculine, [who] are both intimidating and potentially judgmental of her audacious foray into their domain" (Poovey 139–40), but the stylistic range of the Introduction offers another, richer possibility. The glowing testimonials to the famous poets are repeatedly undermined by the immediate descent into a lower stylistic register, where the rhetorical contrast and the dry wit of the plainer prose are apt to make the more elevated phrases seem not just conventional but too neatly formulaic. From the nearly worshipful description of Byron's poetic powers ensues a far more banal observation about the rain, although there is no obvious connection between the two:

> Lord Byron, who was writing the third canto of Childe Harold, was the only one among us who put his thoughts upon paper. These, as he brought them successively to us, clothed in all the light and harmony of poetry, seemed to stamp as divine the glories of heaven and earth, whose influences we partook with him.
>
> But it proved a wet, ungenial summer, and incessant rain often confined us for days to the house. (361)

In other words, all the "glories of heaven and earth" evoked by Byron's poetry cannot overcome Shelley's memory that it rained a lot that summer.

This in itself might not seem like a deliberate deflation of Byronic glory were it not that the same effect is immediately recreated, in a more elaborate form, in the account of the failures of all three of Shelley's competitors in the ghost story contest. The report of Byron's, Percy's, and Polidori's efforts in the ghost story competition casts Polidori as the buffoon in comparison to the brilliant Byron and Percy, but the praise lavished on Percy's poetic talent rings hollow at the end of the story where, for all of his genius, he turns out to be incapable of fulfilling the rhetorical challenge of imagining "a story to rival those which had excited us to the task" (363), and the only successful participant in the contest reappears in terms as unobtrusive as the rainy day that counterpointed Byron's divine poetic powers:

> "We will each write a ghost story," said Lord Byron; and his proposition was acceded to. There were four of us. The noble author began a tale, a fragment of which he printed at the end of his poem of Mazeppa. Shelley, more apt to embody ideas and sentiments in the radiance of brilliant imagery, and in the music of the most melodious verse that adorns our language, than to invent the machinery of a story, commenced one founded on the experiences of his early life. Poor Polidori had some terrible idea about a skull-headed lady, who was so punished for peeping through a key-hole—what to see I forget—something very shocking and wrong of course; but when she was reduced to a worse condition than the renowned Tom of Coventry, he did not know what to do with her, and was obliged to despatch her to the tomb of the Capulets, the only place for which she was fitted. The illustrious poets also, annoyed by the platitude of prose, speedily relinquished their uncongenial task.
>
> I busied myself to think of a story. (362–63; Shelley's emphasis)

The stylistic shifts in this passage are clearly demarcated. It begins on the high side; not "we agreed," but "his proposition was acceded to." Of the "four of us," the "noble author" will properly claim the first place, and Byron's partial success ("a fragment") is politely acknowledged. The level of the diction rises considerably during the description of the second genius, Percy, and it drops sharply when we come to "Poor Polidori," whose ineptness is the stuff of low comedy registered in an extremely chatty style. The reinflation of the prose when the passage returns to "the illustrious poets" does not obscure the bottom line of the narrative: Neither Byron nor

Percy successfully wrote a ghost story. Shelley connects this failure to a stylistic issue; they were "annoyed by the platitude of prose," a difficulty that was overcome by the only member of the company who was able to think in plain prose terms. Thanks to Anne Mellor's meticulous comparative study of Mary Shelley's original manuscript of *Frankenstein* with the revisions added by Percy, we can see that the more elevated diction here ("the radiance of brilliant imagery" etc.) reflects Percy's, rather than Mary Shelley's, characteristic prose style. When Mary Shelley wrote "a long time passed" in the original manuscript of *Frankenstein*, Percy revised it into "a considerable period elapsed"; Mary Shelley's "we were all equal" became, after Percy's help, "neither of us possessed the slightest pre-eminence over the other," and the text of *Frankenstein* contains hundreds of such emendations.[4]

The perfectly conventional, even cliched, rhetoric in which Percy Shelley and Byron are fulsomely praised indicates nothing so simple as an unconscious hostility toward Percy or Byron. The sheer conventionality of the praise serves a double purpose: On a surface level, its opacity enables Shelley to situate herself as a public figure offering praise for other authors of her acquaintance rather than as a participant in a scandalous *ménage*; in a less direct way, the critical distance afforded by the ironic edge of the overblown prose allows Shelley to make the difference between her own storytelling abilities and the poetic imaginations of Byron and Percy an ambiguous hierarchy and not one that automatically privileges the "illustrious poets."[5] When Shelley describes as a breakthrough her realization that "every thing must have a beginning, to speak in Sanchean phrase," she casts herself as the plainspoken Sancho Panza to the quixotic, ineffectual poets.

The elegant evasiveness of the 1831 Introduction is maintained through the construction of a rhetorical tour de force that keeps its readers sufficiently entertained not to notice that the question they have "so very frequently asked" Mary Shelley is never really being answered. Shelley knew that her own celebrity depended not only on her connections with Percy and Byron but with her radical parentage, and the opening of the second paragraph of the Introduction seems to offer the public what it expects: "It is not singular that, as the daughter of two persons of distinguished literary celebrity, I should very early in life have thought of writing. As a child I scribbled; and my favourite pastime, during the hours given to me for recreation, was to 'write stories'" (360). The allusion to Wollstonecraft and Godwin evokes the familial context in which the British public is used to thinking about Mary Wollstonecraft Godwin Shelley, and the immediate transition from the invocation of her parentage to the description of her juvenile writings certainly seems to suggest that the groundwork for the precocious success of *Frankenstein* was prepared by Shelley's childhood training in a literary household. The rest of the paragraph contradicts this story. It says that the origin of *Frankenstein* does not derive from Shelley's early scribblings but from something more ephemeral and private, her childhood daydreams: "Still I had a dearer pleasure than this, which was the formation of castles in the air—the indulging in waking dreams. . . . My dreams were at once more fantastic and agreeable than my writings. In the latter I was a close imitator—rather doing as others had done, than putting down suggestions of my own mind. What I wrote was intended at least for one other eye . . . but my dreams were all my own" (360). The distinction between Shelley's purely imitative childhood writings and her more "fantastic" and original "waking dreams" suggests that the novel owes its origin not to her first scribblings but to these secret fantasies. When the latter part of the Introduction tells us that the origin of *Frankenstein* is "a transcript of the grim terrors of my waking dream" (365), the reiteration of the term "waking dream" seems to confirm that the novel originates in these solitary imaginings. But this very distinction between the public nature of her writings, "intended at least for one other eye" and the private quality of these "waking dreams," which were "all my own," also cautions us that this author is not likely to give an explicit answer to the question of "How I, then a young girl, came to think of, and to dilate upon, so very hideous an idea." These "waking dreams" are not public property: "I accounted for them to nobody; they were my refuge when annoyed—my dearest pleasure when free" (360). This reserved and courteous figure does not confront her publisher with a direct refusal when she is asked to bare her soul before the British reading public, but neither does she open her private life for public viewing.

The next paragraph of the Introduction moves off to Scotland in order to restate the distinction between the author's imitative adolescent writings ("I wrote then—but in a most common-place style") and her "true compositions, the airy flights of my imagination," but it makes no mention of why Mary Godwin spent so much time in Scotland. The impersonal 1818 Dedication (retained in 1831) to "the Author of Political Justice, Caleb Williams, &c" suggests that Godwin's self-absorption contributes to the portrait of Victor Frankenstein, but the 1831 Introduction never mentions Godwin's name, and it gives no inkling that Shelley's periods of adolescent exile in Scotland had anything to do with Godwin's convenience in establishing his new household after his remarriage to Mary Jane Clairmont.

The opening paragraphs of the 1831 Introduction to *Frankenstein* quickly become, without warning, a brief narrative of Shelley's entire (including prenatal) life, but the transition from Scotland to Switzerland, and the most famous events in the life of the "young girl" Mary Godwin, are bypassed in terms laconic in the extreme: "After this my life became busier," and "Travelling, and the cares of a family, occupied my time" (361). The withholding of comment on the period of her life that had become so notorious and "so very frequently" inquired about is more firm than anxious in its deflection of public scrutiny. When Mary Shelley places herself in the lineage of "my Parents and Shelley" in the Introduction, she produces one of the quietest but most definitive moments of self-representation in the entire essay: "My husband, however, was from the first, very anxious that I should prove myself worthy of my parentage, and enrol myself on the page of fame. He was for ever inciting me to obtain literary reputation, which even on my own part I cared for then, though since I have become infinitely indifferent to it" (361). The rhetorical choices in this passage are precise; to be "infinitely indifferent" shades off from more familiar phrases like "completely indifferent" or "absolutely indifferent" to become both more alliteratively elegant and more emphatic, and the noticeable originality of the phrase stands out from its immediate context. Someone who writes of being "infinitely indifferent" cannot be oblivious to the tiredness of the metaphor "the page of fame." The aspiration to an elevated literary style collapses into cliche, but the next sentence declares the triviality of such merely artistic aspirations. It does so with some panache, however, and it is just as Shelley herself emerges from the shadow of her parents and her husband that the passage acquires a style of its own. When one looks back from "though since I have become infinitely indifferent to it" to "which even on my own part I cared for then," even that plain phrase takes on an abyssal quality something like Wordsworth's retrospective sense "of myself / And of some other Being" (*Prelude* 2.32–33).

The core of the 1831 Introduction is Shelley's report of the "waking dream" that enabled her to "think of a story," a report that has been universally accepted as a factual account of the origin of *Frankenstein*. But it is far more likely that this story about a nightmare is a fictional deflection of the demand to account for her ability to "dilate upon, so very hideous an idea." The entire 1831 Introduction is blithely unreliable even about things that are falsifiable, such as the claim that "I have changed no portion of the story, nor introduced any new ideas or circumstances" (366). When the Broadview edition of the novel prints the substantive variants from the 1831 edition in an appendix, the appendix takes up forty-two pages. There is no extant journal for June 1816 and no documented reference to this "waking dream" before it appears in the 1831 Introduction. The shifting point of view within the dream, which slides from Shelley's perception of Victor Frankenstein kneeling beside his creation ("I saw") to the viewpoint of Victor himself ("he sees") awakening to see the nightmare figure standing beside his bed, introduces a literary device that is commonly employed to subvert realism. When a fictional character, such as this "pale student of unhallowed arts," awakens to find a supernatural being standing at his bedside, our confinement within his perception makes it impossible for us to know whether we are meant to believe that he has really awakened or if he is supposed to be dreaming this impossible event. The passage shifts from factual claims to hypotheses and back to assertions of fact; after using the phrase "I saw" three times to assert the visual presence of both "the pale student of unhallowed arts" and his "hideous phantasm," Shelley begins to imagine what "would" happen: "His success *would* terrify the artist; he *would* rush away. . . . He *would* hope . . . that this thing . . . *would* subside into dead matter; and he *might* sleep." After this series of five hypotheticals (four "woulds" and a "might"), Shelley employs present tense verbs to reassert the ocular presence of her vision:

> He sleeps; but he is awakened; he opens his eyes; behold the horrid thing stands at his bedside, opening the curtains, and looking on him with yellow, watery, but speculative eyes.
> I opened mine in terror. (365)

The prose here is too nicely worked to be simply mimetic. The paragraph shift is deft; we leave the nightmare scene as the creature's "speculative eyes" give way to "mine." The apostrophe to the reader—"behold the horrid thing"—is a bit too gothic to be entirely serious, and it is also a stylistic coup; the apostrophic "behold" strains against the mimetic frame of the vision and puts a momentary stress on the syntax of the sentence before "the horrid thing" slides from the object of "behold" into the subject of a declarative clause: "the horrid thing stands at his bedside."

Some version of this scene in which one figure views, and usually tries to revive, another who stands on the border between life and death occurs thirteen times within the text of *Frankenstein*.[6] As Ellen Moers was the first to point out, this terrifying scene reflects the most powerful dream image that is recorded in Shelley's journal in 1815: "Dream that my little baby came to life again—that it had only been cold & that we rubbed it by the fire & it lived" (*Journal* 70). The question that should have been asked by now is whether the account of Victor Frankenstein's dream in chapter 4 of *Frankenstein* emerges from two nightmares, one that occurred in 1815 in London and a second in 1816 at Diodati, or if the central story of the 1831 Introduction is the fourteenth fictional version of the 1815 dream. The evidence strongly favors the latter hypothesis. The evasiveness of the entire Introduction on the most notorious period of Shelley's life, where her laconic comments that "life became busier," and "travelling, and the cares of a family, occupied my time" stand as the only accounts of a period in which freethinking and erotic experimentation led to two suicides and the death of a premature infant, do not suggest that this author is being entirely forthcoming about her private sorrows. Even the first hypothesis, which allows for two nightmares, involves the suppression of the first dream in the public forum of the 1831 Introduction. If we begin to understand how persistently oblique Shelley is throughout this essay about the genesis of her "hideous progeny," we can grasp the metaphoric valence of the moment in which "a piece of vermicelli. . . began to move with voluntary motion." Shelley's concern with the "principle of life" is not an abstraction, and she is not particularly interested in spaghetti. The "voluntary motion" of the vermicelli is a figure for the revival of her dead infant.

The repeated and ambiguous use of the word "might" in 1831 indicates that the account of the waking dream in the 1831 Introduction is not literally mimetic, and that it serves as a supplementary explanation of the imagery of the novel rather than as an account of its genesis. Victor's horrified response to the first signs of the creature's vivification leads to an odd decision that is not very well explained within the novel. Victor tells Walton that he is "unable to endure the aspect of the being I had created," so he leaves the room and goes to sleep, in order, he says, "to seek a few moments of forgetfulness" (86). Taking a nap would not be the first response one would expect from someone who has seen an enormous being of his own creation come to life, but the 1831 Introduction offers a more profound explanation for this behavior than the desire for "a few moments of forgetfulness." In the Introduction, Shelley speculates that "he might sleep in the belief that the silence of the grave would quench for ever the transient existence of the hideous corpse which he had looked upon as the cradle of life" (364–65). The "might" here slips from the simple meaning of a possibility and reaches toward a sense of ethical allowance: Victor hopes he might be allowed to believe that he has not committed a terrifyingly destructive act; that it might all be as unreal as a dream.

The first repetition of the 1815 dream in the novel is also the one that most closely echoes Shelley's journal entry; when Walton and his men pull Victor from the frozen sea, they "restored him to animation by rubbing him with brandy" (58). The following versions of this scene are not always so successful. The next instance portrays a grotesquely prolonged, inverted, and failed pregnancy involving Caroline Beaufort and her father that ends when "in the tenth month her father died in her arms" (64). The novel's central scene, the vivification of the creature, and its conclusion show how easily the roles played in this dyadic structure can be reversed. In the creation scene of chapter 4, Victor wields the power of life and death over the creature: "I collected the instruments of life around me, that I might infuse a spark of being into the lifeless thing that lay at my feet. . . . I saw the dull yellow eye of the creature open; it breathed hard, and a convulsive motion agitated its limbs" (85). But in the novel's final chapter, Walton finds Victor reduced to inanimate matter and the creature hovering over him: "I entered the cabin, where lay the remains of my ill-fated and admirable friend. Over him hung a form which I cannot find words to describe; gigantic in stature, yet uncouth and distorted in its proportions" (242). Victor's transformation from the one who controls the principle of life to one who succumbs to the power of death shows how much of the terror of this scene derives from the fact that the roles of survivor and victim are always in danger of being reversed. Moers was the first to locate the origin of this terrifying chiasmus of birthbed/deathbed in Shelley's own life, specifically in the death of her first infant and in the death of Wollstonecraft at Shelley's birth. The obsessive repetition of this scene throughout the novel points it out as a classic traumatic structure, but the variations Shelley adopts show something far more elaborate than a series of unsuccessful attempts at working through a traumatic event. In the fourteen variations on the central creation scene of *Frankenstein*, Shelley explores the uncertain boundaries that only imperfectly distinguish between victim trauma, structural or survivor guilt, and perpetrator guilt.

The difficulty of distinguishing victims and perpetrators emerges from the gap between intentions and acts; the resulting moral problematic is, for Shelley, a Rousseauean legacy. Whenever Rousseau tries to evade the damage he has done to others, he resorts to the assertion that he never meant to harm anyone, but this rationalization is never entirely successful. The *Confessions* ends with the enigmatic assertion that anyone who claims to know anything contrary to what Rousseau has said, "though he can prove it a thousand times," or who will claim that Rousseau himself is dishonest, should be "stifled." Clearly, the demand for the suppression of evidence does not refute the existence of things that can be proven a thousand times. Both Victor and the creature find a similarly inexplicable gap between the benevolence of their intentions and the outcome of their actions; Victor is stunned to discover that "I wandered like an evil spirit, for I had committed deeds of mischief beyond description horrible, and more, much more (I persuaded myself) was yet behind. Yet my heart overflowed with kindness, and the love of virtue. I had begun life with benevolent intentions, and thirsted for the moment when I should put them in practice, and make myself useful to my fellow-beings" (119). The creature's transformation from a figure who is born "benevolent and good" (128), is nonetheless universally despised, and who turns into the murderer of a child traces this arc from victimization to guilt, but it offers no causal explanation that corresponds in clarity to the moral categories of right and wrong.

Frankenstein is commonly read as a melodrama with clearly defined moral values: Egotism is bad, empathy is good, and Victor is the villain of the piece, the "active author of evil" (Mellor, Shelley 174) for his egotistic self-absorption and neglect of family values. But the gothic scale of Frankenstein leaves the exact nature of Victor's horrible crime ill-defined. Victor is often blamed for spending too much time on his scientific experiments and communicating too little with his family during his college years, but considering that he is working on the principle of life, the "active author of evil" seems a little strong for an unmarried workaholic with no children. Victor perceives his refusal to create a partner for the creature as a sacrifice of his own interests for the protection of humanity at large; blaming himself for the deaths of William, Justine, and Clerval, he tells his father, "A thousand times would I have shed my own blood, drop by drop, to have saved their lives; but I could not, my father, indeed I could not sacrifice the whole human race" (211). The creature's vendetta against the Frankensteins is his revenge for Victor's destruction of his half-formed partner, but Victor claims that he must weigh the private interests of the Frankenstein family against the potential harm to "the whole human race" (211) of a perpetual conflict with a new breed of outcasts. Victor's desire for public glory and his fantasy about the "gratitude" that would be owed to him by his "new species" (82) are often adduced as signs of his excessive egotism, but Victor's motives for investigating the principle of life are given by Shelley as an inextricable mixture of egotism and altruism. Victor imagines that he might not only "bestow animation upon lifeless matter," but that he could go on to "renew life where death had apparently devoted the body to corruption" (83). The primary body in question here is that of Caroline Frankenstein; in Victor's dream, he imagines that "I held the corpse of my dead mother in my arms; a shroud enveloped her form, and I saw the grave-worms crawling in the folds of the flannel" (85). As Victor's fantasy of renewing the life of someone dear to him echoes Shelley's "Dream that my little baby came to life again," it becomes impossible to separate Victor's grandest fantasy from Shelley's own most intimate and empathic desire.

The politics of *Frankenstein* are bound to its representation of domesticity; the creature's murders invoke the revenge of the Jacobin mob, while his haunting of Victor represents Rousseau's children carrying out their revenge on their negligent father (Victor's home town is Geneva) through the vehicle of guilt. But Shelley's talent for "counter argument" makes it impossible to identify her with the anti-intellectualism of family values. Victor's fantasy of the abolition of mortality finds its most impersonal and expansive form in Godwin's *Enquiry Concerning Human Justice*, where Godwin's utopian imaginings lead him to speculate that the scientific process of perfectibility might one day lead to the immortality of the human species and hence to the end of the nuclear family. As Shelley writes in her 1838 journal entry, the "passion for reforming the world" in "my Parents & Shelley . . . makes me respect it," and the opening to her essay on Rousseau is a masterpiece of equivocation on the form of egotism that marks "my parents & Shelley" and Victor Frankenstein. Shelley writes of Voltaire and Rousseau that they "possessed but one quality in common . . . that lively and intimate apprehension of their own individuality, sensations, and being, which appears to be one of the elements of that order of minds which feel impelled to express their thoughts and disseminate their view and opinions through the medium of writing;—men of imagination, and eloquence and mental energy." But her assessment of this quality is marked by an uncertainty that hardly fits the genre of the encyclopedia entry: "It is difficult to know what to call it. In ordinary men it would be named egotism, or vanity" (320). In a letter written contemporaneously with the composition of *Frankenstein*, Shelley signaled her allegiance to the most important historical effect of Rousseau's writings; echoing the proverbial identification of the Revolution as "*la faute de Voltaire et Rousseau*," Shelley praises the "revolution, which his [Rousseau's] writings contributed mainly to mature," and argues that "notwithstanding the temporary bloodshed and injustice with which it was polluted, it has produced enduring benefits to mankind, which not all the chicanery of statesmen, nor even the greatest conspiracy of kings, can entirely render vain" (*Letters* 1.20). This judgment is neither reiterated nor recanted in the essay written twenty years later, in which Shelley offers only her equivocal respect for Rousseau's motives. Her ambivalence toward those whose recognition of their own genius results in a "passion for reforming the world" remained constant throughout her life, and Rousseau serves as the prototype for the trait that recurred in her parents and her husband and that found its fictional embodiment in Victor Frankenstein.

The flip side of the vilification of Victor Frankenstein is a common assertion of Shelley's investment in the ideology of domesticity. In two of the more sophisticated versions of this argument, Kate Ellis argues that Shelley prizes the spirit of "domestic affection" (*Frankenstein* 48) and shows how that spirit is rendered ineffective in the larger social world through the bourgeois separation of public and private spheres, while Anne Mellor sees Shelley as a more conservative thinker whose idealization of the bourgeois family serves as a metaphor for an ideal society with clear class distinctions. In this "polis-as-family," according to Mellor, the lower classes function as "'children' who can be governed" (*Shelley* 86–87). Such clearly bifurcated readings of *Frankenstein*, in which the De Laceys commonly serve as the idealized foils to Victor's selfish vanity, vastly understate the depth of the critique of "domestic affection" in the novel. The De Laceys are, after all, the ones who violently reject the creature and set him on the path of revenge. Families are relentlessly depicted throughout *Frankenstein* as sites of competition, both active and structural, though the rivalries are often as unobtrusively noted as the rainy day of the 1831 Introduction. In the novel's first chapter, Walton is able to embark on his travels, despite the "dying injunction" of his father, when "I inherited the fortune of my cousin" (51). This means that Walton's cousin died as a young man, but the reader of *Frankenstein*, who is interested only in Walton at this point, does not care and probably does not even notice. *Frankenstein* is about this indifference. The creature sees a world of affective hierarchies that originate in familial structures, a world in which he can only be a marginal figure. Throughout *Frankenstein*, Shelley constructs a series of conventional romantic narratives which verge on fairy tales that solicit the reader's sympathy for the central characters of these narratives and then casually allow for the demise of peripheral figures. She then places at the center of her novel a figure who protests his marginalization by the domestic hierarchies that privilege some people over others.

The story of the De Laceys is structured around a romantic narrative, the story of Felix and Safie, which consigns two marginal figures—Agatha De Lacey and Safie's servant—to fates only slightly more visible than that of

Walton's cousin. When Safie tries to find the De Laceys, she needs the help of a stock figure of romantic comedy, the resourceful servant, the Sancho Panza. So, according to the logic of the fairy tale, she has one: "she quitted Italy, with an attendant, a native of Leghorn, but who understood the common language of Turkey, and departed for Germany." Once Safie gets reasonably close to the De Laceys in Germany, there is no further need for this servant, so, in another repetition of the deathbed scene, she dies: "[Safie] arrived in safety at a town about twenty leagues from the cottage of De Lacey, when her attendant fell dangerously ill. Safie nursed her with the most devoted attention; but the poor girl died." The dead servant is barely a bump in the road in the romantic narrative; no one's fault, not very interesting, quickly replaced: "[Safie] fell . . . into good hands. . . . the woman of the house in which they had lived took care that Safie should arrive in safety at the cottage of her lover" (154). The reader who is invested in the romantic story of Felix and Safie finds a happy ending. This is the kind of story in which the creature knows he will never participate.

This unnamed servant is not the only sacrifice to Safie's star turn as the romantic heroine. Familiarity with the novel makes it easy to forget that Agatha De Lacey is introduced simply as a "young girl" (135) and the "companion" to Felix, and Agatha's arrival at the identity of "sister," and nothing more than that, occurs as a result of a two-stage process that reaches deeply into Shelley's life and her reading. In the initial description of Agatha, Shelley restricts herself to the terms of the creature's knowledge, withholding any description other than "the girl" (used four times), "the young girl" (twice), or "the young woman" (four times). Throughout this period, Felix is called "the youth" (eight times) or "the young man" (six times), and such phrases as "the young girl and her companion" (137), "the young man and his companion" (138), and "the youth and his companion" (140) all suggest that this couple may be husband and wife rather than sister and brother. Only when the creature begins to acquire language is Agatha named "sister" (140) (though not "daughter"), and her romantic potential is silently forgotten when Safie arrives with a "musical voice" and a "countenance of angelic beauty and expression" (144) and slides into the narrative position vacated by Agatha as the true romantic companion for Felix. Having read Wollstonecraft's description of the common fate of unmarried sisters who inevitably enter into rivalry with their brother's wives (*Vindication* 65–66), Shelley would not be oblivious to the precarious position in which Agatha De Lacey has found herself. The unfortunately intimate opportunity she had for observing the reactions of Harriet Westbrook Shelley, Fanny Imlay

Godwin, and Claire Clairmont to being relegated to the ancillary role of the sister in Percy's romantic preferences also made the fair-haired Mary Shelley all too aware of the unsatisfactoriness of losing out on the role of being rescued by the handsome poet.[7]

Just as Wollstonecraft locates the rivalry between wives and their husband's sisters in the status of sons as the presumptive heirs of family fortunes, Shelley repeatedly shadows the embedded fairy tales in *Frankenstein* with subtle reminders of gender and economic inequities that disrupt the conventional equation of marriage and eternal bliss. The story of the ship's master and his prospective Russian bride has the basic plot of a successful romance—the young people who love each other overcome the objection of the bride's father, and she is not forced to marry the man he tries to force on her—but the equivocal outcome of the story as it affects the ship's master does not quite fit with the ethos of the fairy tale, in which good things happen to good people. The master nobly gives away his entire property in order to ensure the good fortune of the young lovers, but he seems to be neither happy nor unhappy about this sacrifice. It remains unclear whether the good fortune of the lovers is poetic justice or a kind of theft from a simpleminded, goodhearted victim. In the novel's next fairy tale, Alphonse Frankenstein arrives "like a protecting spirit" (64) to save Caroline Beaufort from poverty and want. In this case, the young girl marries her father's friend, thus contradicting the one convention that anchored the previous romantic tale, but once again the outcome conforms to the only economically viable choice available. These two stories have one feature in common: They show women living at the mercy of men who control their economic means of survival, so that women's domestic destinies depend on the sometimes inexplicable, sometimes self-interested, decisions made by men with money. The happy endings of these two stories are determined by male benevolence, but the women have no ability to affect these outcomes.

In her essay on Rousseau, Shelley made it clear that she remained in accord with her parents' and her husband's disdain for the legal institution of marriage. Of Rousseau's cohabitation with Therese le Vasseur, Shelley finds, "This had been praiseworthy as a proceeding founded on tolerant and charitable principles" were it not for the abandonment of the children; of that, Shelley judges, "when we find that this kindly-seeming society was a Moloch, whom to pacify, little children were ruthlessly sacrificed, the whole system takes a revolting and criminal aspect from which we turn with loathing" (133). As Victor's doubts that he has fulfilled the "duties of a creator toward his creature" (13) are echoed in Shelley's judgments on Rousseau that "our first duty is to render those to whom we give birth, wise, virtuous, and happy, as far as in us lies," and that "Rousseau failed in this . . . the first duty of man by abandoning his children" (335, 365), it is clear that Rousseau is, for Shelley, the prototype of the neglectful parent. But Shelley's critical reading of Rousseau, undoubtedly influenced by Wollstonecraft's critique of Rousseau's primitivism, led her to reject a recourse to the natural feeling of empathy as in itself a sufficient basis for social morality. As *Frankenstein* shows, the natural course of empathy flows from the domestic affections that produce affective hierarchies within the family to the erotic hierarchies that structure social existence and make the creature an outcast, and it becomes as potentially destructive as the egotism that allows Rousseau to "fancy himself the centre, as it were, of the universe" (320).

In Shelley's account of the creature's development from the natural to the socialized state, she adopts a number of Rousseau's descriptive terms; the ontogeny of the creature recapitulates a Rousseauean phylogeny. Shelley's intensification of the Rousseauean problematic of the essential moral nature of the human being takes place as she makes the creature's transition from the natural to the social state even more seamless than it is in Rousseau's *Discourses*, where Rousseau introduces the artificial feeling of *amour-propre* as the defining trait of the fallen, social being. In the *Second Discourse*, Rousseau distinguishes between the natural instinct of *amour de soi-meme*, a "natural sentiment which inclines every animal to attend to its self-preservation" and *amour-propre*, "a relative sentiment, factitious, and born in society, which inclines every individual to set greater store by himself than by anyone else, and inspires all the evils that men do to one another" (226). This factitious feeling emerges in the transition from the utilitarian use of language, when people cluster together for practical purposes, to its recreational use. As Rousseau describes early civilization,

> It became customary to gather in front of the Huts or around a large Tree: song and dance, true children of love and leisure, became the amusement or rather the occupation of idle men and women gathered together. Everyone began to look at everyone else and to wish to be looked at himself, and public esteem acquired a value. The one who sang or danced best; the handsomest, the strongest, the most skillful, or the most eloquent came to be the most highly regarded, and this was the first step toward inequality and vice: from these first preferences arose vanity and contempt on the one hand, shame and envy on the other. (175)

At the simplest level of his text, Rousseau imposes a moral value on this mechanistic process, arguing that "man is naturally good" (208), but that the socialized human being is bloodthirsty and cruel once he becomes capable of seeking revenge when his desire for "public esteem" is thwarted or his sense of *amour-propre* is violated.

Rousseau offers at least five variations on this description of the rupture between the natural and the social state of being. At different points in the *Second Discourse*, he locates this rupture in the economic concept of property and in the acquisition of the concepts of *amour-propre* and of mortality; in the *Essay on the Origin of Languages*, the gap is produced by the emergence of exogamy and in the difference between "southern" and "northern" languages. Shelley weaves all five of these concepts into her account of the creature's acquisition of a social subjectivity, even as she effaces Rousseau's imposition of moral value on a mechanistic process. In the aphoristic opening to Part Two of the *Second Discourse*, Rousseau declares that the difference between natural and social being is not affective but economic, claiming, "The first man who, having enclosed a piece of ground, said 'This is mine,' and found people simple enough to believe him, was the true founder of civil society" (170). The anomaly in the story of the ship's master in *Frankenstein* derives from his lack of this concept of property. Human beings do not just give away everything they own, and his willingness to do so betrays an "ignorance" that places him below the threshold of human "interest and sympathy" (318). The same lack characterizes the creature in his early days; when he enters a house and is attacked by the villagers, he simply leaves, since he is in the natural state described by Rousseau: he "compares the difficulty of prevailing with that of finding his sustenance elsewhere; and since pride has no share in the fight, it all ends in a few blows; the victor eats, the vanquished goes off to seek his fortune, and everything is once again at peace" (*Second Discourse* 209). In Shelley's description of the creature's acquisition of the desire for revenge, she follows Rousseau's link between the concept of property and a sense of *amour-propre*. When the creature is driven from the De Laceys' house, he responds differently than at his first expulsion; now, he finds "for the first time feelings of revenge and hatred filled my bosom" (165). Not only does he wish for better treatment, but he believes he deserves it: "I required kindness and sympathy; but I did not believe myself utterly unworthy of it" (159). As Shelley understood from Rousseau, the concept of justice is the effect of a desire for recognition, and is not a metaphysical reality; there is no reason to expect, in a world without an omnipotent, benevolent creator, that there is such a thing as justice.

While the creature believes that "the utmost limit of his ambition" is "to see their sweet looks turned towards me with affection" (159), he begins to express, though he seems not entirely to understand, the desire that is the final effect of *amour-propre*, the desire for a romantic partner. This desire is more fully articulated when he laments that "no Eve soothed my sorrows, or shared my thoughts" (159). While his conscious wish is simply to become a De Lacey, as Agatha is, he harbors the quintessentially human need to become a central figure in a romantic plot—not just a sibling but a lover. In the *Essay on the Origin of Languages*, Rousseau expands upon the hint in the *Second Discourse* that connects *amour-propre* to exogamy. Writing on the importance of bodies of water as the birthplaces of civilization, Rousseau is drawn into an idyllic rhapsody:

> Here the first ties between families were established; here the first meetings between the sexes took place. Young girls came to fetch water for the household, young men came to water their herds. Eyes accustomed from childhood to see always the same object began to see sweeter ones. The heart was moved by them and, swayed by an unfamiliar attraction, it grew less savage and felt the pleasure of not being alone. Imperceptibly water came to be more needed, the cattle were thirsty more often; one arrived in haste, and left in reluctance. (271)

Contrary to the bleak picture of perpetual conflict that ensues from the desire for attention from others in the *Second Discourse*, the *Essay on the Origin of Languages* imagines a continuity from natural to social affection in the "southern" mode of language that serves as the vehicle of the desire of *aimez-moi*. But the entire *Essay on the Origin of Languages* is riven by a supplementary structure that cannot entirely separate the "southern" discourse of love from the "northern" discourse of fear. Rousseau's speculation on the metaphoric origin of language is drawn from this "northern" discourse. His chapter titled "That the First Language Must Have Been Figurative" explains:

> A savage, upon meeting others, will at first have been frightened. His fright will make him see these men as larger and stronger than himself; he will call them *Giants*. After much experience he will recognize that, since these supposed Giants are neither bigger nor stronger than he, their stature did not fit the idea that he had initially attached to the word Giant. He will therefore invent another name common both to them and to himself, for example the name *man*, and he will restrict

the name *Giant* to the false object that had struck him during his illusion. (246)

In the frozen wastes of the Arctic Sea, Walton sees "a low carriage" with "the shape of a man, but apparently of gigantic stature"; the next day, he finds "a sledge, like that we had seen before," but this time "there was a human being within it. . . . He was not, as the other traveller seemed to be, a savage inhabitant of some undiscovered island, but an European" (57). This equation of "a human being" and a "European," which makes the creature inherently gigantic, will permanently exclude the creature from human companionship. His wish to go off to South America imagines the autonomy of the "southern," primitivist world described by Rousseau, but Rousseau's writings clearly describe the mechanistic process by which the creature and his partner could only become the founders of another, larger race of human beings who would develop all of the failings of "northern" peoples.

The final trait Rousseau describes as distinguishing the human from the natural is the knowledge of mortality; as Rousseau claims in the *Second Discourse*, "the knowledge of death and of its terrors was one of man's first acquisitions on moving away from the animal condition" (150). The creature's lament of the "strange nature [of] knowledge," the burdens of which can only be overcome through "death—a state which I feared but did not understand" (148) shows him beginning to achieve this fully human consciousness, but Shelley also suggests in the scene of the creature's vivification that this incipient sense of mortality is an innate, rather than an acquired, quality. In her most pointed revision of Milton's account of Adam's creation, Shelley takes Adam's remark that he was "untroubl'd" to find himself drowsily "passing to my former state," even though it seemed that he was "forthwith to dissolve" (*Paradise Lost* 8.289–91) and transforms it into the creature's sense of being "troubled" when "darkness . . . came over me" after he shuts his eyes to keep out the painful light (130). Adam's prelapsarian consciousness is indifferent to the prospect of nonbeing, but Shelley's creature is born with the fear that darkness might signify his own nonexistence. In Shelley's revisitings of the nightmare vision that keeps alive this troubling knowledge, the weirdest metarepresentation of this deathbed scene is the painting that sits "over the mantle-piece" in the Frankenstein home: "It was an historical subject, painted at my father's desire, and represented Caroline Beaufort in an agony of despair, kneeling at the coffin of her dead father" (106). Where one would expect a wedding portrait of Alphonse and Caroline, the founding of the Frankenstein family is instead represented by a *memento mori* of Caroline's ancestor. This reminder of his death ("in the tenth month her father died in her arms") foreshadows Elizabeth's picturesque demise: "She was there, lifeless and inanimate, thrown across the bed, her head hanging down, and her pale and distorted features half covered by her hair" (220).

This relentless parade of deaths keeps the knowledge of mortality in the foreground of *Frankenstein*, and just as Shelley makes this knowledge part of the original state of human consciousness, she disallows Rousseau's deferral of the invidious force of *amour-propre* to a post-"natural," postfamilial stage of development. The Frankenstein family is composed, as was Mary Godwin's childhood home, of young people from a variety of parentages, and it is the site of deep affections and equally deep rivalries. Elizabeth is emphatic in her defense of Justine and extravagant in her expressions of praise and affection for her; she speaks of Justine as one "whom I loved and esteemed as my sister" (113), and, writing to Victor before the death of little William, she tells him, "I assure you that I love her tenderly," because "she is very clever, and gentle, and extremely pretty; as I mentioned before, her mien and her expressions continually remind me of my dear aunt" (95). For Elizabeth, who is never entirely sure of her place in Victor's affections, the existence of this "extremely pretty" adopted sister is the sort of mixed blessing that Mary Shelley found in Claire Clairmont. The opening of Elizabeth's letter to Victor contains the resulting ambivalence in a fairly clear subtext. After asking Victor "Do you not remember Justine Moritz? Probably you do not," Elizabeth acknowledges that Victor probably does remember her, since "Justine was a great favourite of your's" (93–94). Elizabeth's letter twice suggests that her rivalry with Justine for Victor's affections is tied up with a competition to replace Caroline Frankenstein as the family matriarch. She notes that Justine thought Caroline "the model of all excellence, and endeavoured to imitate her phraseology and manners, so that even now she often reminds me of her" (94). Since Elizabeth had been the one to receive the injunction from Caroline Frankenstein to "supply my place to your younger cousins" (72), this competition results in a bizarre contest to claim responsibility for William's death. Elizabeth's response to the first sight of William's body is "O God! I have murdered my darling infant!" (100), a response that is doubly inaccurate: Elizabeth has not murdered anyone, and William is not her child.

Justine's confession to the murder and her execution enable her to trump Elizabeth in saintliness and familial devotion; her acceptance of blame preserves the Frankenstein family honor from the taint of scandal by shifting the responsibility for William's death to an outsider. Elizabeth quickly reconciles herself to her more secure place in Victor's affections in terms that are made more self-satisfied, but more haunting, in 1831; writing to Victor after Justine's execution, Elizabeth asks, "Ah! while we love—while we are true to each other, here in this land of peace and beauty, your native country, we may reap every tranquil blessing,—what can disturb our peace?" (340). This question becomes not rhetorical but real when Justine goes the way of Walton's cousin, Safie's servant, Fanny Imlay, and Harriet Shelley—she disappears, and others' lives become less complicated. "What can disturb our peace" is figured in *Frankenstein* as the effect of such events, an outsized, enigmatic force that inexplicably turns from benevolence to viciousness. The knowledge of Justine's demise becomes one of those "shadows of our past actions" that "stalk beside us"; Victor can feel guilty at a conscious level for failing to disclose what he knew, and Elizabeth for having profited from Justine's convenient removal. "That mysterious portion of mind called conscience" can find it difficult to distinguish, in the demise of our rivals, the blamelessness of our accidental survival from an occasion for guilt; it can be difficult to decide whether this mysterious force unjustly afflicts us, or if we fail in our responsibilities to it.

Victor, too, has a rival for primacy of place within the Frankenstein household. As the first child, he enjoys a period of unchallenged bliss; in another passage enhanced in 1831, so long as he "remained for several years their only child," he is his parents' "plaything and their idol" (322). The birth of his first brother, Ernest, changes things very little, since Ernest is "afflicted with ill health from his infancy," which leaves him "incapable of any severe application." The next brother, William, is another matter. While still an infant, William is, according to Victor, "the most beautiful little fellow in the world; his lively blue eyes, dimpled cheeks, and endearing manners, inspired the tenderest affection" (71). By the age of five, Elizabeth reports, William is precociously sexy, "very tall of his age, with sweet laughing blue eyes, dark eye-lashes, and curling hair," and has "already had one or two little *wives*" (95). Like Justine, William is a little too lovely for his own good, and when the creature murders William and places the blame on Justine, he enables Victor and Elizabeth to emerge from the endogamous equality of siblings and to take the "first step towards inequality" as the erotic center of the Frankenstein household.

The 1831 transformation of Elizabeth Lavenza from Victor's cousin into an adoptee of the Frankenstein family, the longest single emendation of the 1818 text, is the most elaborate use of the conventions of the fairy tale as the oblique vehicle through which Mary Shelley examines the meaning of her own survival of the events that claimed so many of her own family and her rivals. This examination involves looking at both her own participation in structures of privilege and at her ugliest prejudices, and it solicits a similar self-examination from readers of the novel. The revised story of Elizabeth's adoption by the Frankensteins has both the conventional plot and the rhetoric of a fairy tale. This little girl with "hair [of] the brightest living gold," the "daughter of a Milanese nobleman" who had given his life for "the liberty of his country" is rescued from poverty and restored to her true station in life as, in fairy tale logic, the signs of her noble birth shine through her dismal circumstances. But the passage that distinguishes this "being heaven-sent" from her more ordinary step-siblings first has to extricate itself from a very different set of sympathies. This is the scene that confronts Caroline Frankenstein:

> She found a peasant and his wife, hard working, bent down by care and labour, distributing a scanty meal to five hungry babes. Among these there was one which attracted my mother far above all the rest. She appeared of a different stock. The four others were dark-eyed, hardy little vagrants; this child was thin, and very fair. Her hair was the brightest living gold, and, despite the poverty of her clothing, seemed to set a crown of distinction on her head. . . . none could behold her without looking on her as of a distinct species, a being heaven-sent, and bearing a celestial stamp in all her features. (323)

The assertions (in Victor's voice) that the golden-haired Elizabeth is "of a different stock" and "a distinct species" from the "dark-eyed hardy little vagrants" who surround her reflect the Anglo bourgeois bigotry that appears in the 1814 sections of the *History of a Six Weeks Tour* and in Shelley's letters from that period, and that resurfaces in a letter written shortly after Percy's death in which the Genovese are described by Shelley as "wild savages."[8] But the story of the separation of Elizabeth Lavenza from her dark-eyed siblings so that Elizabeth can receive the entitlements that flow naturally from her celestial distinction creates a severe interpretive dilemma in *Frankenstein* because of the obvious similarity between Elizabeth's hardy, unattractive, and neglected siblings and the creature doomed by social consensus to be rejected by every human being solely because of his inability to meet minimal standards of acceptability in his physical appearance. The sympathies that draw the reader into an identification with the fate of Elizabeth Lavenza are the same affective preferences that lead to the creature's universal rejection because he exhibits the greatest difference from the conventions of appearance that mark one as an appropriate hero or heroine, as a prince or a princess, in a fairy tale.

The story of Elizabeth Lavenza unsettles the conventions of the fairy tale not only because her adoption leads to her murder rather than to her living happily ever after in the station to which she was born. Even at the outset of this story, the fairy tale rhetoric that justifies Elizabeth's separation from her step-siblings is undermined by the momentary sympathy engendered for the hardworking, hungry peasant family. Juxtaposing Elizabeth's story of being specially chosen to enjoy material and romantic privileges with the creature's account of being specifically excluded from human companionship and forced to scratch out a meager existence complicates the primacy that seems to be accorded to the romantic narrative of the presentation of Elizabeth to Victor. But how many readers pause to reflect that this romantic narrative quickly eclipses the "peasant and his wife, hard working, bent down by care and labour, distributing a scanty meal to five hungry babes"? Does anyone object to how quickly "hardy" replaces "hungry," assuring us that we have not left these dark-eyed vagrants to a hopeless fate? How long do we dwell on sufferings that are not that bad and not our fault?

The stakes of the reading of this passage are high; either Mary Shelley's adolescent racist and classist prejudices so hardened with time that she included in her revision of her most famous work an unwitting refutation of the sympathy engendered by its central figure, or else in a novel that confronts the question of how difference, or otherness, comes to be perceived as ugliness, the conventional rhetoric of "hair of the brightest living gold" is offered not as a validation of the romantic hierarchy of the fairy tale but as a test of the efficacy of such rhetoric in enabling one to forget the dark-eyed vagrants and their hardworking, poverty-stricken, uninteresting parents. In her 1831 revisions, Mary Shelley ties the end of the Elizabeth/Caroline story to its beginning, deepening its moral complexity at the same time as she tightens its psychology. In 1831, when Elizabeth is transformed from Victor's cousin to an adoptee of the Frankenstein family, Caroline's intense, motherly concern for Elizabeth is emphasized from the moment of their first meeting. Caroline's identification with Elizabeth leads to Elizabeth's rescue from poverty, and that same sense of identification impels Caroline into Elizabeth's sickroom in a moment of danger. This single psychological impulse can be read, in moral terms, either as a self-denying altruism or as an other-denying narcissism.

Caroline's next act of benevolence, the adoption of Justine Moritz, jeopardizes Elizabeth's place in the Frankenstein household, a place she regains only through what seem to the Frankensteins like random acts of violence perpetrated against both Justine and little William. The creature's motives for these acts are greatly elaborated in 1831. In the 1818 version of the killing of little William, the creature's account of the second part of his double crime, the planting of evidence on Justine, is brief and straightforward. Justine passes near the creature, and he reports, "I approached her unperceived, and placed the portrait securely in one of the folds of her dress." His motive could be called retribution on principle: "Here, I thought, is one of those whose smiles are bestowed on all but me; she shall not escape" (170). In 1831, the act is rendered more melodramatically and the motive more fully. The moral horror of the scene barely overrides the potential humor of the weird fairy tale parody when the creature hovers over Justine and says, "Awake, fairest, thy lover is near—he who would give his life but to obtain one look of affection from thine eyes: my beloved, awake!" Beseeching the sleeping Justine to "Awake," the creature casts himself as the prince who discovers "Sleeping Beauty in the Wood."[9] But it is precisely his ineligibility for that romantic role that prompts him to punish the innocent Justine. His motive for placing the blame on her for the murder of little William is put in terms that are far more vivid, both in their bitterness and in their malevolence, in 1831 than in 1818. To "she shall not escape," 1831 adds: "not I, but she shall suffer: the murder that I have committed because I am forever robbed of all that she could give me, she shall atone. The crime had its source in her: be hers the punishment!" (346).

In Shelley's depiction of this double crime, the murder of William and the blaming of Justine, she revisits Rousseau's two-part crime, the theft of the ribbon and the blaming of Marion. The structure of substitution that informs this episode in the *Confessions*, in which the ribbon stands both for Marion herself, as the object of Rousseau's desire, and for Rousseau's desire for her, and in which Rousseau and Marion are exchanged for each other in the role of victim (as Rousseau's guilt becomes Marion's revenge), recurs, in every point, in the creature's explanation of his motive for punishing Justine. The passages dovetail so neatly that Rousseau's text explains what neither Justine nor the Frankensteins can understand; Justine wonders of the murderer, "Why should he have stolen the jewel, to part with it again so soon?" (111). Rousseau provides the answer: "I accused her of having done what I wanted to do and of having given me the ribbon because my intention was to give it to her" (*Confessions* 72). When the creature plants the locket on Justine, he fulfills Rousseau's intention; the creature gives Justine the sort of token that he wishes she would give to him. But where Rousseau produces this motive as the proof that he intended no harm to Marion since it shows that his "friendship (amitié) for her was the cause" of his actions, Shelley sees the reversal of love into hate. Rousseau, like the creature, was thwarted in love; when Marion did not reciprocate his desire, he was "deprived of the delights that such beautiful creatures could bestow" (Frankenstein 170). The ribbon was his means of enticing Marion, but if he found himself in jeopardy for having stolen it, and if his love for her is a sign of his capacity for amitié, then who deserves to suffer for this theft? If Marion had returned Rousseau's affection without the need of a bribe, he would not be in this danger. So: "The crime had its source in her; be hers the punishment." Shelley's indictment of Rousseau's candor and his professed purity of motive resonates far beyond the indictment of Rousseau as an individual. As the creature discovers, humans are tied together, in our domestic and our social existences, not only through acts for which we bear individual responsibility but through networks of inequality. The relation between the two central characters in Frankenstein, Victor and his creature, creates a profound ambiguity over which is the victim and which the perpetrator, but as the creature comes to understand, this is a question which is not exhausted in a calculation of personal responsibility.

The logic of indiscriminate retribution that leads the creature to plant the locket on Justine marks an incremental leap in the moral horror story of Frankenstein. Up to this point, terrible things have happened, but they have occurred without malicious intent. It is arguable that Victor can be faulted both for creating the creature and for abandoning it, but in neither case does he deliberately intend to injure anyone. The assaults perpetrated on the creature are all carried out under an honest impression of self-defense, and even the killing of little William is, in the creature's account, more of an involuntary manslaughter than a murder. After the child "loaded me with epithets which carried despair to my heart," the creature claims, "I grasped his throat to silence him, and in a moment he lay dead at my feet" (170). Placing the locket on Justine is a qualitatively different act. In terms of individual ethical responsibility, the creature's behavior is manifestly unfair to Justine, but an appeal to individual responsibility has no relevance for the creature. The intractability of his fate, which is to be permanently excluded from the bonds of human affection, is not the fault of anyone in particular, but is the result of an unspoken but universally recognized social consensus. As the creature deliberately causes harm to Justine not in revenge for any particular action on her part but simply because of her inclusion in a structure of privilege from which he is excluded, his act would be described, in a contemporary Western political vocabulary, as an act of terrorism.

The creature's punishment of Justine closely tracks the arc of Satan's discovery of Eve in Book Nine of *Paradise Lost*, but Shelley's elaboration of the creature's psychology both revises Milton's interpretation of this scene and foreshadows the modern rhetoric of the delegitimation of terrorism. The creature is, like Satan, initially disarmed by the sight of a beautiful woman; the creature's report that "in spite of my malignity," the portrait of Caroline "softened and attracted me" (170) echoes Milton's account of Eve's effect on Satan: "her Heav'nly form / Angelic, but more soft, and Feminine" momentarily "bereav'd / His fierceness of the fierce intent it brought" (*Paradise Lost*, 9.457–462). But Shelley's creature quickly reiterates the Satanic decision that "the more he sees / Of pleasure not for him ordain'd," the only response is to find "all pleasure to destroy," since "other joy / To me is lost" (*Paradise Lost*, 9.469–70, 477–79). Milton's explanation for this decision is that the agent is simply evil; Satan's decision issues from "the hot Hell that always in him burns" (467). Shelley does not rest on metaphysical platitudes. Her creature resorts to a violent, indiscriminate attack on the foundational principles of society only after two unsuccessful attempts to discover a presocial principle that might enable him to escape a traumatic existence. In his attempts to communicate first with the blind De Lacey and then with a child "who might have lived too short a time to have imbibed a horror of deformity" (169), he looks for a prelapsarian world that might predate his perception of himself as deformed. The creature searches for a primitivist, Rousseauean paradise, but there is no such time. His only originary experience is of a "darkness" that functions as a troubling reminder of death, an unacceptable state for a human being. Rousseau's attempts to imagine presocial utopias are, as Shelley shows, evasions of the inescapable moral complexity of the human condition.

Freud suggests that trauma always depends on a missing time; trauma results, he argues, not simply from the fear (*furcht*) of a serious threat to life but from the fright (*shreck*) of an unexpected threat (SE 18:12). In Cathy Caruth's elaboration of Freud's insight, she suggests that the surprise of the traumatic event makes survival an aberrant state; not really knowing what happened in the traumatic event, one never understands why one has survived it (62). The creature experiences trauma and its compulsive repetition in its mechanical form; Felix's sudden entry into the De Lacey home leads to nightmares in which "the horrible scene of the preceding day was for ever acting before my eyes; the females were flying, and the enraged Felix tearing me from his father's feet" (164). But the creature's suprahuman experience of himself as an aberrant being, both as a universal victim and as an indiscriminate terror, never engages the individual responsibility of perpetrator guilt. The creature never experiences a guilt trauma for the deaths of William and Justine; that falls to Victor.

For the most part, Victor's expressions of guilt look past little William and focus on Justine, and the terms in which Victor laments his guilt over Justine echo, in painstaking detail, Rousseau's defensive grief over Marion. Victor, like Rousseau, protests his purity of motive; Victor tells us that his "heart overflowed with kindness, and the love of virtue," (119), Rousseau that "never has wickedness been farther from me than at that cruel moment" (*Confessions* 72) when he accused Marion of the theft. Both displace blame onto others; the judges whose "cold answers" and "harsh unfeeling reasoning" cause Victor's "purposed avowal" to "die away on my lips" (339) play the role of the Comte de la Roque who, Rousseau complains, should have encouraged him rather than frightening him. Like Rousseau, Victor indulges in hyperboles of his own victimization. Even Rousseau's plea to consider "my grief at perhaps having made her worse than myself" (71) barely approaches Victor's claim that he is "seized by remorse and a sense of guilt, which hurried me away to a hell of intense tortures, such as no language can describe" (119). Victor even employs Rousseau's device of having someone else state that he is the greater sufferer; as Marion tells Rousseau, "You make me very sad, but I should not like to be in your place" (71), Elizabeth imagines, "Even if I were condemned to suffer on the scaffold for the same crimes, I would not change places with such a wretch" (122) as the real murderer. Like Rousseau, Victor believes the greatest suffering accrues not to the victim but to the guilty perpetrator. Applying Rousseau's precept that "remorse sleeps while fate is kind but grows sharp in adversity" (72), Victor understands the underlying principle of this aphorism—that guilt prevents one from ever believing that sorrows are undeserved—when he moans that "the tortures of the accused did not equal mine; she was sustained by innocence, but the fangs of remorse tore my bosom, and would not forego their hold" (113).

These hyperboles of victimization in which perpetrators displace their victims are, as Shelley warns in the essay on Rousseau, a caution to us all. Rousseau's inability to "appreciate the real extent of his misconduct" elicits Shelley's condemnation, but she also judges that the suppression of his guilt led Rousseau into "that vein of insanity, that made him an example among men for self-inflicted suffering" (132). Shelley's life first foreshadowed and then mirrored, in a nearly uncanny fashion, the experience of Victor Frankenstein as the perpetual survivor of a relentless series of domestic deaths. Victor is a helpless bystander watching the deaths of Caroline, William, Justine, Clerval, and Elizabeth; when he finally tells a magistrate about the creature, the conversation simply passes as though it never took place, and the next chapter returns to Victor's single pursuit. The effect, as Victor says before the death of Elizabeth, is that "the whole series of my life appeared to me as a dream; I sometimes doubted if indeed it were all true, for it never presented itself to my mind with the force of reality" (204). By the time of the composition of *Frankenstein*, Shelley had the death of her first infant, the knowledge of her mother's death, and the suicides of Fanny Imlay and Harriet Shelley to address, each of which presented her with an ambiguous guilt. She was the material cause of Wollstonecraft's death, and she had survived an infant who, given the circumstances of her elopement, could not have been a wanted child. Her half-sister Fanny Imlay always took second place to Mary in the Godwin household; as Godwin wrote of the two teenagers in 1812, "Of the two . . . my own daughter is considerably superior in capacity to the one her mother had before. Fanny, the eldest, is of a quiet, modest, unshowy disposition. . . . Mary, my daughter, is . . . singularly bold, somewhat imperious, and active of mind" (Spark 15). Godwin's preference for Mary was reenacted in Percy's choice of her from among Godwin's three teenaged daughters. As Mary Shelley was to show in *Frankenstein*, the inequality of domestic affection foreshadows an inequality of romantic destinies, sometimes with life-threatening results.

While the deaths of Wollstonecraft, the premature infant, and Fanny were not caused by Mary Shelley's actions, Harriet Shelley's suicide was a more complicated story. Shelley found it easy to dismiss Trelawny's and Hogg's objections to her excision of the passage about Harriet in the 1838 edition of Percy's poems. In her journal, she speculated on how much Trelawny must have enjoyed sending the volume back to Moxon "in a rage," and mused, "It was *almost* worthwhile to make the omissions if only to give him this pleasure" (560). To Hogg, she wrote that she was becoming used to being "fed on poison" by her friends, and that she "should have been heartily surprised not to have been supplied with a large dose on the present occasion you have mixed the biggest you possibly could and I am proportionately indebted to you" (*Letters* 2:309). This sarcasm consigns Trelawny and Hogg to the status of the "mere drivellers" whose criticism she disdained. Having rejected both of them as suitors in the years after Percy's death, she could easily recognize that their *amour-propre* would require that they find grounds to criticize her thereafter.

Shelley's expression of sorrow over Harriet—"Poor Harriet to whose sad fate I attribute so many of my own heavy sorrows as the atonement claimed by fate for her death"—in the same journal entry in which she scorns Trelawny and Hogg shows that she did not take her moral obligation to Harriet lightly, but her assertion in the same entry that "I never did an ungenerous act in my life" also reflects the limits of the blame she felt she carried for Harriet's death. Mary Shelley was never in a position to repair Harriet's life; just as Victor is helpless to stop the destructive force that decimates everyone around him, Mary Shelley could never have saved the marriage of Percy and Harriet. But Harriet's suicide made the lives of Mary and Percy far less complicated; given the state of divorce law in England in 1816, it could have been a very long time before Mary Godwin became Mary Shelley were it not for Harriet's death.

As one of Rousseau's best readers, Shelley never took at face value such platitudes as the natural goodness of human nature. Instead, she found an author so eloquent in paradox that the counterarguments he inspired often eclipsed his most accessible theses. Reading Rousseau against the grain of the obvious, Shelley teased out the points of impact between the most intimate moments in his autobiographical works and the most compelling theses in his political writings, and she drew a larger Rousseau than one finds in modern academic studies. Shelley herself deserves a more sophisticated profile than simply being cast as a proponent of domestic affection or of natural empathy. Her grasp of counterarguments involved her understanding that natural feelings entail preferences and construct hierarchies; by the time she completed the first edition of *Frankenstein*, she clearly understood the consequences of the fact that affections were, like any other property, finite in quantity and unequally distributed. This knowledge was hard won. Her proposal that Harriet, Percy, and she could all live together, Mary as Percy's wife, Harriet as his sister, nearly replicated Wollstonecraft's unsuccessful offer to Fuseli. When Harriet accomplished what Wollstonecraft had attempted, she became, in effect, the figure over the mantelpiece in the new Shelley household, the sacrificial body that seems like it might at any time come to life and "stalk beside us," tormenting that "mysterious portion of mind termed conscience." If guilt trauma is as real as victim trauma—which is very different from claiming that the survivors are the real victims—then it too is capable of producing survival as an aberrant mode of being. Where mechanical trauma produces an inability to know why one is still alive, guilt trauma, which depends on an ethical debt, produces an inability to believe that one deserves to survive. Since survival always depends on some combination of accident and our own actions, this uncertainty is irresolvable.

Shelley's fairy tale elopement eventually turned out about as badly as Elizabeth Lavenza's upwardly mobile adoption, but as *Frankenstein* relentlessly shows, not only do characters in fairy tales not always live happily ever after, there may not even be any particular reason why they deserve to do so. The assumption by some people of the roles of heroes and heroines of romantic stories means that their rivals, who are excluded from those roles, can only play ancillary parts in the lives of the privileged few. When happiness depends on receiving the love that accrues to romantic identity, and convention decrees that romantic heroines fit definable patterns, either exotically glamorous or blond and thin, this is a tough verdict for "dark-eyed hardy little vagrants," let alone those who recoil at their own reflections. *Frankenstein* does not willingly sacrifice the Sancho Panzas of the world, but it does narrate the grim story of the consequences of their exclusion from the realms of privilege. *Frankenstein* turns from a fairy tale going awry through bad luck, mixed motives, misunderstandings, and lack of foresight into a story of deliberate mayhem when one creature comes to the conclusion that he will never be loved, so he sees no reason why anyone else should have it any better. The 1831 Introduction and revisions to *Frankenstein* highlight Mary Shelley's critique of our willingness to accept the fictional cover that novels provide in order to indulge our identifications with figures of privilege, especially if those figures are clothed in romance, to overlook the dispossessions that their privileges entail, and to do so even as we read a novel wherein the central figure is a victim of those conventional preferences. In the oneiric relays of *Frankenstein*, the creature's punishment of Justine carries out the revenge of the dark-eyed little vagrants on Caroline Frankenstein, even though this is manifestly unfair to Justine. As the 1831 revisions to *Frankenstein* knit together, through the story of Elizabeth Lavenza and her dark-eyed step-siblings, the domestic affairs of the Frankenstein and De Lacey families, the revised novel reinforces the warning that we cannot safely exonerate ourselves from responsibility for the exclusions that arise from structures of social privilege just because those decisions are not our fault.

The terror of *Frankenstein* is not a matter of gothic special effects; the book's ability to inspire fear resides in its subversion of the very possibility of ethical behavior by fallible beings in an utterly contingent world. Shelley confronts Kantian imperatives, which ask us to imagine principles that can act as universal moral truths, with a materiality that ruins the efficacy of any such principles. The scope of Shelley's ethical critique can be measured against the other texts considered in this study; Wordsworth and Jane Eyre aspire to a Kantian condition of exemplarity, while Rousseau and Humbert Humbert honor Kantian principles by asking for tolerance for their inability to measure up to those standards. But *Frankenstein* fractures the Kantian imperative altogether. When the creature commits an act of terrorism, his action can neither be endorsed nor condemned. His conduct is not a guide for us, but to condemn him for his behavior requires a willful obliviousness to the conditions of power to which he responds. The actions of Victor Frankenstein and his creature, who challenge natural and social norms, are no better and no worse than the passivity with which the rest of the characters in *Frankenstein* (and its readers) accept the norms that legitimate an indifference to the lives of the creature and of the four hungry, hardy stepsiblings of Elizabeth Lavenza.

4

From Jane Eyre to Villette

The Autobiography of a Writer

⋮

IT is not immediately obvious why an author who based the plots of two of her novels on events in her own life would subtitle an intervening novel, the plot of which bears far less resemblance to her experience, "An Autobiography." Yet this is what Charlotte Brontë did in "*Jane Eyre. | An Autobiography. | Edited by Currer Bell.*"[1] The stories in *The Professor* and *Villette* of expatriate English teachers in Brussels who enter into student/teacher romantic entanglements are clearly based on Brontë's involvement with Constantin Heger, but the novel that Brontë subtitled "An Autobiography" was *Jane Eyre*.

The simplest explanation of this paradox would be to describe *Jane Eyre* as the work that provides the most direct reflection of Charlotte Brontë's inner life, an impression that has arisen frequently throughout the novel's reception history. In such touchstone moments as William Makepeace Thackeray's introduction of Brontë to his guests as "Jane Eyre" and Virginia Woolf's belief that Jane's voice expressed Brontë's intense, demanding sensibility, we find the central presumptions that inform the reception of the novel in our own time. The popularity of *Jane Eyre* has been established through a current of identification that seems to bind the desires of both the author and the reader of the novel to the fate of its main character. The external world of *Jane Eyre* coheres not as a representation of an actual place (mid-nineteenth-century England) but as the set of circumstances that at first unfairly cause the heroine to suffer (bad weather, hostile relatives, terrible food) and finally serve as a recognition of her innate value, but the exaggerated scale of the obstacles she faces, and the perfection of her triumph over those impediments, require some degree of irony toward its fantasy structure. And while all three of Brontë's first-person novels, *The Professor*,

Jane Eyre, and Villette, deal with stories of romantic passion, the work that most often employs the vehement first-person rhetoric of Brontë's letters to Heger is Villette.

Before transferring the subtitle of "autobiography" from Jane Eyre to Villette on the presumption that Brontë's final work provides the fullest revelation of her inner life, it would be helpful to consider how Brontë would have seen the relation between autobiographies and novels. As Patricia Meyer Spacks observes in her study of autobiography and the novel in the eighteenth century, there is an "intrinsic unnaturalness" (195) to autobiography; the central figure of an autobiography is not simply a person who has lived a series of events that are to be recorded in a text but the self that is created in the telling of the story. Spacks concludes that the difference between an autobiography and a novel can be found in the different rhetorics of the two genres. While novels employ a "dramatic rhetoric" in order to "express character through adventurous imagery," autobiographies "rely on a rhetoric of explanation, shading often toward self-justification" (313–14).

The recent reception history of Jane Eyre has shown that the structural relation between Jane and Bertha Mason is central to the novel's legitimating narrative, in which conjugal identity ratifies the virtue of individual desire. Sandra Gilbert and Susan Gubar's identification of Bertha as Jane's angry double absorbs Bertha's identity into Jane's, making Bertha's anger into an immature stage that Jane passes through in her progress toward "a marriage of true minds" (367). Gayatri Spivak effectively adopted Gilbert and Gubar's reading of the novel but gave it a political spin when she chastised Brontë for using "an unexamined and covert axiomatics of imperialism in Jane Eyre" (257) in order to produce "a self-immolating colonial subject for the glorification of the social mission of the colonizer." In what became a cornerstone of the critique of white feminism for its blindness to other modes of oppression, Spivak charged that in Brontë's work, "the woman from the colonies is . . . sacrificed as an insane animal for her sister's consolidation" (251).

Nancy Armstrong recasts the moral polarity between Jane and Bertha as a matter of class, rather than race, so that the expulsion of Bertha Mason serves to protect the bourgeois family from its aberrant others. Even if, as Armstrong contends, the images of the "monster and angel worked discursively as a team," she finds that they did so only rhetorically in order to "suppress other notions of sexuality—namely, those attributed to the aristocracy and the laboring classes—that did not adhere to the ideal of legitimate monogamy" (253). In Foucauldian fashion, Armstrong describes Jane's desire as both properly disciplined and deeply personal; her plain appearance marks her distance from the "standardized surface" of the conventionally desirable Blanche Ingram, and Rochester's preference for her indicates the "highly personalized" (194) nature of their bond. In Armstrong's account, Brontë presents desire as a deeply individuated counterforce to the "aesthetics of the surface" (191) delineated by Jane Austen, which could reconcile social form and personal desire. Through Brontë's elaboration of the depths that she felt were missing in Austen, the repressive hypothesis, with its presumptive opposition of personal desire and social convention, is fully developed.

While Armstrong focuses on Brontë's use of a normalizing discourse of sexuality to efface class conflict, Spivak makes it clear that race also functions as a normalizing discourse in *Jane Eyre*, and the "axiomatics of imperialism" described by Spivak are far more visible in the novel than is the allegory of class struggle identified by Armstrong. When one recalls that the other woman in Rochester's past, Céline Varens, is French, it becomes clear that race functions in the novel as a hyperbolic form of nationalism; the identification of Bertha Mason as "creole" extends and intensifies her distance from the English norm. While the resolution of the novel seems to assert a thematic hierarchy in which characters assume their value through the exercise of "highly personalized" desire, this thematic balance is nonetheless secured, as Armstrong and Spivak show, by discourses that differentiate subjects through normative discourses of sexuality, class and national origin. Within the novel's nationalist discourse, Jane's inheritance does more than afford her the means of establishing her economic independence. Through her reattachment to "her father's kinsfolk," who are "as much gentry as the Reeds are" (*Jane Eyre* 100),[2] Jane escapes her orphan status and is installed at the heart of true Englishness as a rightful member of an old family. The nationalist sentiment evoked by this discovery of Jane's roots supplements the sympathy that her character generates through her many struggles and helps to reassure the English reader that the death of the Spanish Creole Bertha Antoinetta Mason is an acceptable price to pay for Jane's happiness. Gilbert and Gubar's description of Bertha as nothing more than a phase in Jane's development unfortunately completes the work of this normalizing discourse that makes the non-English subject something less than a person.

Still, as the critiques of the novel by Spivak and Jean Rhys show, the thematic resolution of *Jane Eyre* becomes vulnerable on grounds that are fundamentally ethical: In what terms, and on behalf of what values, is the death of Bertha Mason good news? If this autobiography is viewed not as an axiomatic celebration of the normalized, individuated subject but as an exercise in the rhetoric of self-justification, the sacrifice of Bertha Mason leads into a series of ethical questions, none of which is entirely answered by Jane's satisfied summary of events at the novel's conclusion. Bertha is not the only sacrifice to the happiness of the new Rochester household; Adele Varens, despite her "frantic joy" at seeing Jane again and at being released from her boarding school, is once again sent away, not for her own good but because Jane finds that "my time and cares were now required by another—my husband needed them all" (438). And Adele is not the only child to be deprived of Jane's attention. Although Jane had promised the children of Morton school that "never a week should pass in future that I did not visit them, and give them an hour's teaching in their school" (380), these impeccably English children are forgotten without a mention after Jane returns to Rochester. Bertha's death makes it possible for the novel never to confront the position argued so passionately by Rochester, that Bertha's incapacity gives him the right to remarry—i.e., to form a sexual union with Jane—while his wife is alive. The novel finesses this question, which in practical terms would require an examination of the legal difficulties of divorce in nineteenth-century Britain, without quite tying up every loop in the plot; when Jane sets off from Moor House to rejoin Rochester, she does not know that Bertha is dead. And the most forcefully unanswered ethical question in Jane Eyre is raised by Gilbert and Gubar's insight into the figural doubling of the two characters: Does Jane or Bertha have the right to set Rochester on fire?

These questions are eclipsed, but not answered, by the autobiographical narrative that binds the reader to Jane's voice. The reappearance of Adele in the novel's conclusion is framed as a reminder to the reader: "You have not forgotten little Adele, have you, reader?" The chiding of the reader, as if we are the ones guilty of neglecting Adele, displaces the responsibility for the fact that Adele is not allowed to remain within the Rochester household. That Adele requires this mention, while the children of the Morton school silently disappear, reflects the demands of narrative conventions and readerly expectations. Adele and the Morton children fill the role in Jane Eyre of the "five hungry babes" Mary Shelley introduces into Frankenstein, only to immediately forget about four of them. Brontë, like Shelley, calculates precisely how little attention peripheral characters will require when readers are given a strong romantic narrative with which to identify. Jane's response to Rochester's plea that he should be allowed to remarry operates within the melodramatic conventions of the gothic novel, but in realistic terms it is only a radical short-circuiting of the debates over divorce in nineteenth-century England. Rochester asks whether it is "better to drive a fellow-creature into despair than to transgress a mere human law—no man being injured by the breach?" Jane's answer, that she "will keep the law given by God; sanctioned by man" (312), hardly addresses the fact that the grounds for divorce had been a matter of deep disagreement within Protestant churches for centuries and that the Church of England had been established for the purpose of authorizing a divorce.

Jane's account of the happy resolution of her story depends on the premises that (1) it had once been utterly impossible for her to marry Rochester but that the single impediment is removed in the only way possible by the death of Bertha Mason and (2) that the only reason that she was unable to marry Rochester in the first place had nothing to do with his character or her desires but resulted only from this single external obstacle. Most readers have realized, since Gilbert and Gubar's groundbreaking work, that these premises are not entirely true and have seen that Jane's initial reluctance to marry is based on her uneasiness with the dynamics of power between herself and Rochester. This realization has not resulted in a general suspicion of Jane as an unreliable narrator, but it should. Brontë foregrounds the unreliability of the narrators of *Villette* and *The Professor*, Lucy Snowe and Edward Crimsworth. Lucy Snowe's deliberate withholding of information forces us to look outside her narrative for the truth of her story, and Crimsworth's judgment is clearly held out as dubious in *The Professor*. The most obviously problematic decision Crimsworth makes is that his son Victor must go to Eton in order to learn a masculine toughness that is endangered by his mother's "congenial tenderness" (*Professor* 289). Heather Glen suggests that when *Jane Eyre* begins with a sympathetic focus on a child's need for love, the juxtaposition of Victor's fate and Jane's need reveals Brontë's social agenda; her critique of Crimsworth's arid "ideal of independence," Glen argues, shows that "it is in its treatment of childhood that the essential nature of a society is revealed" (Introduction, *Professor* 30). But when Adele Varens, like Victor and young Jane herself, is banished from the domestic scene at the novel's end, the reader who has been chilled by the ballad of the "poor orphan child" has reason to wonder why the happiness of the nuclear family cannot be extended by a single degree.

Gilbert and Gubar's assent to Jane's depiction of her marriage to Rochester as an egalitarian marriage of true minds requires a channeling of the novel through the individualist focus of autobiography. Jane's doubles, Bertha Mason and the "baby-phantom" (221) that Jane dreams of at Thornfield, become, in Gilbert and Gubar's reading, mere images of Jane's angry, immature self, and their exorcism is a positive development in Jane's "pilgrimage toward maturity" (366). But in the dream logic within which these night-figures appear, they are thoroughly overdetermined. They are both aspects of Jane and, just as fully, themselves: Bertha Mason and Adele Varens. As the wife of Edward Rochester and his adopted child, Bertha and Adele are the people who are displaced by his union with Jane Eyre. For Adele, the marriage means that she is deprived of the gift-bringing father figure and the affectionate surrogate mother once they become entirely devoted to each other. For Bertha, the introduction of the young governess into the house signals the threat of her replacement as Rochester's wife. Her response is to rip Jane's wedding veil in half and set Rochester on fire. While Rochester is terrified by the possibility that Bertha will attack Jane and orders her to sleep in the nursery with Adele, the "mad" Bertha actually offers a precisely measured response to the threat of supplantation. She warns Jane and reserves the fuller measure of retaliation for Rochester.

The answers to the ethical questions that the narrative raises—such as, Is setting your husband on fire a justifiable response to his taking up with a young governess?—depend on shadings of the background story of the novel. In Rochester's account, Bertha is a madwoman who was foisted on him by their conniving families, a story that legitimates his desire for Jane. But when Jane worries whether she can "enjoy the great good that has been vouchsafed to me, without fearing that any one else is suffering the bitter pain I myself felt a while ago"—that pain being her jealousy over Blanche Ingram—the functional value of Rochester's story becomes clear. Rochester assures Jane, "That you may," because "there is not another being in the world has the same pure love for me as yourself" (261). The hyperbolic story of Bertha's madness is just another version of the excuse "my wife doesn't understand me," which allows Rochester to argue that an affective affinity should supersede a legal contract. Jane's demand that she must have both is ultimately satisfied by Bertha's death, but the legal status that becomes available to Jane through Bertha's demise is no guarantee against the threat that leads Jane to leave Rochester in the first place. Bertha and Adele, the abandoned wife and child, become Jane's oneiric doubles because they represent her fear of occupying the dependent, potentially infantilized, place of a wife. A wealthy husband can always bring in a new governess or a woman servant; Jane can always become the next Bertha, consigned to a spare room. That this inequity can only be overcome by the radical solution of the mutilation of the husband shows that *Jane Eyre* does not, as Armstrong argues, present desire and power as external to each other. From the outset, *Jane Eyre* shows desire as a scene of power; in fact, for Jane, the primary appeal of desire is that it initiates a game of power.

The precondition of that game is erotic possibility, and the entire relationship between Jane and Rochester exemplifies, from its outset, Foucault's principle that sex is an "especially dense transfer point for relations of power" (HS 103). Jane is dissatisfied with the placid femtopia that greets her at Thornfield, and she is pleased to discover that the house "had a master." As a result, she declares that "for my part, I liked it better" (125). The question of Jane's power arises in her first encounter with Rochester when he wonders aloud whether Jane somehow caused his fall, a perplexity which suggests that Jane's desire could somehow collapse their status difference. In their first extended conversation, Jane and Rochester quickly fall into the confessional roles and the "spirals of power and pleasure" of the ritual of the confession as it is explicated by Foucault. Rochester's disingenuous question "Are you fond of presents?" initiates the game in which he acts as "a power that questions, monitors, watches, spies, searches out, palpates, brings to light" and Jane offers the reciprocal "pleasure that kindles at having to evade this power, flee from it, fool it, or travesty it." Jane's ability to deflect Rochester's questions with four perfectly composed replies demonstrates her power to win this game from below, but, as Foucault shows, the subordinate position has its intrinsic pleasures that mean so much more than winning the game: "[S]o many pressing questions singularized the pleasures felt by the one who had to reply. They were fixed by a gaze, isolated and animated by the attention they received" (HS 45). Rochester's gaze is transferred from Jane's person to her portfolio of drawings, and his question as to whether her "head" has "other furniture of the same kind within" (131) signals his recognition that this artistic labor serves as a truer sign than Jane's physical appearance of her essential value. Yet his approval is not enough to bring about a happy ending; in order for the domestic novel to complete its work, it becomes necessary for the power of surveillance to be transferred to Jane. Rochester's blinding accomplishes this transfer, and the partial abatement of his blindness is allowed only after he demonstrates, through his repentance, a proper deference to Jane's rule.

Jane Eyre thus seems to fit neatly within Armstrong's paradigm of the domestic novel. As the power of the gaze is transferred from Rochester to Jane, it is deeroticized; the gaze is transformed from voyeurism to surveillance, and the narrative shifts from scandalous tales of a libertine sexual history to the demonstration of exemplary virtue. But Armstrong's story of the modern individual who is "first and foremost a woman" (8) is the story of a desire that is profoundly anti-erotic, of a subject that finds no pleasure in the friction of exhibitionist display and voyeuristic power, and of a cultural narrative that seeks only to establish the normativity of its passionless supremacy. This domesticated desire anchors Jane's unreliable summary of her autobiography, but it does not account for the force that binds Jane to Rochester as a matter of irrevocable destiny. What makes it impossible for Jane to marry St. John Rivers, or anyone in the world except Rochester, originates in the volatility of the eroticized discourse that passes between Jane and Rochester. Jane is animated in her initial encounters with Rochester not by his approval but by her ability to disrupt his power. After the first fire, when Jane presses to know more of the story of Grace Poole, she tells the reader, "It little mattered whether my curiosity irritated him; I knew the pleasure of vexing and soothing him by turns . . . on the extreme brink I liked well to try my skill" (161). After the revelation of Bertha's existence, when Jane is in the midst of telling Rochester that she must leave him forever, she confides to the reader, "The crisis was perilous; but not without its charm: such as the Indian, perhaps, feels when he slips over the rapid in his canoe" (299). There is no such peril or charm in Jane's dealing with St. John Rivers. When Rivers remains imperturbable after her rejection of his proposal, Jane's frustrated response that "I would much rather he had knocked me down" (400) indicates her desire that Rivers would enter into the contest of wills that opens both sides to the dangers of indecent exposure.

The reason Jane gives for her rejection of Rivers's marriage proposal is precise; the rejection is based on "one item—one dreadful item" (395). The call of religious duty overcomes Jane's fears that her own identity would be eclipsed as Rivers's helpmate, or even that that role would be fatal to her. Both Jane and Diana Rivers imagine that Jane has not the constitution to survive the Indian climate; Diana worries that Jane would be "grilled alive in Calcutta," while Jane calculates that "if I go to India, I go to premature death" (399, 395). Still, she is not dissuaded. "Consent," she argues, is still "possible," except for that "one dreadful item": She cannot "endure the forms of love," which she has no doubt that St. John "would scrupulously observe" (395). The convention that places a woman's sexual virtue above her material existence is given a new twist. What Jane must resist is not rape but loveless sex, even in the support of a missionary husband. This refusal becomes necessary on behalf of an idea of sex as the core of one's being;

Jane's characterization of Rochester as her other half (389, 395) and her insistence that she is "absolutely bone of his bone, flesh of his flesh" (439) equates her sexual relation to Rochester with her identity. The construction of this "fictitious point of sex" (HS 156) that is the truth of the self makes sex more important than life itself. Jane is willing to die a premature death to support St. John's religious mission, but she cannot give him her sex.

The conclusion of *Jane Eyre* folds this idea of sex into a natural symbiosis with domesticity by constructing sexuality in Aristophanic terms as binary, passive, and exclusive. In doing so, it affirms interior virtues of character over social values of status. But this construction belies everything that the book has shown about sex as an active battle for power. The fires that afflict Thornfield are Jane's retaliatory gambits against Rochester's attempts to dictate the terms of their sexual relationship. The first fire follows Rochester's explanation of the presence of Adele through his confession of his affair with Céline Varens. The agency and the cause of this first fire are overdetermined; Bertha sets Rochester on fire over Jane, but within the dynamic of Jane and Rochester, the fire is a figure for Rochester's inappropriate passion for Céline, and the cold bucket of water thrown over the sleeping Rochester is the penance imposed by Jane after Rochester's confession. Since Rochester knows what Jane only suspects, that there is a more disturbing reminder of his sexual past in the house than little Adele, he prepares for the revelation of that secret by diminishing Jane's power. He makes her jealous over Blanche Ingram, a woman whose availability to him is meant to remind Jane of the greater range of possibilities open to a man of his social status. The result is that Jane's loss of power makes her more forgiving; as she relates, "I was growing very lenient to my master; I was forgetting all of his faults" (190). Rochester notes the change in her and enjoys it: "If . . . I lacked spirits and sank into inevitable dejection, he became gay . . . alas! never had I loved him so well" (246). When Rochester's secret is revealed at the church, it becomes clear to Jane why the wedding is so small and why Rochester was so pleased that she "has no kindred to interfere." When she had told him of her lack of family, his response was "that is the best of it" (254). Contrary to the romantic narrative that Jane presents, Rochester never actually chooses Jane over Blanche Ingram because he never had that choice. A man with a wife locked away in the attic cannot marry into a powerful family; when the secret breaks, all hell will break loose with it. But the owner of a large estate who minimizes the number of witnesses to a wedding with an orphan governess might well be able to sustain that union even beyond the revelation of a mad wife in the attic.

As Richardson's Mr. B says to Pamela (in a book Jane has read; 21) after he attempts a sham marriage ceremony: "We might have lived for years, perhaps, very agreeably together; while it would have been in my power to confirm or abrogate the marriage as I pleased" (305). The second fire, the one that destroys Thornfield and mutilates Rochester, is a joint effort by Bertha and Jane to punish Rochester for attempting to perpetrate this fraudulent marriage.

Rochester's inability to marry Blanche Ingram, and the misleading portrayal of that impossibility as a choice, is the equivalent of Jane's return to Rochester without knowing that he is not still married. In each case, the idea that sexual desire constitutes a truth that transcends all social and practical considerations is able to obscure the existence of contradictory material in the background story of the novel. Jane's assertion of the "perfect concord" of her marriage transforms the novel's subtext of a battle fought out through the possibilities available in the social world into the pretext of two minds fused in an ontological union, where "to talk to each other is but a more animated and an audible thinking" (439). The pretext of *Jane Eyre: An Autobiography* is that Jane's story is essentially intrinsic; it says that Jane stands on a principle "given by God" when she refuses to join herself to Rochester and that she is rewarded with the fulfillment of a desire that is immune to the vagaries of social value. That Jane's happiness actually depends on a series of events that are outside her control—an inheritance from a distant relative, the death of Bertha Mason, and the mutilation of Rochester—shows this fabricated interiority to be not only an ideological effect but an attempt to address a moral scandal in the most profound sense of the term. When virtue is rewarded, rather than serving as its own reward, the very concept of morality is endangered by the potential metalepsis of intrinsic value and extrinsic events. The dependence of intrinsic moral value on extrinsic factors that are outside the control of the subject introduces the paradox that ethical theorists have called "moral luck," a concept that, as Bernard Williams warns, threatens to make intuitive notions of innate moral value, such as the one that anchors Jane Eyre's narrative of self-justification, "radically incoherent" ("Moral Luck" 36).

The essentialist, or Kantian, notion of moral value that supposedly informs Jane's principled abandonment of Rochester presumes that moral value is, in Kant's term, "unconditioned." As Thomas Nagel explicates Kant's categorical imperative, "The good will is not good because of what it effects or accomplishes . . . it is good of itself" (57). When Jane leaves Rochester, she argues, "Laws and principles" are "inviolate" (313) and not dependent on circumstance; Jane contends that she does what she must do, regardless of the consequences. But as Williams argues, this intuitive sense that morality reflects an inner integrity that transcends circumstance actually depends on a contingent relation between choices and uncontrollable events ("Moral Luck"). Jane's decisions are justified by their seemingly fortunate consequences, but they do not lead inexorably to the novel's eventual conclusion. If Rochester had committed suicide and Bertha had been delivered by uncaring distant relatives from the relatively benign one-on-one care of Grace Poole to Bedlam, where she was sexually abused and starved, Jane's decision would look like a cold acquiescence to a rigid and uncaring social code. It is only luck—manifested in an inheritance, a suicide, and a mutilation—that connects Jane's principled stand to her destiny as a happy wife and a satisfied autobiographer. It is only in retrospect that the fire that destroys Thornfield is transformed from the vehicle of Rochester's punishment into the condition of possibility, through the removal of Bertha, for the happiness of Jane and Rochester.

The scandal of the concept of moral luck is that it leads to the disappearance of the subject through the evacuation of moral agency. The Kantian notion that true moral agency is immune to the contingency of circumstance or consequence gives it, as Williams suggests, a "supreme kind of dignity or importance" ("Moral Luck" 36) in defining the character of an individual. Jane's principled stand in the first part of the novel is meant to demonstrate that she is the kind of person who deserves the happiness that finally falls to her, but, as Nagel argues, when any moral choice is reintegrated into the web of antecedent circumstances and resultant consequences in which it plays the role of a single event, "the area of genuine agency, and therefore of legitimate moral judgment, seems to shrink to an extensionless point" (66). If Jane's abandonment of Rochester is the only possible response to his attempt to dupe her into a sham marriage that affords no legal status, it hardly qualifies as a self-sacrificing stand on principle. Jane Eyre attempts to repair this void of moral subjectivity with normative discourses of nationality, class, and gender that offer the roles of English, bourgeois, and wife as identities that are imbued with genuine moral character, but, as Williams and Nagel argue, when the source of morality is external to an individual, it becomes entirely a matter of luck. The difference between a philanthropist and a terrorist is not a matter of individual moral character but is primarily the result of what Nagel calls "circumstantial luck," defined as "the kind of problems and situations one faces" (60). That Jane acts philanthropically, albeit within a small circle of kin, is a matter of luck—she receives an abundant inheritance. That she does not have to decide, in the novel's conclusion, whether to take up with a married man is also a matter of luck. Luckily enough, his wife commits suicide.

As Williams argues, the notion of moral luck is not simply a vehicle for the critique of specific hypocrisies; its internal contradiction constitutes a challenge to the Kantian notion that morality claims a privileged place in defining individual character. *Jane Eyre* juxtaposes two discourses—a discourse of unconditioned ethics and a discourse of sexuality—both of which claim to define the essential character and worth of a subject in intrinsic terms. While Jane claims to define the truth of her own identity through this combination of unyielding principle and the integrity of desire, the novel shows how her ultimate moral status depends on the effects of circumstantial and resultant luck. In *Jane Eyre*, marriages acquire the status of artworks; some are more successful, and hence more valuable, than others. The greater success of some affective unions, where "to talk to each other is but a more animated and an audible thinking," gives them a greater moral value. Exactly how much better one union has to be before it can claim the dissolution of another is a question that the novel simplifies through the hyperbolization of the mad, bestial Bertha, and the responsibility for making even that assessment is neatly avoided through the circumstantial luck of Bertha's suicide.

The ability of Jane's triumph to so reliably satisfy readers makes *Jane Eyre*, in Gilles Deleuze and Felix Guattari's terms, Brontë's major novel, the work that affirms the majoritarian "power [*pouvoir*] of constants." In comparison, *Villette* is her "minor" novel, which employs the "power [*puissance*] of variation" to deconstruct the central myths of *Jane Eyre* (101). These myths include the purity of English identity, the natural and inevitable exclusivity of romantic love, and the central narrative premise of the realist novel: the implication that life is composed of a logical sequence of events and that mastering its causal principles can lead to living happily ever after. The hypercanonicity of *Jane Eyre* is an effect of the ease of access offered through the replication of convention. The more intensely polarized reception history of *Villette*, beginning with George Eliot's judgment that it is "a still more wonderful book than *Jane Eyre*" and Matthew Arnold's complaint that it is a "disagreeable" book proving that "the writer's mind contains nothing but hunger, rebellion and rage" testify to the greater interpretive challenges posed by literature that operates in a minor key, always within sight of conventions, but never explicable through them.

Villette opens with a sly subversion of the myth of the organic unity of the English nation. The eponymous Brettons of Bretton recall the pun that secures Jane Eyre's identity as a true heir of authentic Englishness; the very name "Bretton" suggests an aboriginal lineage, as though this family might claim its origin in the ancient Britons who preceded the Saxon invasion. But the immediate disclaimer that this eponymy may be only a "coincidence" (5) with no real historical significance denies the antiquarian satisfaction that Jane Eyre had found in the discovery of her lineage, and the name Bretton is itself ambiguous; if it means anything at all, it may be that these Brettons are not Britons but Bretons, descendants of the Normans who conquered the native Saxons. The Brettons stand throughout the novel as exemplars of English virtues, but the early and emphatic identification of Graham Bretton's appearance as "Celtic (not Saxon)" (16) severely tries the premises of authentic Englishness. Graham is later referred to as a "true young English gentleman" (63) with an "English complexion" (96) and a "fair English cheek" (103), but the descriptions of him as both "Celtic" and "English" fly in the face of the dominant racial mythology of the period, which emphasized the Saxon origins of the English character.

Saxonist mythology of the mid-nineteenth century located the origin of a peculiarly English capacity for self-government in the ability of Saxon freemen in the fifth century to evolve a system of customs that regulated the use of both private and communal property (Macdougall 101; Curtis 9–12, 31–32, 76–80). In the racialistic versions of this myth that were used to argue against granting self-rule to the Celtic Irish, it was claimed that the English had received as a genetic inheritance from their Saxon ancestors a national character that was "superior to every other in the love and possession of useful liberty" (Curtis 76). The contrast between Saxon and Celtic character was outlined by Goldwin Smith: "The Teuton loves laws and parliaments; the Kelt loves a king" (Macdougall 97). The Celtic Irish, according to Saxonist historians, both needed and liked to be subjected to a strong authority. As Robert Knox put it in 1850, "The Celt does not understand what we Saxons mean by independence. . . . As a Saxon, I abhor all dynasties, monarchies and bayonet governments, but the latter system seems to be the only one suitable for the Celtic man" (Curtis 70).

Villette makes much of the opposition between the independent Englishwoman Lucy Snowe and the servile inhabitants of Labassecour, but it is never entirely clear whether that difference is the effect of social circumstances or the manifestation of innate national traits. Lucy Snowe is liable to contrast "quick French blood" with the "marsh-phlegm" (82) of the Labassecourians, but the mixed background of Lucy's family circle makes her a problematic representative of Englishness. If Graham is at least partly

144 : Sex, Lies, and Autobiography

Celtic, then so is his relative Lucy. The Brettons' extended family includes the "Caledonian and Gallic" (280) Home/de Bassompierres, which largely obliterates any possibility of genetic purity of the Brettons of Bretton. Brontë's use of ethnic identifiers draws on, without reifying, the mythology of the Celtic revival of the 1830s and 1840s that arose in response to Saxonist historiography. Lucy describes Graham Bretton's features as not only Celtic but Greek, claiming that his "chin was full, cleft, Grecian and perfect" (96). Graham is thus the literary descendant of St. John Rivers, whose "Greek face," Jane Eyre observed, had "quite an Athenian mouth and chin" (338). The mid-century Celticist revival provided the basis for this equation of the Celtic and the Greek. Celticists of the period tried avidly to produce an ancient genealogy for the Irish that would be even more impressive than the supposed fifth-century Saxon origins of the English. Based on references to the Celts in the Mediterranean area by ancient writers such as Tacitus and Herodotus, Celticist historians variously traced the origins of the Celts in Ireland to migrations led by King Milesius of Spain sometime before 1000 BC or to Greek settlers anywhere between the sixth and third centuries BC.

The identification of the Celts as Greeks was not universally accepted, and Elizabeth Gaskell mixes the terms oddly as she attempts to distance the Brontës from their Irish origins in her description of Patrick Brontë's features: "He never could have shown his Celtic descent in the straight Greek lines and long oval of his face" (22). Patrick Brontë's "Greek" appearance, Gaskell suggests, effaces his "Celtic descent," and in the ensuing narrative it seems that Patrick's true English character emerges the moment he enters St. John's College at Cambridge. Brontë offers a similarly paradoxical account of Graham's ethnicity. Polly is entranced by Graham's "straight Greek features" (424), but her father charges that Graham's red hair and "tongue of guile" betray the fact that "there is a trace of the Celt in all you look, speak and think." Graham's response shows how ethnic identifiers are used ex post facto: "'Sir, I *feel* honest enough,' said Graham; and a genuine English blush covered his face with its warm witness of sincerity" (433). To the English readership of *Villette* that warms to the "English" hearth fires Lucy encounters throughout her stay in Labassecour, Graham's handsome appearance is Greek, his eloquence Celtic, and his sincerity English.

While both Madame Beck and Paul Emmanuel see Lucy Snowe's self-reliant character as quintessentially English, Brontë had good reason not to take any such identification too literally. If Charlotte Brontë had, in the manner of Jane Eyre, recovered her connection to the fallen gentry of her father's kinsfolk, she would have come up with the Irish Ó Pronntaighs

(Chitham 55). Lucy Snowe's fervent attachment to her English identity in a foreign land reenacts what Nancy Armstrong and Leonard Tennenhouse have argued is the prototypical form of the English novel: the New World captivity narrative. While race typically serves in the captivity narrative as the reifying term that definitively separates the (usually female) English captive from her American Indian captors, in *Villette* the hyperbolic accounts of the evils of Roman Catholicism serve a similar function in making the distinction between Englishness and its other into a moral opposition. Lucy Snowe has abundant reason to denounce Roman Catholicism; these denunciations affirm her English identity against the suspicion that her brooding temperament is stereotypically Celtic. Celts were characterized at midcentury, in opposition to the self-disciplined English, as emotional and particularly susceptible to mood swings. In one of the more benign versions of Celtic stereotyping, Thomas Babington Macaulay suggested that the Irish "were an ardent and impetuous race, easily moved to tears or to laughter, to fury or to love. Alone among the nations of Northern Europe they had the susceptibility, the vivacity, the natural turn for acting and rhetoric which are indigenous on the shores of the Mediterranean Sea" (1.69) Lucy Snowe's insistence that she is "guiltless of that curse, an overheated and discursive imagination" (12), and her "firm resolution" after her single dramatic appearance that, having "tried my own strength for once," she would never again take to the stage (141), both exhibit and deny traits that are stereotypically Celtic.

Lucy Snowe's struggles with Hope, Imagination, and Feeling are, she realizes, terribly un-English, and Lucy's description of Louisa Bretton and herself as two ships measures the distance between Lucy's character and proper Englishness. Mrs. Bretton is "the stately ship, cruising safe on smooth seas," while Lucy is "the life-boat, which most days of the year lies dry and solitary in an old, dark boat-house, only putting to sea when the billows run high in rough weather, when cloud encounters water, when danger and death divide between them the rule of the great sea" (181). The difference between the godmother and goddaughter cannot be genetic but only circumstantial; Louisa seems to be comfortably ensconced at the center of the Bretton clan while Lucy ekes out her existence in the midst of an alien culture whose children are forbidden to speak to her outside the classroom. Some commentators see not just a resultant gulf but an active antagonism in Lucy's relation to her native culture. Rosemary Clark-Beattie argues that in Lucy's dealings with the Brettons she is "[t]reated with a bland affection that is in some ways more horrifying than actual cruelty" (826) while Amanda Anderson suggests that when the "Brettons' serene behavior issues in neglect," as it does when Mrs. Bretton renews contact with Lucy after a seven-week lapse, "the letter's breezy kindness carries an almost sadistic edge" (56). But the difference between Lucy's desperation and the "mild, drowsy maternalism" (Anderson 50) of Louisa is less secure than it seems, and the perception of a clear polarity is largely an effect of style. Lucy's melodramatic self-description as a lifeboat in a storm is characteristic of one of the great accomplishments of *Villette*, namely, Brontë's ability to fill such highly charged rhetoric with a sense that the rhetoric itself is straining to capture some portentous truth. Lucy's desire is often expressed in this dramatic rhetoric while her attempts to suppress exorbitant feeling produce a contrasting rhetoric of understatement. In the novel's opening chapters, for example, there is simply no mention of Lucy's attraction to Graham, a palpable reality that is conveyed only through Lucy's observation of her rival and double, little Polly Home.

The oblique understatement of the letter from Louisa Bretton is immediately overshadowed by the hyperbolic rhetoric in which Lucy expresses her desperate loneliness. Lucy's response to the letter quickly shifts from a brief acquiescence in its superficial cheer ("Now, a letter like that sets one to rights!") into an anguished arabesque on the theme of solitude:

Perhaps few persons can enter into or follow out that [process] of going mad from solitary confinement. They see the long-buried prisoner disinterred, a maniac or an idiot!—how his senses left him—how his nerves first inflamed, underwent nameless agony, and then sunk into a palsy—is a subject too intricate for examination, too abstract for popular comprehension. Speak of it! you might almost as well stand up in an European market-place, and propound dark sayings in that language and mood wherein Nebuchadnezzar, the imperial hypochondriac, communed with the baffled Chaldeans. (273–74)

This eloquent plaint clashes with the serene opening of Mrs. Bretton's letter: "It occurs to me to inquire what you have been doing with yourself for the last month or two?" If one presumes that Louisa Bretton has been leading a merry round of parties within the Home/de Bassompierre circle, the contrast between Lucy's precise calculation of "seven weeks as bare as seven sheets of blank paper" (267) and Louisa's vague "month or two" can certainly sound insensitive. But Mrs. Bretton's letter does not suggest that her life has been a lively one. She describes no regular activity except waiting through the days for Graham to return home in the evenings, and she summarizes this existence in a brief metaphor worthy of Lucy: "I seem to live in a moral antipodes, and on these January evenings my day rises when other people's night sets in" (272). The image of early January evenings functions like Lucy's use of storm metaphors and her white cap on white hair, as a portent of impending mortality. After ascribing this importance to Graham's arrivals, Louisa offers only one instance of an evening in the Bretton household, in which Graham, after a day of struggling with "the ordeal of fifty sorts of tempers, and combating a hundred caprices, and sometimes witnessing cruel sufferings" comes home, and promptly, "To my great delight . . . dropped asleep." To someone whose "day rises" with Graham's arrival, the notion that she would be delighted to see him come home and immediately fall asleep is a moment of self-denial as perfect as any practiced by Lucy herself.

Louisa could easily imagine that Lucy has "been just as busy and happy as ourselves" during this period; Lucy is actively earning a living while the only activity in which Mrs. Bretton engages besides waiting for Graham is to deal with her "old Bretton agent," in an attempt to "regain for Graham at least some of what his father left him." Having created the necessity for Graham to endure daily the tempers, caprices, and sufferings of others, Mrs. Bretton can hardly upbraid him for not being the best of company every evening. The letter's final address to Lucy as "my wise, dear, grave little god-daughter" is far more than empty rhetoric in the light of Louisa's actions before the seven-week hiatus. Louisa was the one who put Lucy into a pink dress and had her accompany Graham and herself to a concert, where she then kept her seat at intermission in order to send Graham and Lucy off together (220). Before the "Vashti" performance, Louisa claims that "an arrival" prevents her from joining them (she could hardly plead illness to her son the doctor), so, once again, she sends Graham and Lucy off alone. In the nuanced, nearly opaque rhetorical mode that the novel employs when unrequited desire is forced to remain inexplicit, Louisa operates as a matchmaker, trying to bring about a kin marriage that would help to maintain the insularity of the Brettons of Bretton. But once Graham rediscovers his attachment to Paulina after the Vashti evening, a decent interval needs to elapse before Lucy can rejoin the Brettons in a less central role.

The perception of a more definitive contrast on the novel's surface than in its subtext between Lucy and her godmother is not only the effect of the different levels of explicitness brought about by a division between the work's rhetorical modes. *Villette* repeatedly suggests that there should be a clear opposition between inner worth and the superficiality of conventional value, a theme that culminates in Lucy's furious response to the prospect of Paul Emmanuel's prospective marriage to Justine-Marie:

> This was an outrage. The love born of beauty was not mine; I had nothing in common with it: I could not dare to meddle with it, but another love, venturing diffidently into life after long acquaintance, furnace-tried by pain, stamped by constancy, consolidated by affection's pure and durable alloy, submitted by intellect to intellect's own tests, and finally wrought up, by his own process, to his own unflawed completeness, this Love that laughed at Passion, his fast frenzies and his hot and hurried extinction, in this Love I had a vested interest; and whatever tended either to its culture or its destruction, I could not view impassably. (468)

The difference between Lucy and Justine-Marie, or between Lucy and Ginevra Fanshawe, was the difference in *Jane Eyre* between Jane and Blanche Ingram. But in *Villette*, Brontë introduces a middle term, Paulina Home de Bassompierre, who is not an empty-headed, mercenary coquette but a rich, beautiful woman of exceptional intelligence and admirable character. When Paulina's father expresses consternation that his "wealth and position" may be of any interest to Graham, Lucy contradicts him, insisting that Graham simply "values them as any gentleman would—as *you* would yourself, under the same circumstances" (429). The moral polarity between intrinsic virtue and the arbitrary fortune of social status dissipates; there is a difference in kind, but not of moral degree, between Lucy's relation to Paul Emmanuel and the love of Graham and Polly.

The difference between inner virtue and superficial conformity is thematized in *Villette* as the opposition between English Protestantism and Continental Catholicism, a theme that draws on several centuries of Protestant anti-Catholic polemics. In the interwoven romantic plots of *Villette*, the shuttling of characters through different roles subverts the essential nature of this opposition between the intrinsic and the superficial. The initial triangle that allows for a clear polarity, that of Ginevra, Graham and Lucy, is dissolved at Madame Beck's fête into two triangles: Graham/Ginevra/Hamal, and Graham/Lucy/Paul. After this dispersion, both Graham and Lucy reverse roles. Graham goes from playing the part of the lover who is unable to discern the proper value of Lucy's true worth over Ginevra's insubstantial charms into the victim of Ginevra's refusal to value his substance over Hamal's appearance. Lucy is transformed from the figure of plain appearance and sterling character into someone who is reluctant to choose between the superficial values at which she railed (now embodied by Graham) and a figure who owns the qualities assigned to her in the first configuration (Paul). Lucy remains enamored, throughout the narrative and even in retrospect, of Graham's "countenance, beautiful with a man's best beauty" (190), and for this she is chastised by Paul Emmanuel in terms that recall Lucy's characterization of Graham as Ginevra's "slave": "Your judgment is warped . . . you are indifferent where you ought to be grateful—and perhaps devoted and infatuated, where you ought to be as cool as your name" (345). The realignment of characters and roles occurs in the wake of a performance in which Lucy deconstructs a role and makes it into something other, and better, than it is ("plus beau que votre modele . . . mais ce n'est pas juste" [141]). As she performs the *fat*, Hamal's role in the Ginevra triangle, and outplays the *ours*, she displays the inessentiality of these roles; in different circumstances, the same person, Graham Bretton, can be either an unappreciated *ours* or an overvalued *fat*. There is no reason to believe, however, that every person blessed with wealth and social position, is, by an axiomatic logic, a *fat* morally inferior to every poor earnest *ours*. There is simply no correlation, positive or negative, between social value and moral worth.

A powerful support for the premise that there should be a negative correlation between the two is the influence of Protestant polemics, beginning in the sixteenth century, that emphasized the superiority of Protestantism as a religion of deep faith over the supposed Catholic demand for only a superficial obedience to form. This influence has been strongly felt in British and American autobiographical studies, which have often presumed a Protestant origin of autobiographical writing. Such a presumption, as Peter Burke argues, is "undermined by the many Catholic examples" of "introspection and self-examination" that "were part of the preparation for confession" (27). Lucy Snowe's visit to a Catholic confessional forges the link between Catholic confession and moral introspection; Lucy is driven to the confessional by the impossibility of expressing her desire within the conventions of English Protestant culture. As Clark-Beattie puts it, "the Brettons have no desire to know" Lucy's torment; "unlike Père Silas, they do not wish to plumb the depths of Lucy's soul" (830). Lucy's unwillingness to admit to the reader that she even recognizes Doctor John as Graham Bretton suggests the gap between her desire and the possibility of its fulfillment among the Brettons of Bretton. Lucy's subsequent oscillation between her attraction to Graham Bretton and her interest in Paul Emmanuel restructures, and comes close to reversing, the Protestant/Catholic opposition, which becomes not a moral hierarchy that opposes interiority to surface but a difference between a socially recognizable form of desire and the volatile dyad engaged in intimate combat that Foucault describes as the effect of the technology of the confession. The erotic intimacy of the Catholic confession is effaced in studies that locate the origin of modern subjectivity in eighteenth-century conduct books and the contemporary novels that replicated their ideology. Armstrong's modern subject, who is "first and foremost a woman," is also essentially a Protestant: a figure who has learned to discipline and deeroticize her desire and to ground her identity on her unconditional virtue.

In Foucault's "Catholic" genealogy, sex inherits the role played by love at the beginning of the early modern period as the site of a "value high enough to make death acceptable" (HS 156). Foucault's complaint that this "fictitious" idea of "sex-desire" has usurped the claims of "bodies and pleasures" revises Denis de Rougemont's classic analysis of romantic love as a concept that is religious in origin and antagonistic to the idea of sexual pleasure. De Rougemont's description of romantic love as the desire for an all-encompassing, transcendent value is sharpened in Foucault's characterization of sex as "the general and disquieting meaning that pervades our conduct and our existence . . . a general signification, a universal secret, an omnipresent cause" (69). This vague disquietude both initiates the romantic plots of *Jane Eyre* and *Villette* and steers those plots away from immediate resolution. In both novels, as soon as the female protagonist extricates herself from an economic predicament and settles into a comfortable situation controlled by women, she begins to look beyond the boundaries of her setting. Jane's trips to the roof of Thornfield and her reluctance to leave her searching view of "the horizon bounded by a propitious sky" in order to re-enter an "attic [that] seemed as black as a vault" (114) foreshadows her less than despairing account of her first steps outside Thornfield as she leaves Rochester: "A mile off, beyond the fields, lay a road which stretched in the contrary direction to Millcote; a road I had never travelled, but often noticed, and wondered where it led: thither I bent my steps" (316). Similarly, as soon as Lucy Snowe establishes her occupancy of *l'allée défendue*, she begins to listen to the "far-off sounds of the city," to look at the moon that she imagines shining over "an old thorn at the top of an old field, in Old England," and she "long[s] . . . for something to fetch me out of my present existence, and lead me upwards and onwards" (108–9). That "something" becomes the two figures who fill the role of Jane Eyre's "master." Lucy looks first at Graham, the universally observed and observing male presence in the female *pensionnat*, whose entry is marked by a distinctive ring, "quick, but not loud" (112), and the "hum" of whose "man's voice pervaded, I thought, the whole conventual ground" (115). But from the very start, Graham's masculine presence is shadowed by another voice whose "lectur[es] with open doors, and his name, and anecdotes of him, resounded in one's ears from all sides" (129). Paul Emmanuel's ring, too, is individuated; its "particular peal had an accent of its own," and it has an immediate effect on Lucy: it "chased my dream, and startled my book from my knee" (133).

The union that Lucy could form with Graham was the one rejected by Jane Eyre with St. John Rivers: a comfortable kin alliance supported by friendly female relatives. The effect when "We Quarrel" (188) is a laughably weak tea, infinitely blander even than Rivers's refusal to show any anger at Jane; after one harsh comment from Lucy about his becoming Ginevra's "slave," Graham thanks her for being so interested in his welfare. The quasi-courtship that takes place after Graham realizes that he is an object of ridicule to Ginevra is conducted primarily (like Graham's later courting of Paulina) by letter. This Protestant courtship is soon interrupted by a Catholic intervention; when Lucy retires to the garret to savor Graham's first letter, her happiness at finding it both "long" and "kind" is interrupted by the appearance of the Nun, the ghost of a woman buried alive "for some sin against her vow" (106). This presumably sexual sin suggests a far more risky and exciting form of sex-desire, one that requires that we be willing to die for it. Lucy reads Graham's letter in the attic, where she practiced the dramatic part she found herself "warming" to (141), and Graham's appreciation of this performative warmth is tested when Lucy and Graham attend the Vashti performance. This episode inspires some of Lucy's densest, most self-referential prose ("Scarcely a substance herself, she grapples to conflict with abstractions" [258]) and forces her realization of Graham's limits: "For what belonged to storm . . . he had no sympathy, and held with it no communion. . . . Cool young Briton" (259).

While Graham inherits the unerotic role of St. John Rivers, Paul Emmanuel's Spanish features recall both Rochester's "dark eyes and swarthy skin" that make him "the very model of an Eastern Emir" (*Jane Eyre* 186) and Zamorna of the Angrian tales, who was like "the Grand Sultan of Turkey surrounded by his seraglio" (Alexander 118). This dominant mode of erotic attraction in Brontë's work fits the model described by Daryl Bem as exotic/erotic attraction.[3] Paul Emmanuel's foreignness sparks an ambivalent reaction of fear and "curiosity" (324) in Lucy. One of their first quarrels results from her reluctance to sit too near him on a bench; when she repairs this "misunderstanding" at a later opportunity, she discovers that "I was losing the early impulse to recoil from M. Paul" (347). Paul's most widely recognized trait in the *pensionnat* is his ability to inspire fear, and Lucy's assertion that he is capable of frightening Ginevra "almost into hysterics at the sound of his step or voice" (129) fits Lucy's pattern of representing her own feelings toward men through female surrogates. From the outset of Lucy's dealings with Paul, she recognizes the inevitability of entering into a struggle for power with him ("this little man was of the order of beings who must not be opposed, unless you possessed an all-dominant force sufficient to crush him at once" [137]), but she also sees a depth that others do not: "in his vexed, fiery, and searching eyes," she finds "a sort of appeal behind all its menace" (134). The pleasure of display and the power of surveillance circulate between Lucy and Paul from the outset of their acquaintance. Paul's power of surveillance seems monolithic in their first encounter when he examines Lucy's face and allows her to enter the *pensionnat*, but his judgment that her face contains "*bien des choses*" suggests that he confronts an enigma that is not transparent to scrutiny. Paul occupies a position of detached observation during Lucy's performance as the *fat*, but Lucy is able to turn display into both a power and a pleasure. Thinking of "nothing but the personage I represented—and of M. Paul, who was listening, watching, prompting in the side-scenes," Lucy discovers that "feeling the right power come . . . having accepted a part to please another: ere long . . . I acted to please myself" (140–41). The satisfaction of "pleasing myself" is less autonomous than it appears; Lucy's divided focus between the personage of the *fat* and M. Paul suggests that her pleasure lies in proving, as much to him as to herself, her ability to so far outshine expectation.

Jane Eyre presents the opposition between companionate love and passionate desire as the difference between the unacceptable (St. John Rivers) and the necessary (Rochester). *Villette* reproduces this opposition but vastly diminishes the stakes of the difference. Graham is never disdained, as Rivers was by Jane, as an offense to Lucy's personal integrity. Even after the rapprochement of Lucy and Paul is well underway, Graham remains a sensual presence for Lucy: "his voice still kept a pleasant tone for my name; I never liked 'Lucy' so well as when he uttered it" (362). Graham's affective potential remains a reality even in retrospect, in the mental space the white-haired narrating Lucy maintains for him that, she imagines, "released . . . from hold and constriction . . . might have magnified into a tabernacle for a host" (457). The sex-desire that joins Lucy and Paul is not a metaphysical force that transcends material separation but the effect of the friction the two are able to generate in their constant quarrels. When Lucy decides, like Jane, to try her skill at vexing her master ("M Paul was so tragic, and took my defection so seriously, that he deserved to be vexed" [340]), she finds that he is more than willing to abdicate the role of the master and enter into this contest on equal terms. He counterattacks, trashing the English and their icons, until Lucy breaks out in indignant protest: "Vive l'Angleterre, l'Histoire et les Heros! A bas la France, la Fiction et les Faquins!" Paul's response shows that he has no interest in the relative merits of the French and the English; he laughs, and Lucy realizes, "He now thought that he had got the victory, since he had made me angry" (341). While the arc in *Jane Eyre* from Jane's principled stand to the matrimonial imagery of "flesh of my flesh" suggests that desire shares an essential, interior space with a moral character whose acts inevitably affirm inviolable principles, *Villette* denies the inevitable nature of erotic cathexis and exemplifies Foucault's principle that interiority itself, the "fictitious point of sex," is the effect of eroticized display. Paul Emmanuel understands the performative basis of this interiority that mixes abjection and defiance. Recalling the game of surveillance and display of Lucy's vaudeville performance, Paul asks her to consider how many times in their daily lives those roles have been reversed: "How often, in your insular presence, have I taken a pleasure in trampling upon, what you are pleased to call, my dignity; tearing it, scattering it to the winds, in those mad transports you witness with such hauteur, and which I know you think very like the ravings of a third-rate London actor" (366). Paul not only acknowledges that Lucy has the power to judge his histrionic performances; he knowingly continues to sacrifice the authoritative persona that he so carefully cultivates for all other eyes in order to convince her that he is not "some species of tyrant or Bluebeard" (137).

While *Jane Eyre* is structured on the seemingly ethical opposition between the impossible (Rivers) and the ineluctable (Rochester), *Villette* offers in its place an opposition between the fictional and the real, with *Jane Eyre* serving as a crucial reference point as the exemplar of the fictional. Jane's three-day swoon is followed by her resurrection into her true English identity as an "Eyre"; Lucy reawakens from a similar faint to the movable furniture of England but with no more intimate connection to her homeland or to the Brettons of Bretton than she had had before. The reintroduction of Paulina Home de Bassompierre in Lucy's new setting recapitulates Lucy's displacement in the novel's opening chapters and derails the Cinderella fantasy of *Jane Eyre*, in which hidden merit ultimately triumphs over unearned advantage. The ethical subtext of *Jane Eyre*, which legitimates the various injuries suffered by Rochester, is revisited in *Villette* in allusions that suggest that the reader, the writer, and the characters of *Villette* have read the novel titled *Jane Eyre*. Miss Marchmont's lifelong identity as a grieving widow is established with a tweak of the first encounter between Jane and Rochester; Miss Marchmont's Frank, unluckily, falls off his horse headfirst rather than feetfirst. Paul Emmanuel's response to Lucy's accidental breaking of his glasses suggests that he is a particularly astute reader of *Jane Eyre*, one who recognizes the motive and the stakes of this "accident"; holding his broken spectacles, he exclaims, "You are resolved to have me quite blind and helpless in your hands!" (326). *Jane Eyre* represents romantic love as an unmistakable and inexorable force through which desire is cathected onto a single object that is differentiated, to an infinite degree, above all others. Replicating the romantic conventions of *Jane Eyre*, Miss Marchmont is fated to a solitary life when she loses her other half, but when Paul Emmanuel is able to make a joke about Rochester's blinding, those conventions seem to lose much of their fateful power. In *Villette*, the heroine is unable to make a clear choice not only between two objects but between two modes of romantic love: either one, she seems to feel, might lead to a happy life. Even after the loss of both, Lucy Snowe does not entomb herself in a posthumous existence. She runs her own school through her middle years, and she retires not to provincial solitude but to the city of London, where, in a perpetual present, "you are deeply excited" (49). Love is not quite, Lucy's diegetic existence suggests, a matter of life and death.

Jane Eyre properly merges its mimetic and diegetic temporalities at its conclusion, in a fully conventional form; all problems are resolved, and the reader is left with the prospect of the protagonists living happily ever after. In *Villette*, the single, early, unelaborated image of Lucy's urban self-reliance does not entirely subsume the novel's baroque excursions, often framed in the rhetoric of the Christian sermon, on desire and loss. The beginning of chapter 17 uses the story in John's Gospel of the healing pool at Bethesda as its text: "A great multitude of impotent folk, of blind, halt, withered, wait[ed] for the moving of the water. / For an angel went down at a certain season into the pool, and troubled the water: whosoever then first stepped in was made whole of whatever disease he had" (John 5:3–4). As the Gospel passage continues, it describes how a lame man had been unable, for "eight and thirty years," to be the first into the waters after the angel's visitation, and how he was finally healed by a miracle wrought by Christ. As a parable, the passage is meant to emphasize the importance of Christ for human redemption. Brontë's sermon makes no mention of

Christ, and focuses not on the single healed figure but on the "Thousands" who "lie round the pool, weeping and despairing, to see it, through slow years, stagnant" (179). The spectacle of this despairing multitude results in a meditation on the gap between divine and earthly temporalities: "Long are the 'times' of Heaven; the orbits of angel messengers seem wide to mortal vision; they may en-ring ages: the cycle of one departure and return may clasp unnumbered generations; and dust, kindling to brief suffering life, and, through pain, passing back to dust, may meanwhile perish out of memory again, and yet again." The embedded allusion to Genesis ("dust thou art, and unto dust thou shalt return" [3:19]) frames an entire human cycle within the longer, oblivious "times" of angel messengers, but the passage as a whole highlights the trouble with angels: The uncertainty of their arrival makes them unreliable messengers, but the rare blessings they confer inevitably raise our hopes that this life should be more than a painful preparation for the next. The image of capricious angelic visitation repeatedly knits the novel's theological imagery to its uncertain romantic plots. Graham's letters are figured as the deposits of "a passing seraph" (244) or "some angel" (271), while the books left in Lucy's desk by Paul Emmanuel issue from "the brownie's work," whose results can be seen although one can never "detect the hours and moments of his coming" (343). In a more elaborate use of this angelic imagery, while Lucy waits and hopes for Paul to see her before he leaves Europe, she imagines an angel who enters Hades offering "a doubtful hope of bliss to come, not now, but at a day and hour unlooked for," and she judges that this dubious gift is "suspense—a worse boon than despair" (446).

While John's Gospel uses the healing of the body as a metaphor for the redemption of the soul, Brontë uses the soul's redemption as a figure for romantic fulfillment. The biblically resonant language of the unknowable "hours and moments of his coming" and the "bliss to come . . . at a day and hour unlooked for" inflates the image of redemption beyond the moment of individual judgment into the universal finality of the Second Coming, of which Matthew's Gospel warns that "of that day and hour knoweth no man, no, not the angels of heaven," and that "Ye know neither the day nor the hour wherein the Son of man cometh" (Matt 24:36; 25:13). Brontë was confident that in the "times of Heaven," suspense would not be eternal; her belief in the doctrine of universal salvation (Barker 264) offered redemption to all, even priests (*Villette* 420). But within the finite cycle of dust passing to dust, the certainty that "at some hour, though perhaps not *your* hour, the waiting waters will stir; in *some* shape, though perhaps not the shape you dreamed, which your heart loved, and for which it bled, the healing herald will descend" (179) carries only a dubious promise. *Some* angel will arrive, suspense will end, but its termination may not be an earthly fulfillment: "To how many maimed and mourning millions is the first and sole angel visitant, him easterns call Azrael"—the angel of death in Muslim theology. The deliverance from suspense can take two forms, each of which acquires an equivalent theological significance in Brontë's imagery: the fulfillment of sex-desire or death.

Lucy's struggle with "Feeling," which occasions this hyperbolic outburst, is prompted both by her proximity to Graham and by her first skirmish, at the vaudeville, with Paul Emmanuel. Paul's choice of Lucy as the only one who could learn the part of the *fat* in the allotted time, despite her disadvantage as a foreign speaker, introduces the possibility of a bond formed through the "submi[ssion] by intellect to intellect's own tests," and the hint of triangular rivalry in Zelie's attempt to force Lucy into masculine dress shows both that the bond between Lucy and Paul is potentially erotic and that this intellectual eroticism is never safe from compromise by arbitrary external impediments. After the vaudeville, Lucy looks to overcome the principal impediment to a union with Paul in her first journey outside the space of the *pensionnat* when she ends up in a Catholic confessional after passing "beyond cemeteries, Catholic and Protestant" (158). Bringing the doctrine of universal salvation into an earthly context, Lucy imagines that if God can redeem the souls in all of those cemeteries divided by sect, she could be equally ecumenical in her romantic prospects. But the experience of the confessional proves otherwise; the opportunity for the explicit articulation of desire produces the faint that drives Lucy back into the arms of Englishness.

If the problem with the Brettons is that they do not recognize the depths of Lucy's interior torment, the danger of Catholicism is that it is actually less superficial than it seems. The ritual of confession promises absolution on the condition of pure interiority; an act of perfect contrition requires entirely selfless remorse. Père Silas, like Paul Emmanuel evaluating his actors, is able to distinguish Lucy's true feeling from confessions that have become "formal and trivial with habit" (162), and he considers Lucy a special prize because she seems to understand the Church's doctrine of the infinite significance of the soul's depth. When Silas reappears as part of the Catholic conspiracy in the book's final chapters, he attempts to enforce the implications of this doctrine; he rules that Justine-Marie's death imposes on Paul Emmanuel a requirement of perpetual celibacy because to do otherwise would violate the monotheistic nature of a value "high enough to make death acceptable." While Foucault complains that the transferal of this value to "the agency of sex" has exerted a monolithic force in usurping the claims of our bodies and pleasures, what is dazzling and unsettling about *Villette* is that it shows how this hyperbolic desire can exist alongside the knowledge that it is not necessarily so; that cathected desire is not an inexorable metaphysical force that comes into being through the unmistakable recognition of one's other half but a deliberate and tortuous fabrication that exists, as Lucy puts it, only "after long acquaintance, furnace-tried by pain, stamped by constancy, consolidated by affection's pure and durable alloy, submitted by intellect to intellect's own tests, and finally wrought up, by his own process, to his own unflawed completeness." Foucault's thesis that a general deployment has spread this hyperbolization of sex-desire throughout the bourgeoisie would require the entire class to value passionate commitment over companionate comfort. *Villette* suggests that this agonistic construction has only a few aberrant participants while the rest are content to enjoy it voyeuristically as fiction.

Lucy Snowe, the strange nobody, is unwilling to accept either the Catholic or the Protestant circumscriptions of her extravagant desire. Her rejection of the ritual of the Catholic confession takes a doctrinally orthodox Protestant form in the repudiation of the standing of priests to intervene between the individual soul and God: "As to what lies below, leave that with God. Man, your equal, weak as you, and not fit to be your judge, may be shut out thence." But Lucy's "heretic narrative" immediately passes from reformation to rebellion: "take it to your Maker—show Him the secrets of the spirit He gave—ask Him how you are to bear the pains He has appointed" (179). This is not an appeal for God's forgiveness or approval but a protest against the obdurate nature of the desire He must have created. As this passage asserts the privilege of the "strong native bent of the heart" to demand that the surveillant authority disclose His motives, the narrative leaves behind the penitential form of the early modern spiritual autobiography and acquires the self-justifying, fully modern form of the post-Rousseauean autobiography. Despite the evidence of Brontë's own strong religious belief, the "Maker" here crosses from tenor to vehicle, becoming the imaginary form through which the narrator attempts to understand the ethical nature of her own desire. When He is called to account for the paradoxes of His creation, His presence becomes no more literal than that of Azrael.

The metaphoric field of *Villette* is pervaded by this fluid and collapsible relation of tenor and vehicle. The figure of the angel-troubled water of

Bethesda hints at the image that haunts the text like a traumatic obsession, the storm, which generally functions as an image of passion but ultimately becomes the final, literal plot event that terminates the engagement of Lucy and Paul. The two dominant sources of *Villette*'s imagery are the theological and the natural sublime, and both inform the final, foreboding image of the storm that takes Paul Emmanuel: "The skies hang full and dark—a rack sails from the west; the clouds cast themselves into strange forms—arches and broad radiations; there rise resplendent mornings—glorious, purple as monarch in his state; the heavens are one flame; so wild are they, they rival battle at its thickest—so bloody, they shame Victory in her pride. I know some signs of the sky; I have noted them ever since childhood" (495). These "signs of the sky"—the purple, flaming, bloody clouds—are the proverbially dreaded "red sky at morning," a wisdom at least as old as the Christian Bible: "And in the morning, It will be foul weather today: for the sky is red and lowring" (Matthew 16:3). This is not a supernatural sign but a materially explicable one; since storm systems in the midlatitudes travel west to east, a red morning results when the sun can be seen in the east and reflects off gathering clouds to the west. The image of Bethesda is reinvoked in the description of the storm as the "perfect work" of the "destroying angel of tempest," and in the "thousand weepers, praying in agony on waiting shores," who "listened for that voice" to say "Peace, be still"—the words with which Christ calmed the waters that terrified the faithless apostles. This time, though, the words are "not uttered till, when the hush came, some could not feel it: till, when the sun returned, his light was night to some" (495). This "sun" is a pun, the redemptive promise of which is obliterated by—take your pick—a destroying angel or a force of nature.

This diminution of the Son is characteristic of Brontë's work. As Marianne Thormahlen notes, there is a "singular discrepancy" between Brontë's fiction and the Protestant theology of her time; although even Brontë's favorite preacher, F. D. Maurice, insisted that we "could not think, breathe, live a single hour" without being "joined to Christ," Brontë's work "accords very little space to the figure of Christ" (Thormahlen 64). Lucy Snowe confronts the forces, represented as storms, that make it impossible for her to live a quiet life, to "escape occasional great agonies by submitting to an whole life of privations and small pains" (38) with no sense of mediation; these forces are both "a Fate [that] was my permanent foe" (157) and a part of her nature, "the being I was always lulling . . . a craving cry I could not satisfy" (109). The storm that takes Paul Emmanuel's life marks the third arrival in Lucy Snowe's life of the keening Banshee. The second visitation had been for Miss Marchmont, and Lucy's "mourning-dress" (36) at her initial meeting with Miss Marchmont indicates that the prior event had been a recent one. This first event receives only the most opaque representation, in Lucy's invitation to the reader to imagine its opposite: "I will permit the reader to picture me, for the next eight years, as a bark slumbering through halcyon weather, in a harbour still as glass" (35). As the metaphor is extended, its tenor is reversed; the narrator has "somehow . . . fallen over-board, or . . . there must have been a wreck at last." This dreamlike uncertainty is extended into the next stage of the extended metaphor, where the relation between literal event and imaginary representation becomes doubly wrong; the metaphoric vehicle becomes literal, but the literal experience does not belong to the narrator: "To this hour, when I have the nightmare, it repeats the rush and saltness of briny waves in my throat, and their icy pressure on my lungs." These physical sensations could reassault a near-drowning victim as traumatic repetition, but they are not Lucy's experience, and they do not belong to this first appearance of the Banshee but to its third appearance, when Paul Emmanuel did feel the waves in his throat, and their icy pressure on his lungs.

This assertion of the terror of drowning as Lucy's own experience invokes the continued presence of the lost other as something as real as the physical world. In Freud's description of melancholia, it is the response of the morbid temperament that refuses to find more value in reality than in the lost object. The restoration of Paul Emmanuel's physical presence is accomplished throughout the text in apostrophes ("You should have seen him smile, reader" [321]; "his figure (such as it was, I do not boast of it)" [338]) that lure the reader into a fictional temporality. Having been introduced to Lucy Snowe as the solitary, white-haired inhabitant of the city, the reader is invited to imagine that if the romantic plot reaches its expected conclusion, these will be moments drawn from a lifelong union. That prospect is already lost to Lucy when the words are written, and the rereader of Villette rediscovers these nostalgic moments as acts of incredible rhetorical discipline, which leave inexplicit the depth of loss they hide. As divine redemption becomes a failed hypothesis and Paul Emmanuel a physical presence, Villette adopts the theological sublime as the rhetorical vehicle of material loss.

A similar reduction of the supernatural to the material occurs in the exorcism of the Nun, a transformation that diminishes the threat of Catholicism from a metaphysical evil into a seemingly manageable economic problem. The demand of the Catholic conspirators that Paul Emmanuel must spend three years tending to Mme Walravens's plantation is drawn from anti-Catholic literature of the period, in which the Church is liable to thwart the sexual desires of its members in ways that lead to its own enrichment (Clark-Beattie 841). Lucy is content to allow Paul to fulfill this obligation since it seems finite in nature, and, she asks, how can one fault a person who feels bound to honor even a spurious claim? While she waits for Paul in his New World exile, a final allusion to Jane Eyre produces yet another transformation of the supernatural into the economically quantifiable: Lucy receives a windfall of a hundred pounds from a relative of Miss Marchmont. The magical power of Jane's inheritance to transform her from orphan castoff to the lady of an estate becomes, in the antimythic world of Villette, simply an opportunity for Lucy Snowe to expand the size of her school.

When Lucy uses her windfall to turn her externat into a pensionnat, this plain economic event acquires a biblical resonance. Lucy becomes one of the good servants in the parable of the talents, those who increase the bequest left them during the master's temporary absence and present him with the surplus on his return. Where Jane's desert seemed to depend on an innate commitment to principle, Lucy earns her good fortune by incremental labor and luck. But the parable, in which the least-privileged servant buries the one talent left to him and is punished for not having added to it, has a Calvinist quality that presents Brontë with a theological conundrum. Matthew's Gospel makes the meaning of the story clear: "For unto every one that hath shall be given, and he shall have abundance: but from him that hath not shall be taken away even that which he hath" (25:29). The passage legitimates bourgeois values of hard work and material increase, and it takes these external signs of prosperity as markers of divine election. Lucy Snowe's terror that, for some inscrutable reason, "some must deeply suffer while they live, and I thrilled in the certainty that of that number, I was one" (157) reflects Brontë's youthful fear that her belief in a merciful God who offers universal salvation might be unduly optimistic, and "if the doctrine of Calvin be true I am already an outcast" (Barker 154). In Calvinist terms, not just Lucy's desires but her suffering mark her as reprobate. Rousseau's paradox of suffering and conscience suggests the psychological basis of this fear; when suffering prompts the self-examination of conscience, it raises the doubt that suffering may be in some way deserved.

Foucault offers two alternatives to the melodramas of self-accusation that result from the conflation of Christian and bourgeois ethics of sacrifice. At the conclusion of the first volume of The History of Sexuality, he calls for the reinstatement of the claims of "bodies and pleasures" over the deflection of those pleasures into the hyperbolic and fictitious "agency of sex." In later essays and interviews, he argues that a cultivation, rather than an abnegation, of the self can be inherently ethical. Only those who have improperly lost control of their own desires, Foucault contends, are liable to impose modes of domination on others. Thus, he concludes, "Care for others should not be put before the care of the self. The care of the self is ethically prior in that the relationship with oneself is ontologically prior" (EST 288). Foucault's second principle affirms the Protestant ethos of Jane Eyre; Rochester's attempts to manipulate others only occur, the ethic of the "care of the self" suggests, because he was unable to control his improper desire for Bertha and Céline. Jane's ability to discipline her own desire makes her into a proper guide for Rochester as she teaches him how to "keep from being carried away by the appetites and the pleasures" (UP 31).

The disappearance of Bertha Mason, Adele Varens, and the Morton School children at the conclusion of Jane Eyre indicates the limited scope of this individualist ethos; Jane's self-discipline creates only a limited obligation within the immediate sphere of marital and genetic bonds. The closing chapters of Villette return to the ethical questions that are too neatly resolved in Jane Eyre, and they offer a less secure and less egoistic account of the ethical state of the autobiographer. The gothic horror of Rochester's mutilation first recurs in a miniaturized reverse image in Villette. When Lucy can think of no other way to conciliate Paul in one of their last quarrels except to "cut my own finger—half on purpose" (416) while sharpening a pen, this self-mutilation, which recalls the production of Polly's dutifully bloodstained handkerchief in the book's opening chapters, acknowledges what Jane Eyre pretended was not necessarily true: that in any union between a man and a woman in a patriarchal society, it is far more likely that the woman will be the one to suffer a disfiguring of identity. One reading of Villette, expressed most flamboyantly by Kate Millett, takes this realization as the central theme of the book and describes the death of Paul Emmanuel as the fulfillment of Lucy Snowe's fantasy of escape. But this privileging of the value of work over love belies the extravagant rhetoric with which Villette mourns Paul's loss. Brontë had examined the bourgeois ethos of hard work and self-reliance in The Professor, in which she averred that "my hero was to work his way through life as I had seen real living men work theirs—he was not to get a shilling he had not earned" (37). She then repeatedly broke this rule in the course of the novel, where Crimsworth's material success depends more on luck than on work or desert. Crimsworth's belief that his final prosperity is the result of his own efforts reveals a willful blindness to the fact that he is actually bailed out by the interventions of Hunsden and Vandenhuten every time his principled stands throw him into destitution. When Lucy's hard work does not lead to domestic bliss, *Villette* inverts the story of Crimsworth's unearned prosperity, and *Villette* is left without a causal principle. Is Lucy Snowe's romantic privation somehow a matter of desert, or is she just unlucky? *Villette*'s unwillingness to reward virtue offers no basis on which the future could avoid the sufferings of the past.

Paul Emmanuel's disappearance into the world of Bertha Mason, the New World plantation which was the source of Jane's magical fortune, indicates the wider ethical range of *Villette* to that of *Jane Eyre*. The New World plantation is a recurrent marginal presence in Brontë's novels, beginning with *The Professor*. One of the crudest of Crimsworth's students looks forward to rejoining "her father in the —— Isles," and "exult[s] in the thought that she should there have slaves, whom, as she said, she could kick and strike at will" (130). Spivak presumes that Brontë is simply incapable, as a matter of historical condition, of addressing the moral problematics of imperialism, but the reversal of the representation of the New World from *Jane Eyre* to *Villette*, its transformation from miraculous source of unexpected plenitude to the land of no return, employs the relation of colonial plantations to Europe as a systematic trope for an inquiry into the nature of obligation. When Paul Emmanuel goes off to the New World, he cannot repay one obligation without engaging in a system of exploitation and incurring an even greater debt. *Jane Eyre* draws on the European fear that no one comes back from New World plantations untainted; *Villette* locates that fear not in a reification of race but in economics. The refiguration of Jane Eyre's inheritance as Lucy's receipt of a bequest from a relative of Miss Marchmont suggests the moral problem of imperialist profits. Lucy's windfall is not a confirmation of genetic identity but the effect of a bad conscience; Lucy somehow knows that the money from Miss Marchmont's relative "was a peace-offering to his conscience, reproaching him in the matter of, I know not what" (493). *Villette* approaches the Marxist realization that all money is, ontologically, other people's money, and when it comes flying in over the threshold it brings with it the history of its production and its accumulation.

Lucy's place among the thousands who wait, in equivalent suspense, for the ships laden with bounty from colonial plantations splinters the individualist ethos of *Jane Eyre* that is able to make Bertha, Adele and everyone outside the nuclear Rochester family dwindle into insignificance. *Villette* shares with *Jane Eyre* the autobiographical focus on interiority, but it parses that space differently. It reaffirms, in the intensity of its style, the belief that passion is a matter of infinite importance, and it demands that it be honored with a theological reverence, but Villette is never able to support the fantasy that a trust in one's intrinsic value will lead, by an inevitable moral law, to a privileged place in the extended kingroup of the national family, or even to the satisfaction of individuated desire. Villette does not, finally, affirm the ontological priority of the self in erotic or economic terms. It finds the most intense eroticism in an overlap of charged subjectivities, while its economic subject exists within a worldwide web of interdependence, and exerts only a minimal control over her own destiny.

In Armstrong and Tennenhouse's argument that the English novel evolves from the New World captivity narrative, they contend that when the English subject returns to the English community, she is never entirely re-assimilated. Having defended her Englishness in an alien environment by asserting her distinctness through the vehicle of the English language, this now strongly individuated subject cannot resume a seamless relation to her own culture. Lucy Snowe's return to her native English culture is shadowed by such a deracination. Throughout Villette, Lucy's identity is repeatedly tied to language and, in particular, to writing. Lucy's Reason chides her not to allow her writing skills to foster unrealistic expectations in her correspondence with Graham. When Lucy pleads that "surely there cannot be error in making written language the medium of better utterance than faltering lips can achieve" (229), Reason responds that Lucy's "inferiority" in the presence of speech should remind her of how she will be valued in person. The courtship and the combat between Lucy and Paul are centered on Lucy's intellectual, and particularly her literary, abilities. Paul is initially dubious of Lucy's right to "a knowledge of my own" (355), but his pride in her ability is manifested when he boasts of the quality of her dicteé and creates the show-trial where she produces her tour de force on "Human Justice." The letters that Lucy exchanges with Paul during the three happiest years of her life are an attenuated version of the mythic intersubjectivity of Jane Eyre, where "to talk to each other is but a more animated and audible thinking." Such perfect communication is, as Jacques Derrida argues, precisely what does not exist, and the admission that communication is dependent on writing ultimately has to acknowledge Derrida's metaphor in The Post Card that a letter can always not arrive.

Lucy's response to this unavoidable lack is to retire to London and to write an autobiography. Although she has presumably spent most of her life in Villette by the time of her retirement, she finally settles in her own linguistic community, in the world where people speak English. Lucy's choice of residence in the city of London, rather than in a Marchmont-like provincial seclusion, revises the moves of Crimsworth and Jane Eyre, who take their fortunes into pastoral settings that show a proper reverence for sentiment and tradition. In *Jane Eyre*, Englishness is an essential matter of blood and breeding; in *Villette*, it is a performed linguistic identity. While *Jane Eyre* creates the effect of amateur performance, as if the written text is simply the transcript of Jane's continuous monologue restructured by the professional efforts of Currer Bell, the overt investment in style throughout *Villette* signals the self-conscious professionalism of an author who struggles with language as a recalcitrant medium. One of the most harrowing passages in *Villette* is Lucy's description of the agonies of composition as a battle with "the most maddening of masters . . . all cold, all indurated, all granite, a dark Baal," an anti-muse who only relinquishes a small morsel at "some long-trembling sob of the wind" when "the irrational demon would wake unsolicited" and "rush from its pedestal like a perturbed Dagon, calling to its votary for a sacrifice" (356). The invocation of the Banshee and the comparison of this figure to Paul Emmanuel when Lucy calls this Baal "the most maddening of masters (him before me always excepted)" shows that, for Lucy, autobiographical writing becomes a repetition of the eroticized combat of display and surveillance that she lived with Paul.

Despite Lucy's repeatedly stated preference for a quiet life, the imagery with which she describes her placid existence before the first arrival of the Banshee suggests the drive that continually propels *Villette* beyond the homeostatic conclusions of *The Professor* and *Jane Eyre*. The sunny prospect of "basking, plump and happy, stretched on a cushioned deck" is, Lucy imagines, the equivalent of being "buried, if you will, in a long prayer" (35). As the metaphoric vehicle slips from an air of comfortable indolence into the deadly suffocation of being "buried" in an uncertainly long prayer, Lucy tries to contain her uneasiness with a rhetorical question that assimilates the theologically vast to the culturally proper: "A great many women and girls are supposed to pass their lives something in that fashion: why not I with the rest?" The question refuses to remain rhetorical; immediately after Miss Marchmont's death, "a keen, low breeze," punning the sound of the Banshee, tells Lucy to "Leave this wilderness . . . and go out hence" (44). Faced with the choice between "the passionate pain of change" and "the palsy of custom" (237), Lucy's choice not to bury herself in a long prayer casts her into the perpetual excitement of the exotic/erotic. *Jane Eyre* ends where it does because its narrative has been entirely assimilated to the repetition of custom, where bourgeois virtue is rewarded with material prosperity. *Villette* presents a life not as the teleological unfolding of knowable principles but as something lived in the interims of traumatic events. Lucy Snowe lives on in the uncertain but always exciting world of strangers; her everyday dealings with the anonymous citizens of London form the mundane backdrop for the intimate display of self to the even more unknowable community of readers of English autobiography.

5

From Seduction to Fantasy

"Lolita, or the Confession of a White Widowed Male"

⋮

APART from a few dissidents, the first generation of Lolita's readers did not perceive the book to raise significant ethical issues. Lionel Trilling's pronouncement that "Lolita is not about sex, but about love" (15) set the tenor for the initial reception of the work, and Vladimir Nabokov's grouping of pedophilia with the two other themes he claimed were taboo for American publishers—happy interracial marriage and unpunished atheism—suggested that it would be vulgar to focus on the obvious sexual content of the novel. Critics generally supported Nabokov's claim that free artistic expression should trump community standards, and Martin Green offered the fully politicized form of this defense when he compared Lolita to didactic "Soviet art":

> The obligation of the critic is a necessary correlative of the freedom of the artist, and we of the liberal tradition are committed to that freedom. Nabokov is a fine example of the free artist. . . . He refus[es] all allegiance to non-aesthetic schemes of value . . . he is anti-ideological. . . . Lolita is a brilliant and beautiful experience, satisfying our most purely moral sense as well as all the others. What is there in Tolstoy's "art of the future," Soviet literature, that can compare with it? (376–77)

In the immediate aftermath of the Second World War and the Holocaust, this effortless synthesis of aesthetics and morality—the unforced assumption that a commitment to the aesthetic is in itself morally satisfying—indicates how quickly the combination of formalism and anticommunism enabled American critics to overcome any spasms of doubt about the moral behavior of civilized nations. Humbert's weary reference to "yet another World War" (32) is barely more narcissistic than the general complacency of his adopted culture. If there has been surprisingly little debate about the moral standing of Lolita in more recent criticism, this may be because the ethical positions that the book stakes out seem to be so clearly polarized. Either it is still possible to celebrate Nabokov's "lyrically mourning" prose (Wood 141), or else it is necessary to denounce the aestheticization of pedophilia. Neither alternative would seem to be very productive for a consideration of the ethical force of the novel.

In a departure from the critical norm, Richard Rorty has made an ambitious attempt to make Lolita morally palatable to a contemporary sensibility. Rorty argues that Nabokov did recognize an inevitable contradiction between ethical and aesthetic values and privileged the ethical. Rorty takes the four terms that Nabokov attributes to "art" in the Afterword to Lolita—"curiosity, tenderness, kindness, ecstasy"—and he concludes that "Nabokov knew quite well that ecstasy and tenderness not only are separable but tend to preclude each other" (158–59). When Rorty offers to summarize Nabokov's ethical message in Lolita, he produces a dictum that begins with an echo of Trilling: "The moral is not to keep one's hands off little girls, but to notice what one is doing, and in particular to notice what people are saying. . . . Insofar as one is preoccupied with building up to one's private kind of sexual bliss, like Humbert, or one's private aesthetic bliss . . . people are likely to suffer still more" (164). Rorty shares Trilling's confidence that Lolita is not about sex; "sexual obsessions," he contends, "are just handy examples of a more general phenomenon" (162), the "effects of our private idiosyncrasies on others" (141).

The ability to marginalize the sexual content of Lolita depends, to a very great extent, on believing one of its major characters over the other on an important plot point. Although Dolores Haze threatens to "call the police and tell them you raped me" (141) and later refers to "the hotel where you raped me" (202), the dominant critical reception of Lolita has accepted, explicitly or implicitly, Humbert's claim that "it was she who seduced me" (132). Rorty's judgment of the ethical balance of the novel exemplifies the implicit acceptance of Humbert's version of the story; Rorty's contention that Humbert's greatest flaw is a general inattentiveness to others would not really cover the case of a coercive rapist. The presumption that Humbert's story—"she seduced me"—is truer than Dolores's story—"you raped me"—marks a general acquiescence in the truth that orthodox Freudians consider the foundational moment of psychoanalysis: the supplanting of the "seduction theory" of sexual abuse by the fantasy theory of childhood desire.

Despite Nabokov's lifelong disdain for Freud, there is a striking parallel in their depictions of incest: Lolita's description of Dolores Haze as a sexually precocious twelve-year-old who lusts after middle-aged men revises Nabokov's earlier account of stepfather/stepdaughter incest in the same way that Freud reverses his original seduction theory. Freud's "seduction theory," outlined in The Aetiology of Hysteria (1896), described the sexual abuse of children by adults and traced adult pathologies to that childhood trauma. Soon afterward, Freud renounced the seduction theory and joined the consensus of Viennese analysts who characterized such stories from their patients as lies or delusions. Freud's innovation in the fantasy theory was to contend that these delusions arose from his patients' own repressed desires for their male elders. There is a similar trajectory of revision in Nabokov's accounts of stepfather/stepdaughter incest. In The Enchanter, a novel written in the late 1930s and not published until 1986, the stepfather's exposure of his penis produces cataclysmic results; seeing his erection as "some monstrosity, some ghastly disease" (91–92), the stepdaughter screams, the police come running, and the stepfather commits suicide by throwing himself in front of an oncoming truck. The transformation of the daughter from horrified victim to willing participant makes possible a very different conclusion for Lolita. Instead of the grisly scene of self-mutilation which concludes The Enchanter, Lolita ends with a flight into romantic sublimity that ratifies Nabokov's claim that the novel is really about "aesthetic bliss" (314).

The most straightforward irony in this parallel between Freud and Nabokov is that the term "Lolita" is now cultural slang for the figure invented by Freud: a teenaged or prepubescent girl who is erotically drawn to her male elders. In the modern reception of both Freud and Nabokov, the occlusion of sexual abuse by an account of imaginative fantasy is perpetuated by some unusually forceful interventions by the orthodox interpreters of each author. In Freud's case, the standard account of his renunciation of the seduction theory is that Freud announces the change in a letter to Wilhelm Fliess on 21 September 1897. To keep this story straight in the compilation of Freud's correspondence with Fliess, which was released under the title The Origins of Psychoanalysis, Anna Freud and her coeditors removed, without ellipses, passages in which Freud expressed misgivings about the fantasy theory after September 1897. The deletions included a letter of December 1897, in which Freud told Fliess that "my confidence in the father-etiology has risen greatly" (Masson, Assault 114). These elisions were not accidental. Anna Freud explained to Ernst Jones in 1954 (in an unpublished letter) that the inclusion of such material would be "bewildering to the reader" (Masson 55). When Jeffrey Masson secured access to the Freud archive in the 1980s and asked Anna Freud about the omissions, she replied, "Keeping up the seduction theory would mean to abandon the Oedipus complex, and with it the whole importance of phantasy life, conscious or unconscious phantasy. In fact, I think there would have been no psychoanalysis afterwards" (Masson 113).

A similar suppression has taken place in Nabokov studies about the very existence of *The Enchanter*. The work Nabokov claimed in the 1956 Afterword to *Lolita* had been "destroyed . . . sometime after moving to America in 1940" (312) quickly rematerialized when *Lolita* became a commercial success. In 1959, Nabokov offered the manuscript to his publisher, but publication did not follow at that time. Nabokov seems not to have shared this information with Alfred Appel in 1970; Appel says in the notes to the 1970 *Annotated Lolita* that "the story . . . unexpectedly turned up among his papers in 1964. . . . Nabokov informs me that he will never publish this reclaimed story" (438). *The Enchanter* was subsequently published, in a translation by Dmitri Nabokov in 1986, and this edition included Nabokov's 1959 letter to Putnam's. But when the "Revised and updated" *Annotated Lolita* was released in 1991, Appel went beyond the call of duty in maintaining more of the original story than the facts would allow. In the revised footnote on this point, Appel notes the "newly translated version" of *The Enchanter*, but he reiterates the claim that the manuscript "unexpectedly turned up among [Nabokov's] papers in 1964" (453), and he never mentions the existence of the 1959 letter that belies this story of an unexpected find in 1964.

A skeptical reader might suspect that the manuscript of *The Enchanter* had never really gone missing but that Nabokov had initially been wary of publishing two works about a man's obsessive desire for his twelve-year-old stepdaughter. Both Nabokov and Appel have been adamant in maintaining that Nabokov had no particular interest in pedophilia; as Nabokov loftily said of Humbert, "there are many things, besides nymphets, in which I disagree with him" (*Lolita* 315). But in *Speak, Memory*, the autobiography Nabokov revised during the same year he composed *Lolita*, he described his own molestation as a child by his Uncle Ruka: "When I was eight or nine, he would invariably take me upon his knee after lunch and (while two young footmen were clearing the table in the empty dining room) fondle me, with crooning sounds and fancy endearments, and I felt embarrassed for my uncle by the presence of the servants and relieved when my father called him from the veranda" (68). The similarities between Uncle Ruka and Humbert, and some of the more indirect links between Uncle Ruka and Humbert's Uncle Gustave, have been described by Brandon Centerwall. There is a twenty-five year gap between Uncle Ruka's age and that of young Vladimir; Humbert Humbert is thirty-seven when he begins sexually abusing the twelve-year-old Dolores Haze, and both Ruka and Humbert die of heart disease in their forties. The story of Ruka and Vladimir ends, according to *Speak, Memory*, on Nabokov's fifteenth birthday, when Ruka takes him aside and, prefiguring the "four thousand bucks" (279) that Humbert gives to Dolores at their parting, informs his nephew that he will be his sole heir. Centerwall suggests that Humbert's vomiting when he sees Quilty as his Uncle Gustave, "a great admirer of le découvert" (139), indicates that uncle Ruka's molestation of young Vladimir went beyond the semipublic fondling described in *Speak, Memory*. Centerwall's description of the transformation of Nabokov's personal trauma into art is a simple variation on the standard etiology of pedophilia. In Centerwall's account, the abused Nabokov, instead of becoming an active pedophile, was able to sublimate his reaction into literary expression.

Even if Centerwall's claim that *Lolita* originates in Nabokov's childhood experience is entirely correct, the story of Nabokov's personal life does not explain why this novel has been so popular, nor why it would seem so important not only for Nabokov but for his critics to distance it from the more unadorned story of pedophilia in *The Enchanter*. The feminist answer to this question is clear. The story of *The Enchanter* is unacceptable for the same reason that the seduction theory is unacceptable; both illustrate sexual abuse by male authority while *Lolita* and the fantasy theory hide that reality behind a fantasy of desiring daughters. What is at stake in the choice between the seduction theory and the fantasy theory is, as Anna Freud puts it, Oedipal identity—"the Oedipus complex," which dictates that a normative male subject will sexually desire women and identify with male authority. But while the reception history of *Lolita* has been almost entirely composed of aestheticized readings that ratify Humbert's robust Oedipality, the novel's narrative is actually bifurcated into two stories that explicate both of Freud's theories: the "seduction"/rape theory, in which "you raped me," and the fantasy theory, in which "it was she who seduced me." Beginning with Nabokov's own comments on the novel, Humbert's wit and his lyrical talents have been marshaled into the fantasy story that concludes with "aesthetic bliss" ("aurochs and angels," "durable pigments," etc.), but the shadow narrative of a paranoid and compulsive pedophile actually demonstrates a much greater degree of not only psychological acuity but of literary originality.

In the tension between these stories, Lolita outlines the route by which Freud proceeds from the material of the seduction theory to the fiction of the Oedipus complex. It is a common critique of Freud that he engaged in a logically tendentious validation of cultural norms when he fabricated the Oedipus complex—the story of the son's desire for the mother—out of case studies that mostly involved accounts of father/daughter incest. Oedipal identity in its most familiar form—what Freud calls "the simple positive Oedipus complex"—is only a particularly reified formation that Freud himself conceded "is by no means its commonest form . . . but rather represents a simplification or schematization" that "is often enough justified for practical purposes" (SE 19:31–33). In broader terms, Oedipality refers not simply to a son's desire for his mother but to the triangular structure through which male subjects acquire masculine identity by competing with other men for women. Humbert's self-depiction as a highly cultured, "intensely virile" (49) individual and his condescending aggressivity toward other men he imagines ogling Dolores Haze ("which I kissed five minutes later, Jack" [157]) establish his Oedipal credentials. At the same time, Humbert provides the clues for a very different interpretation of his character. His impotence dreams (malfunctioning pistols, riding a carousel and discovering no horse between his legs) and his admissions of failure in ordinary sexual performance with mature women—his second encounter with the young prostitute Monique is "less successful" (23), he is "never very successful" on the Arctic expedition with Dr. Anita Johnson, and he anticipates disappointing Charlotte on their wedding night (72)—portray an impotent homophobe who suspects himself of latent homosexual tendencies. Humbert insinuates that these clues are deliberate misdirections designed to punish the psychoanalytically inclined reader when he claims that he torments his psychiatrists by fabricating dreams that lead to a false diagnosis of "potentially homosexual" and "totally impotent" (34), but the text of Lolita offers no definitive basis for deciding which of these portraits is true. After all, why does Humbert spend so much of his time in psychiatric institutions in the first place? Does he really "have to be an artist and a madman" (17) because he is misunderstood by a vulgar, normative culture that just does not understand that "Grant Wood or Peter Hurd was good, and Reginald Marsh or Frederick Waugh awful" (199)?

The dominant, Oedipal story of Lolita is anchored at two points, neither of which is necessarily true. The first is Humbert's claim that "it was she who seduced me," and the second is his claim that he murdered Clare Quilty. In each case, the text calls attention to the possible fictionality of Humbert's assertions. Dolores Haze twice refers to the encounter in the Enchanted Hunters as a rape, and, as a number of readers have noted, the precise calendar that Humbert provides for the novel calls into question whether the events of the final ten chapters (beginning when Humbert supposedly receives a letter from Dolores in chapter 27) ever really take place.[1] Humbert reports that he received the letter from Dolores on 22 September 1952; he says on the final page of the novel that he has been writing this memoir for fifty-six days; and John Ray reports that Humbert died on November 16, which is exactly fifty-six days after September 22. There is therefore no time, these readers contend, for Humbert's visits to Dolores and Quilty, and they suggest that the events of the novel's final chapters are either fantasized by Humbert or fabricated in order to manipulate the reader's sympathy. The most thorough and emphatic response to this reading has come from Nabokov's biographer Brian Boyd, whose objections are both editorial and ethical. Characterizing the attempt to fictionalize the final chapters of the novel as "revisionist," Boyd first suggests that the dating in the text may be a misprint; perhaps Nabokov or the typesetter misprinted November 16 for November 19, a date which would allow for the three days it takes for Humbert to reach Dolores and Quilty. But Boyd's most vigorous argument is an ethical one. Boyd argues that if the visit to Dolores and the murder of Quilty did not take place, the central moral principles of the novel would be compromised. In making both Quilty's death and Dolores's final appearance into Humbertian fantasies, Boyd maintains, the revisionist argument obliterates the moral significance of both love and murder, and he argues that to lose the image of "Lolita in her final proud but abashed independence" is to "gain nothing and to lose everything—and all for the sake of one reversible digit" ("Homais" 86).

Unfortunately for Boyd's editorial argument, there is no reason to suppose an author's error here, and the compositional record strongly suggests that Nabokov was careful about the precision of the dates in the novel. When Nabokov prepared the Russian version of *Lolita*, he made the date of September 22 more prominent as the date of Humbert's receipt of the letter from Dolores, and he left November 16 and the "fifty-six days" as they were (Dolinin, "Lolita" 327). When he subsequently revised the English edition for American publication, he adjusted a passage from "early September" to "late in September" (264) in order to bring it into accord with the September 22 date, and he left September 22, November 16, and "fifty-six days" in place. Boyd's suggestion that the text of *Lolita* should be altered by changing a date within it from November 16 to November 19 joins Appel's manipulation of the footnotes as another attempt to change the documentary record in order to maintain the integrity of the Oedipal narrative. Undoubtedly, both Appel and Boyd believe that they are defending the novel's aesthetic integrity, but when they identify the literary value of the text with one particular story—that of the intensely virile, highly cultured individual who bestows artistic immortality on himself and his paramour—they make *Lolita* into a far simpler work than it really is.

Both the orthodox majority and the revisionist minority of *Lolita*'s readers have looked for a single story in the text: Either "you raped me" or "she seduced me," either Humbert kills Quilty or Quilty is a figment of Humbert's paranoid imagination. In narratological terms, these contradictions occur at the level of story, which Gerard Genette describes as the "signified or narrative content" (27) of the text. As Genette explains, the temporal precedence of story (*histoire*) strictly applies only in the case of a nonfictional narrative where the story consists of actual events; the act of the historian, the narrating, comes second; and the narrative, the record of events, is the final product. Thus the nonfictional narrative is composed in the straightforward sequence, Story/Narrating/Narrative. But in the fictional text, Genette contends, the true order can only be represented in the following diagram:

where story and narrative—the fictional events and their representation—are produced simultaneously by the act of the narrator (15). In terms of this clear distinction between fiction and nonfiction, it might seem that all of Nabokov's interpreters have been overly literal-minded. When critics assert either that Dolores Haze seduced Humbert or that he raped her, or when they try to ascertain whether Humbert killed Quilty or imagined doing so, or if Humbert died on November 16 or November 19, the presumption that the story is bound to a preexistent set of events belongs, Genette suggests, to the realm of nonfiction. But Genette's model of fictional discourse allows for a refinement that would delineate a difference between realist and nonrealist fiction. For realism, the sequence would be

where "realism" describes a set of conventions regarding the laws of physics and probability in the material world, and "story" is required to conform to those conventions. Within these conventions, either Humbert murdered someone named Quilty or else he has paranoid delusions of having done so; the name "Quilty" either refers to a character or to an imaginary projection of Humbert's guilty feelings. But if the realist convention is removed, the entire sequence is changed. Without the constraint of realism, there could be any number of stories, or plots, emerging from one narrative, such as:

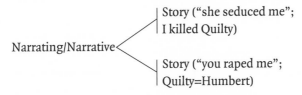

Lolita's critics have regularly tried to bring the narrative of the text within the bounds of realism, but there is no narratological reason why a novel that disdains realism could not produce at least two simultaneous but contradictory stories, one in which the novel's final chapters represent the central character's fantasy and another in which he exists at the same level of story as every other character. Such a structure accommodates the logically contradictory narrative effects that suggest that Quilty is both Humbert's double and an independent character. While Humbert murders Quilty in the dominant story, in the revisionist story the destruction of a doppelganger figure who carries off Humbert's excess guilt reenacts the concluding suicide of *The Enchanter.*

These two stories within *Lolita* unfold two etiologies of Humbert's pedophilia. In the orthodox story, Humbert's pubescent affair with Annabel initiates his precocious sexual development. In the learned historical disquisition on pedophilia that follows this episode, Humbert suggests that his desire for "nymphets" is a sign of a libidinal excess that is both sexual and intellectual. Humbert and Annabel discuss "infinity, solipsism and so on," and he later wonders whether this childhood affair was the cause of "the rift in my life" or if "my excessive desire for that child [was] only the first evidence of an inherent singularity" (13). This Humbert is always infinitely above the American rubes who think he has written a book about a poet named Rainbow; he is "exceptionally handsome," full of "exceptional virility," and capable of getting "at the snap of my fingers any adult female I chose" (25). He appears to Dolores Haze as "two eyes and a foot of engorged brawn" (283). But the impotence dreams and the unsuccessful performances with mature women suggest a different, more clinical etiology: Humbert as the semi-impotent male subject who seeks a young, inexperienced partner who will not recognize his inadequacy.

The aesthetic sensibility of the virile Humbert, the artist and madman, is marked by a exceptionally fine capacity for "focal adjustment" (17) that enables him to see "nymphets" where the normals see only children, but the reliability of this visual sense is cast into doubt when Humbert describes how some of his voyeurist adventures "ended in a rich flavor of hell": "It happened for instance that from my balcony I would notice a lighted window across the street and what looked like a nymphet in the act of undressing before a co-operative mirror. . . . But abruptly, fiendishly, the tender pattern of nudity I had adored would be transformed into the disgusting lamp-lit bare arm of a man in his underclothes reading his paper by the open window in the hot, damp, hopeless summer night" (20). This is not an isolated incident but a recurrent event, and it recurs to Humbert's imagination when (in the dominant narrative) he carries the letter from Dolores back to his apartment on September 22. As he wearily climbs the stairs, Humbert recounts how "the ever-alert periscope of my shameful vice, would make out from afar a half-naked nymphet stilled in the act of combing out her Alice-in-Wonderland hair," but, as he attempts to masturbate, "the lighted image would move and Eve would revert to a rib, and there would be nothing in the window but an obese partly clad man reading the paper" (264). Within the dominant narrative, this is simply a record of Humbert's disappointment; his exceptional sensitivity is, as usual, unrequited by the vulgar world. But in the revisionist story, the man in the undershirt is a recurrent symptom. As the traumatized subject attempts to master his trauma through repetition, what emerges from the unconscious is a hallucinatory image of the tormentor. It is at the second occurrence of this image that the narrative bifurcates: at this point, Humbert either overcomes his recurring disappointment, opens the letter from Dolores, then goes off to meet with her and kill Quilty, or else he is institutionalized for the last fifty-six days of his life and writes a memoir ("Lolita, or the Confession of a White Widowed Male") liberally laced with fantasy.

While the dominant story of Lolita is structurally Oedipal—one man kills another in a rivalry over a woman—it departs from the simple positive Oedipus complex in that the woman being pursued is not a mother but a daughter. This triangular structure surfaces throughout the novel as Humbert expresses his hostility toward imaginary male rivals. In a preliminary erotic episode with Dolores, he addresses "my learned reader (whose eyebrows, I suspect, have by now traveled all the way to back of his bald head)" (48), where the combination of erudition, baldness, and shock all suggest a competitor who is more timid, and less masculine, than Humbert despite their shared desire. But the scope of this rivalry ultimately undercuts Humbert's claim to erotic singularity. The attention he claims Dolores draws from nearly every man they encounter on their cross-country trips ("garage fellows, hotel pages, vacationists, goons in luxurious cars, maroon morons near blued pools" [159]) suggests that his is actually quite an ordinary sexual preference. By identifying the daughter, rather than the mother, as the object of desire, *Lolita* targets a central promise of Oedipal heteronormativity: the promise that sexual maturity consists of a single, successful repression of aberrant desire. Both the seduction theory and the fantasy theory are premised on incest, in fact or imagination, but while the Oedipal theory suggests that a single act of repression can leave aberrant fantasy behind in the transition from childhood to maturity, Freud's original seduction theory implies that repression necessarily forms a perpetual resistance to a force of nature.

By identifying a pubescent girl not only as a universal object of male desire but as a willing partner, *Lolita* reconnects Freud's account of normative Oedipal subjectivity and the originary fiction of the fantasy theory, the fantasy of the daughter's desire. In the episode that is meant to shock the "learned reader," Dolores Haze enters Humbert's room and stands near him while he luxuriates in her "adorable profile, parted lips, warm hair." Humbert imagines that "I could kiss her throat," but he does not do so until "the knowledge came to me"—though "I cannot tell . . . how"—that Dolores wants him to do so: she was "waiting . . . for the glamorous lodger to do what he was dying to do." This imaginary knowledge of Dolores's desire then secures Humbert's identity as "a handsome, intensely virile grown-up friend" (48–49). Humbert's "intensely virile" identity, which stands in contrast to that of the bald, bookish reader, is produced in this episode as an effect of Dolores's desire for him, but the text raises the question of whether her desire exists as anything other than a projection of Humbert's fantasy. In the next, more elaborate, erotic episode, the couch masturbation scene, Dolores's desire is both projected and denied. In the midst of the act, she is described as an active participant: "she wiggled, and squirmed, and threw her head back, and her teeth rested on her glistening underlip as she half-turned away," but Humbert nevertheless reassures himself a moment later that "she had noticed nothing" (61). The contradictory descriptions of Dolores as eager partner and as oblivious object register the

competing erotic and ethical demands of the passage, and the irreconcil-
ability of the two portraits highlights their fictionality. In the uneroticized
bridge between these two episodes, Humbert admits the impossibility of
finding "a singularly knowing, cheerful, corrupt and compliant Lolita be-
having as reason knew she could not possibly behave" (54). Reason and
possibility can be overcome only when the couch masturbation scene reaches its erotic climax, and what was inconceivable in an unaroused state now
seems perfectly natural: Dolores Haze is presented to the learned reader as
the ideal object of patriarchal desire, the desiring daughter.

The competing image of Dolores as the "safely solipsized" object who
"had noticed nothing" is equally detached from reality. This imaginary
obliviousness is the standard excuse of the pedophile, as Sandor Ferenczi
explained: "Almost always the perpetrator acts as though nothing had happened, comforting himself with the thought: 'After all, this is only a child,
who still knows nothing, and will soon forget everything again'" (290). But
the production of this rationalization is neither entirely cynical nor simple.
In Ferenczi's analyses of patients who reported sexual abuse, he discovered not a universal hostility to the abuser but, more often, an identification
that was produced both affectively and intellectually. On the one hand, a
child who is overwhelmed by a sexual advance from a family member for
whom she feels affection will try to "maintain the former situation of tenderness." This produces an "introjection of the guilt feelings of the adult"
and a consequent identification with the abuser. But Ferenczi also discovers
a less immediate path of identification; as the child realizes that the adult
abuser is helpless to resist his own compulsion, "Fear of the uninhibited
and therefore as good as crazy adult turns the child into a psychiatrist, as it
were. In order . . . to protect himself from the dangers coming from people
without self-control, he must first know how to identify himself completely
with them" (293). While the figure of the desiring daughter obviates any
need to understand pedophilic desire—because, according to the fantasy
theory, this desire does not exist, it is only her fantasy—as Ferenczi explains the rationalization process of the pedophile, he enacts the necessity
of identification as the only means of understanding this process when he
ventriloquizes the voice of the pedophile ("after all, this is only a child").

The focalization of Nabokov's two narratives of pedophilia, The Enchanter
and Lolita, through the perspective of the pedophile solicits this degree of
identification from the reader, who is led through the painstaking precau-
tions taken by Arthur and Humbert to protect their objects of desire from
harm. Arthur's slow, careful approach to his sleeping stepdaughter's body

("slowly, with baited [sic] breath, he was inching closer and then, coordinating all his movements, he began molding himself to her, testing the fit" [Enchanter 91]) foreshadows Humbert's attempted use of knockout drops on Dolores and his hope that she might "notice nothing," that "my ecstasy would have been all softness, a case of internal combustion of which she would hardly have felt the heat" (Lolita 131). Ferenczi shows how the transformation of the daughter into a willing partner becomes the most effective assuagement of the pedophile's guilt, and he also suggests how Humbert's hallucinatory projections of male tormentors emerge as traumatic symptoms. When identification with the abuser has been completed, Ferenczi writes, the result is that "the aggressor disappears as external reality and becomes intrapsychic . . . in accordance with the pleasure principle, it can be shaped and transformed into a positive or negative hallucination" (290). Humbert's apparitional "Uncle Gustave" first appears in the lobby of the Enchanted Hunters as a figure Dolores thinks looks "exactly, but exactly, like Quilty," (121) but Humbert finds that he "resembled a little my Swiss uncle Gustave" (139). In the orthodox, realist story, this figure is Quilty, and Dolores recognizes him because she has met him before and she has an advertising poster of him on her bedroom wall alongside another poster whose model she has christened "H. H." (69). In the revisionist story, not only is Quilty Humbert's double, but, in a hallucinatory proliferation, Quilty has two doubles of his own: both Humbert's uncle Gustave and his own writing partner, Vivian Darkbloom, with whom he shares a gender ambiguity deliberately promoted by Dolores ("Vivian is the male author, the gal author is Clare" [221]).

This gender and identity confusion ripples across the hotel lobby when Humbert and Dolores first arrive and see "an ancient lady swathed in violet veils" (118). If the "violet veils" are not in themselves enough of a hint of Vivian Darkbloom (why is the "lady" so carefully hiding her face?), the hotel clerk, abetted by "my [Humbert's] static," suggests the interpretive path: "One crowded night we had three ladies and a child like yours sleep together. I believe one of the ladies was a disguised man." The text provides ample clues that the veiled lady is in fact the disguised Quilty; she is the owner of the cocker spaniel that reappears with Quilty later in the novel, and she takes the opportunity to speak to Dolores out of Humbert's earshot. In the realist plot, they are planning Dolores's escape from Humbert. When Humbert returns to the hotel lobby the next morning, he finds Dolores being watched by a figure who reminds him not only of his uncle Gustave but of himself, "A fellow of my age in tweeds" (138). But the shifting identity borders that allow Vivian to metamorphose into Clare, Quilty into Trapp, Gustave into Gaston, and all into Humbert resist reduction to a single story. These blurred identities subvert the psychological and moral clarities of both the seduction theory and the fantasy theory by invoking both the psychologically permeable border between the sexual abuser and the victim and the moral problematic that derives from the standard etiology of sexual abuse: a high percentage of abusers were, once, victims.

The essential elements of the lobby scenes at the Enchanted Hunters—the dog, an ambiguous figure of Quilty, and Dolores actively engaging in a display of "legshow"—recur in the poolside scene in the second half of the novel when the Quilty figure is fully consolidated as Gustave Trapp and Humbert vomits at this recognition (237). Within the realist narrative, Dolores and Quilty are projected as erotic conspirators. Her flamboyant display ("her obscene young legs madly pedaling in air") is put on for his benefit, and Humbert is disgusted and marginalized by their play of exhibitionism and voyeurism. But this passage repeatedly careens beyond the bounds of the realist story. Humbert's description of Quilty graphically establishes the competitive terms of their Oedipal rivalry—"his tight wet black bathing trunks bloated and bursting with vigor where his great fat bullybag was pulled up and back like a padded shield over his reversed beasthood"—but as Quilty becomes Gustave, Humbert's discourse takes on the logorrheac quality of hysteria: "He was no longer the satyr but a very good-natured and foolish Swiss cousin, the Gustave Trapp I have mentioned more than once, who used to counteract his 'sprees' (he drank beer with milk, the good swine) by feats of weight-lifting—tottering and grunting on a lake beach with his otherwise very complete bathing suit jauntily stripped from one shoulder." The description of Quilty has a discernible focus, a threatening masculinity, but the claim that cousin Gustave drank beer with milk has no obvious referential value. And the central sentence in this passage that describes Quilty watching Dolores does not exactly say what the context would lead one to expect; as Humbert angrily watches Quilty/Gustave watching Dolores, he discovers that "what I had recognized him by was the reflection of my daughter's countenance—the same beatitude and grimace but made hideous by his maleness." This "reflection" does not simply involve the fact that each of these figures knows that the other is looking, but identifies "the same beatitude and grimace" in Quilty that Humbert sees in Dolores, and it says that this is how Humbert recognizes Quilty as his relative Gustave. The paradoxical conjunction of "beatitude and grimace," and the even more strained attribution of "beatitude" to this figure whose sexuality has just been described in hyperbolically bestial terms, demand a reading that goes past the specular reality of the moment. Beatitude should not belong to the hideously masculine Quilty, nor should the child Dolores be identifiable by a grimace. The unwieldy combinations construct the entire disorderly cycle of abuse: the beatitude of childhood becomes a "hideous" predatory "maleness" through the experience of a grimace. In the dominant narrative of Humbert's achievement of Oedipal maturity, his rival's eventual loss of his exceptional virility is ultimately accomplished through the clinical reduction to impotence. But in the revisionist story in which Quilty is Humbert's double, the doppelganger structure indicates that Humbert himself both claims an identification with Dolores's childhood beatitude and experiences a disgusted sense of his difference from her in his culpability for her grimace.

This full-blown, up-close appearance of Gustave Trapp culminates a series of ambiguous and partial identifications of Trapp as Quilty that lead Humbert to wonder if he is really being followed or if "all those identical detectives in prismatically changing cars were figments of my persecution mania" (238). The revisionist story in the second half of Lolita follows the arc of Rousseau's paranoia in the second half of the Confessions. Humbert's conviction that he is pursued by enemies who know his secrets, his doubts that these pursuers might be imaginary symptoms of his madness, his immediate relapse into the grip of the delusion that he has just identified as madness, and his expectation that the reader can identify the central agent of the plots against him rehearse all of the stages of Rousseau's paranoia. Humbert's most spectacular symptom—his belief that "the astute reader has guessed long ago" (272) Quilty's identity—recalls Rousseau's request for the reader to reread three chapters of the Confessions in order to discover the "impelling hand" (493) behind his persecution. As in Rousseau's case, Humbert's paranoia is not simply a clinical condition but an effect of guilt. The Jesuits in Rousseau's paranoid fantasies were, as Mary Shelley suggested, the displaced figures of his own abandoned children, while Quilty/Trapp embodies the guilt that drives Arthur to suicide in The Enchanter.

Alongside the rhetoric of intimidation, in which Nabokov forbade his readers to pursue any connections between his depictions of pedophilia and his personal life,[2] he provided an abundance of clues that suggested biographical sources for both of the etiologies of pedophilia outlined in Lolita. Humbert's tryst with Annabel echoes Nabokov's encounter at the age of ten with "a little French girl named Colette" recorded in chapter 7 of Speak, Memory. But the story of Colette also appeared in The New Yorker (as

"Collette") and in a short story collection titled *Nabokov's Dozen* (as "First Love"), and in the story collection it is accompanied by a "Bibliographical Note" that states that it is "(except for a change of names) true in every detail to the author's remembered life" (158). Given the repeated admissions throughout *Speak, Memory* of the frailty of memory and of the need to repair its "amnesic defects" by "great effort" (9), it is not clear how much latitude Nabokov allows himself to invent details that fill in the gaps in his "remembered life."

Speak, Memory also offers the cryptic description of the young Vladimir's fondling by Uncle Ruka, but the memoir never hints at any resentment on Nabokov's part toward his uncle. Nabokov always speaks of Ruka affectionately, even protectively, such as when he says that he thought so little of the inheritance he received from his uncle, since it was almost immediately rescinded by the Bolshevik revolution, that he is left with a "sense of having been ungrateful to Uncle Ruka" (55). Nabokov's enduring affection for Uncle Ruka corresponds to the symptomatology described by Ferenczi when Nabokov sympathetically describes Ruka's troubled life. Nabokov writes of the "other, stranger torments that beset" Uncle Ruka that "he sought relief—if I understand these matters rightly—in religion, first in certain Russian sectarian outlets, and eventually in the Roman Catholic Church" (53). The exact nature of these "torments" is discreetly unnamed, but Humbert's protest against the sexual determinism of psychoanalysis— "It is not the artistic aptitudes that are secondary sexual characters as some shams and shamans have said; it is the other way around: sex is but the ancilla of art" (259)—redeems Ruka's character far more effectively than it does Humbert's. Nabokov describes Ruka's "artistic aptitudes" ("He wrote music himself, of the sweet, rippling sort, and French verse") and his limitations: "His was the kind of colorful neurosis that should have been accompanied by genius, but in his case was not" (53). The source of Ruka's neuroses is not far afield: "he had been intensely disliked by his father . . . whose uncontrollable temper was rumored to have been a threat to the boy's very life" (54). Nabokov's idyllic descriptions of his relationship with his own father offer a sharp contrast to Ruka's plight, and Nabokov further differentiates himself from Ruka through the inner strength of the "genius" he implicitly possesses and that Ruka explicitly does not.

Centerwall's straightforward biographical interpretation of *Lolita* suggests that the stories of Annabel and Collette are screen memories that hide the real trauma behind Nabokov's repeated depictions of pedophilia, the "dark truth" (481) of young Vladimir's abuse by his Uncle Ruka. But the nonrealist story of *Lolita* offers a more complicated and dispersed account of cause and effect in which the figure of uncle Gustave channels both the biographical introjection of Uncle Ruka and the novelistic projection of Humbert's guilt into Clare Quilty. Before Uncle Gustave begins to metamorphose into Quilty, he makes a momentary appearance as a slip of the tongue when Humbert misstates the name of the homosexual pedophile Gaston Godin and immediately corrects himself ("Gustave's—I mean Godin's" [202]). The identification of Gustave with Gaston, who is not a child molester but an impotent, harmless "invert" (183), and not even a very good chess player, charts one arc of sexual abuse, in which the victim is completely debilitated—like Uncle Ruka, Godin is "potentially homosexual" and "totally impotent" (34). Humbert's Oedipal narrative follows a different arc. Once Humbert identifies Quilty as his rival, Quilty absorbs the figure of Gustave; Humbert finds that he has "lost contact with Trapp's image" as it is "engulfed by the face of Clare Quilty" (291). In the final stages of this story, moral categories acquire the distinctness of personal identities. Dolores's pregnancy restores her wounded innocence when she refuses to describe her sexual past "with that baby inside her" (277), and Humbert's killing of the abjected Quilty, who claims to be "practically impotent" (298), becomes a duel in which Humbert's defense of Dolores's honor proves that he is at least a better man than Quilty.

The murder of Quilty forms half of the expiatory logic of the dominant story, while the novel's sublime conclusion provides the other half. In reparation for the years he stole from Dolores's childhood, Humbert confers on her aesthetic immortality in the world of "durable pigments," as an art object: as Lolita. Both Humbert's and Dolores's implicit deaths, conveyed by the requirement that this memoir could only be published once both were "no longer alive" (309), neatly address Humbert's guilt for exploiting his position as Dolores's guardian. The sentimental discovery of Dolores's premature death in a remote outpost in Alaska suggests that some metaphysical force—time, fate, nature—took more from her than Humbert did, and Humbert's own death supplements the guilty torments he suffered during the period of abuse. Humbert emphasizes, like Rousseau, that his awareness of the suffering he caused is itself a misery. Humbert's account of his anguish during his travels with Dolores is as self-serving as Rousseau's example; his poignant evocation of Dolores's sorrow, "her sobs in the night—every night, every night—the moment I feigned sleep" (176) focuses not on Dolores's sobs but on his awareness of them and echoes Rousseau's plea concerning Marion: "If my remorse at having perhaps made her unhappy is unbearable, what can be said of my grief at perhaps having made her worse than myself?" (*Confessions* 71). But as Rousseau realized, material harm requires a material penance; in order for this contrition to satisfy the terms of poetic justice, Humbert's remorse, like Rousseau's, has to terminate in a retributive end. When Humbert enables Dolores/Lolita to transcend a greater harm than that which he visited on her (he stole a few years of her childhood, but death takes many more years from her), his recompense to her exceeds the damage he has done, and his own death provides the necessary penance for his actions. Humbert's death wraps up the package of Quilty's murder and the transformation of Dolores Haze into Lolita and completes his compensation to Dolores for his hours of sexual bliss.

Looking at the narratives of *The Enchanter* and *Lolita* in biographical terms leads to constructing the sort of ratio that Centerwall offers, a ratio of confession to repression through which Nabokov ultimately transcends his own traumatic experience. But the reception history of the novel, in which readers almost unanimously accept Humbert's claim that "it was she who seduced me," illustrates the efficiency with which the Oedipal story interpellates subjects who become simultaneously oblivious to their own repressed histories and to other people who do not share those histories: that is, non-Oedipal subjects, such as women. It should be obvious, but it is apparently worth saying, that the reader of *Lolita* in Rorty's essay, the "one" who has to learn the danger of "building up to one's private kind of sexual bliss, like Humbert" (164), is not a universal subject but the masculine— that is, Oedipal, male-identified—reader. In the doubling of Humbert and the semi-impotent, sexually ambiguous Quilty, *Lolita* illustrates the proximity of intensely virile, fully accomplished Oedipal identity to its nightmare double, a proximity that Freud explains through the castration complex. The general effortlessness with which *Lolita* is read as a book that is "not about sex," and the occasional need for emphatic reminders of this truth, testify to the success that the Oedipal narrative enjoys as the exemplar of heteronormativity. The premise that Quilty's death is a murder rather than a suicide shields both Humbert and his learned reader from both the stigma of pedophilia and the requirement of self-mutilation that afflict Arthur in *The Enchanter*.

In the Afterword to *Lolita*, Nabokov's derisive comments about pornography firmly separate his "aesthetic bliss" (314) from Humbert's "incomparably . . . poignant sexual bliss" (18), presenting an aestheticism that is purified not only of John Ray's didactic moral concerns but of erotic satisfactions. The parodic borrowings of pornographic cliche throughout the novel establish a discreet distance between the reader of Lolita and the world of common porn, and the resulting bond of urbanity eclipses the terror that haunts The Enchanter: the recognition of the point of view of the daughter. When Arthur is confronted with his stepdaughter becoming "fully awake and looking wild-eyed at his rearing nudity," his fanciful descriptions of his "magic wand" and "enchanted yardstick" are smashed by his realization of "how it appeared to her: some monstrosity, some ghastly disease" (91–92). In Lolita, this monstrousness is erased in the final synthesis of the aesthetic and the moral into the sublime. But the gravity of Lolita's conclusion is undercut by the book's truly last words, the posthumous preface delivered by John Ray, Jr., Ph.D. John Ray's final paragraph on the "ethical impact the book should have on the serious reader" is subverted by a voice from the dead, an irrelevant intrusion that sabotages any degree of ethical vigilance with an image of monstrosity: "In this poignant personal study there lurks a general lesson; the wayward child, the egotistic mother, the panting maniac—these are not only vivid characters in a unique story: they warn us of dangerous trends; they point out potent evils. 'Lolita' should make all of us—parents, social workers, educators—apply ourselves with still greater vigilance and vision to the task of bringing up a better generation in a safer world" (5–6; my emphasis). In the midst of John Ray's normative rhetoric, a "panting maniac" appears, from a far less solemn rhetorical field, to mock the collective efforts of parents, social workers, and educators.

When John Ray's homily is interrupted by a voice from nowhere (since the "panting maniac" can only be the wry self-description of the Humbert who slyly informs us "I am writing under observation" [10], and that Humbert is dead), this lunatic excess trumps the vigilant supervision of parents, social workers, and educators, but Nabokov's distancing of aesthetics from erotics enables an orthodox reading of Lolita to reestablish norms that make this maniac into a mere fiction. Rorty's translation of pedophilia into a "handy example" of idiosyncrasy, like Trilling's argument that pedophilia is now the only form in which the "intensity and grace" (17) of passion-love can still be recognized, takes the Freudian turn: pedophilia becomes not a real thing but only a hyperbole of aberrancy and a fantastic misrepresentation of the norm. The manifest story (the rape of the daughter) is only a representational fantasy that reflects yet another fantasy: the daughter's desire. Neither fantasy is the fantasy of the panting maniac, who is only a harmless joke.

When Martin Green characterizes Lolita as a book that is about freedom from ideology, he indicates how deeply the aesthetic pleasures of Lolita are bound to a wider set of pleasures that constitute, in Green's formulation, freedom itself. In the orthodox story of Lolita, that freedom is manifested in the spontaneity of the Oedipal subject. The orthodox story of Lolita offers both the freedom of the fantasy theory and the referentiality of the simple positive Oedipus complex. The nonrealist surface of the novel operates as a marker of pure aestheticism that distances the reader from its pedophilic content and licenses the spontaneity of both eroticism and scandalous humor. The ability to simultaneously assert, as Nabokov did, that Lolita "has no moral in tow" (Lolita 314) and that the book is a "highly moral affair" (Karlinsky 331) depends on the perception that there is, alongside an ethos of pure freedom, a moral core to the book. When the Oedipal narrative absorbs the entire focus of interpretation, freedom itself is that moral core. Rorty identifies a potential contradiction at the thematic level of the text between this unalloyed freedom and ethical responsibility (between "ecstasy" and "tenderness"), but he nevertheless offers the cheerful assurance that tenderness can easily win out in this conflict if we would all just become better listeners.

Rorty's ethical optimism rescues the orthodox story of Lolita, which minimizes the book's sexual horror, through his description of Humbert's pedophilia as only a metaphor, a "handy example" of our "private idiosyncrasies." His confident iteration of John Ray's call for "greater vigilance" ("notice what one is doing" and "notice what people are saying" [Rorty 164]) presumes that the purely fictional "panting maniac" can be consigned to what Rorty calls the "parasitic" realm of "literary language," which, as the "nonstandard, nonpredictable use of words," will "always will be parasitic on ordinary language" just as "literary interest will always be parasitic on moral interest" (167). Rorty's ethical reading of Lolita simultaneously denies the specificity of both pedophilia and literary language; pedophilia is just a metaphor, and literary language is simply a derivative or "parasitic" way of knowing a world that can be known more directly through "ordinary language." The revisionist story of Lolita, as it spills out of the realist frame that ends on 16 November 1952, as it believes Dolores's claim that "you raped me," and as it recognizes Quilty as Humbert, contests the sufficiency of the ordinary as it constructs a more potent reality that is fabricated out of the ordinarily unspeakable. The recognition that Dolores's matter-of-fact reference to "the hotel where you raped me" is truer, in an exemplary and a moral sense, than Humbert's self-justifying claim that "it was she who seduced me" acknowledges that sexual perversion is the perversion of power, and it shows that the perception of Lolita as a deeroticized story of "idiosyncrasy" and "aesthetic bliss" depends on an obliviousness to the circulation of power through sexuality.

Freud's resistance to the seduction theory was based on an assertion that ordinary life could not be pervaded by such abuses of power; as he wrote to Fliess in the letter of 21 September 1897, "surely such widespread perversions against children are not very probable" (Masson, *Letters* 108). But as Ferenczi reminded Freud, pedophilia emerges in "respected, high-minded puritanical families" (Ferenczi 288) as often as anywhere else, and it sometimes overcomes good people, like Uncle Ruka, despite their best intentions. Even the worst case, the bestial Quilty, is not really that exceptional. Quilty looks like Uncle Gustave, thinks like Humbert, and is easily within the comprehension of the learned reader. The revisionist story of Lolita problematizes ethics as it problematizes referentiality; it effaces intrapsychic borders and realist boundaries, making Quilty, Gustave, and all of Humbert's other imaginary rivals into symptoms of his sexual hysteria. Unlike Rorty's subject, for whom a successful ethical relation is always available through a good faith effort to understand others, the traumatized subject who enters the cycle of sexual abuse—the molested child who becomes an abuser in turn, who progresses from beatitude to monstrosity—suffers, Ferenczi argues, from an excessive understanding of others. The full understanding that results from identification and countertransference emerges from the recognition that abuse does not proceed from a lack—from a purely unconscious mechanical repetition of trauma, or from an intellectual deficit that can be addressed through an exertion of good will—but results from an excess of knowledge, from a realization that seemingly secure limits can be transgressed.

Rorty contends that the ethical issues posed by Lolita can best be addressed in "ordinary language," and he suggests that Humbert's greatest ethical failing, a moral solipsism, is recreated in the reader who overlooks the importance of peripheral characters in the novel such as the son of the Kasbeam barber and Dolores's brother who died at the age of two. But Rorty's dismissal of the specificity of pedophilia as simply a "handy example" of a more general lack of sympathy obscures the most specific ethical questions that Lolita presents. When the Oedipal desire of Lolita is focused on a pubescent girl, it suggests that the simple positive Oedipus complex is itself a screen narrative that obscures the real Oedipal fantasy: the fantasy of a "cheerful, corrupt and compliant Lolita." If Lolita shows that pedophilia is a hyperbole of a norm, rather than a deviation from it, then the novel suggests a question about mainstream norms: At exactly what point does an adult male obsession with younger women constitute an individual or a social pathology and not just a private idiosyncrasy? This question has been obscured in the reception history of the novel by the power of the Oedipal narrative to compel the reader's identification. The conclusion of Lolita asks to be read in the same terms as the ending of Jane Eyre, as a moment of fulfillment in which the narrator has overcome the temptations of the past and is now able properly to cathect his desire onto a single object. Embodied in this fulfillment is a promise; Jane Eyre makes the conventional promise of a couple living happily ever after, while the conclusion of Lolita promises that, because of the redemptive power of his love for Dolores Haze, Humbert is no longer the compulsive and opportunistic pedophile who lusts after children in orphanages, his friend's younger sisters, and his stepdaughter's schoolmates. The hyperrealist calendar of Lolita belies this promise; Humbert begins his narrative on 22 September 1952, and his delighted accounts of his pedophilic adventures are all narrated after his realization on September 23 that he "loved her more than anything I had ever seen or imagined on earth, or hoped for anywhere else" (277).

The Oedipal story of Lolita encourages the reader's identification with this witty and virile brother in desire ("Reader! Bruder!" [262]), and it mocks those figures who have fully completed the cycle of countertransference: the psychiatrists who "wake up shrieking" (34) in terror as their dreams incorporate the implications of identifying with Humbert Humbert. In Humbert's battles with psychiatrists, he repudiates their attempts to make him into an object of scrutiny and insists that he is the ultimate connoisseur of sexual knowledge. But his account of his victories in these battles indicates that what he is able to transmit in the most intimate intellectual struggles is not pleasure but terror. The prioritizing of aesthetic over moral or political readings of literature presumes that an aesthetic reading involves a close, engaged understanding of the internal logic of the text, while a moral reading is only a distanced abstraction of a work into its most generalized ideas. The tradition of aesthetic readings of Lolita has claimed to operate in these terms, by bracketing off moral concerns and entering into the pleasures of "aesthetic bliss." But Ferenczi argues that an aestheticized sympathy with the pedophile or his victim is inadequate to understanding; to really identify with the internal logic of the narrators of The Enchanter and Lolita is to take on a moral burden that leads to Arthur's suicide and Humbert's paranoia.

Lolita and *Speak, Memory* offer two avenues for mitigating this terror. In *Speak, Memory*, Nabokov identifies his own sensitivity to lost time with that of Uncle Ruka in an extended anecdote: "Once, in 1908 or 1909, Uncle Ruka became engrossed in some French children's books that he had come upon in our house; with an ecstatic moan, he found a passage he had loved in his childhood, beginning: "'Sophie n'était pas jolie . . .' and many years later, my moan echoed his, when I rediscovered, in a chance nursery, those same 'Bibliothèque Rose' volumes, with their stories about boys and girls who led in France an idealized version of the *vie de chateau* which my family led in Russia" (57; ellipsis in original). This memory issues into an evocation of domestic harmony: "A sense of security, of well-being, of summer warmth pervades my memory." And when a bumblebee, in a nearly perfect iteration of Proust's flies, enters the adult Nabokov's room, the recovery is complete: "nothing will ever change, nobody will ever die" (57). The image of tender family values in a perpetual summer may reflect, as Brian Boyd suggests, Nabokov's view of the "kindliness of life" (*Nabokov* 7), but at the same time, as it airbrushes the "uncontrollable temper" of Ruka's father and the "colorful neurosis" of Uncle Ruka himself, it restores, as Ferenczi describes it, the child's needed sense of familial security.

Speak, Memory offers a gesture of forgiveness that can only come from the victim as it suggests that Uncle Ruka does not deserve to be labeled a sexual predator. The poolside scene in *Lolita* presents a more problematic blurring of the distinction between Quilty/Gustave/Humbert and Dolores. To see both Dolores and Quilty as active participants in this scene says nothing about the distribution of power between them. The suggestion that Dolores recognizes and enjoys the attention she can compel through flirtation does not necessarily lead to the conclusion that she is the agent of seduction rather than the victim of rape. The perceived necessity of choosing one of these stories as true and rejecting the other, instead of weighing out the exact distribution of power in this particular situation, and the perception that a transcendent moral value—love, freedom, or the ethical coherence of the ordinary—is at stake in this choice, reflects an intolerance for the premise that power inhabits the most intimate transactions of everyday life. As Foucault suggests, this may be the condition of the acceptability of power, that it should only be perceived as an external limit, leaving a "measure of freedom" within us (HS 86).

Lolita outlines the attainment of sexual maturity through the achievement of a fully cathected libido, and it turns the object of that cathexis, Dolores Haze, into a piece of American sexual mythology: the original Lolita. That this achievement can be so easily defended as purely aesthetic, and hence ethically inconsequential to our daily lives, suggests how tenaciously the Oedipal narrative defends its claims to freedom. The reception history of *Lolita* displays a resistance to power but not in the positive, political sense of a struggle against the encroachments of an oppressive force. This resistance takes the form of a double repression: a denial of its own love of power, and a refusal to know the price of its freedom.

Afterword

Politics Is the Future, Ethics Is Now

⋮

ETHICS and politics do not, at the moment, enjoy an easy cohabitation in literary and cultural studies. Critics who overtly profess their political allegiances often describe ethics as an individualist discourse that obscures broader structures of power while those who continue to trust in the ethical value of Kantian universals charge political critics with grounding their work in unarticulated ethical norms. The reception histories of the widely popular works I have looked at in this study suggest that the problems in the discourses of ethics and politics run even deeper than their critics have claimed. In virtually every case (except for *Frankenstein*), readers easily identify with the central narrators of these stories and overlook the impact of their actions on others. Both the norms of ethical discourse and the norms of political discourse contribute to this myopia. Ethics legitimates a narcissistic self-absorption through the interpellation of the self as an exemplary figure, while the most optimistic works in this study—*The Prelude*, *Jane Eyre*, and *Lolita*—show how the political prospect of imagining a more perfect future enables the deferral of present responsibility to that imaginary potential.

The occultive properties of both discourses, ethics and politics, have exerted a dominant and disfiguring influence in Rousseau studies. In a representative analysis, Christopher Kelly sets out to explain the gap between Rousseau's philosophical principles and the behavior he chronicles in the *Confessions* by adducing a crucial distinction between Rousseau's concepts of "goodness" and "virtue." According to Kelly, Rousseau can claim to be a good person because he never sets out to hurt anyone, but when circumstances put him in a position where he must choose between harm to himself and harm to another, this requires a higher power than goodness: "This something," Kelly claims, "is virtue." In Kelly's formulation, "Goodness allows one to follow one's inclinations without (usually) harming anyone else. Virtue allows one to overcome one's inclinations on those occasions when they would lead to harming someone else" ("Introduction" 23).

Kelly's thesis that, for Rousseau, something called "virtue" enables altruistic behavior regardless of circumstances survives an explicit refutation of this idea in the *Confessions*. When Rousseau describes how his father stole his inheritance, he nonetheless defends the "virtues" of his father's character, claiming that Isaac Rousseau "had one of those strong souls which make great virtues" (*ces ames fortes qui font les grands vertus* [Pléiade 55]). Rousseau is unwavering in his contention that his father's moral fiber is composed of "tenderness and virtue" (*tendresse et la vertu*), and the fact that he behaved badly in this instance leads Rousseau to a general conclusion on the relative lack of power of virtue: "whatever sincere love of virtue (*sincére amour de la vertu*) one brings to such situations, sooner or later one weakens . . . and becomes unjust and bad in fact, without having ceased to be just and good in the soul." Citing the word "virtue" three times in this passage, Rousseau maintains the distinction between inner goodness and unscrupulous actions, but he does not claim that there is a degree of virtue that enables us to behave ethically in the face of temptation. He draws precisely the opposite moral, concluding that perhaps the only "maxim of morality" that is of any "use in practice" is "to avoid situations that put our duties in opposition with our interests" (47).

It is not at all clear, at least to me, what "great virtues" consist of, or what it means to be "just and good in the soul" if, in a conflict between interests and duties, it is inevitable that interests will win out. The premise that interests will always trump duties provides a more compelling rationale for Rousseau's thesis in the *First Discourse*—that advances in the arts and sciences have not produced a corresponding improvement in morals—than the pastoral fictions of the *Discourse* itself. If interests will always predominate in the motivation of human behavior, then new technologies will simply be put in the service of power, and modes of domination will become increasingly efficient. If one accepts the cynical implications of what Rousseau actually says in the *Confessions* about interests and virtue, Rousseau becomes the forerunner of Foucault. His antimodernism is not a naïve nostalgia but a justifiably paranoid resistance to the advancing efficiency of power.

Rousseau's rationalization of his father's behavior serves his own interests in fairly transparent ways that operate, as Paul de Man would say, both metaphorically and metonymically. Isaac Rousseau's mistreatment of

Jean-Jacques parallels Rousseau's neglect of his own children, a comparison which suggests that if Rousseau can be so forgiving to his father, then perhaps he too should be judged by a similarly lenient standard. Isaac's behavior is not only analogous to that of Jean-Jacques, it could be construed as the cause, offering an implicit excuse for Rousseau's greatest fault. This structure of rationalization in no way mitigates the cynicism of Rousseau's comments on virtue; if he is praising his father only in order to excuse himself, then he is practicing what he describes, the exercise of personal interest. Perhaps it would be scandalous to suggest that Rousseau is as ironic here about the rhetoric of virtue as he is about the rhetoric of sentimentality in the story of his affair with Sophie d'Houdetot, but such a reading would lead into a coherent and contrarian view of Rousseau's work in which there really is an irreconcilable conflict between Rousseau's political and philosophical works and his autobiographies—in other words, between morals in books and morals in life. Kelly's reconstruction of the efficacy of virtue serves the supplementary function of sustaining the viability of Rousseau's most influential political and philosophical theses—that "man is naturally good" and that "Man is born free, and is everywhere in chains"—by suggesting that there is some reservoir of interior virtue that promises a future in which people would be better behaved if they were freer than they are in the present. In the retrospective focus of the *Confessions*, this political promise becomes a discursive fantasy that has no relevance to real life.

If we were to look for empirical evidence of whether our work in the arts and sciences has made us any better, ethically, than our predecessors, we might take some encouragement from the most recent developments in the reception histories of these hypercanonic works, and we could legitimately attribute these improvements to advances in the dissemination of political discourse. The sentimental appeals made by Rousseau and Wordsworth are more likely to be seen today as the self-referential expressions of a cult of sensibility than as proof of exemplary character. It is difficult to imagine Meyer Abrams's claim that the central ethical value of Romantic literature is that "the norm of life is joy" (431) enjoying the currency today that it had a generation ago. Readers sensitized by a generation of criticism focused on the links between material reality and symbolic representation would be likely to search for the material bases for distinguishing between those whose lives are constituted by "joy" and those who experience a higher proportion of suffering. In the cases of *Frankenstein* and *Jane Eyre*, the critical rehabilitation of the creature and the revival of Bertha Mason signal a heightened recognition that a deviation from a norm is not automatically a monstrosity. And I think it is safe to say that readers of Lolita today are more aware than critics were in the 1950s about the need to recognize the separate reality of Dolores Haze. If fictional characters have imaginary rights, Dolores Haze should soon find her Jean Rhys.

But there is something missing in this story of progress, and it appears in the scapegoating of Victor Frankenstein. Even when critics of Frankenstein see the necessity of sympathizing with the creature's plight, they do not see that his troubles have anything to do with them. Victor Frankenstein is still blamed for "playing God" for bringing an aberrant creation into being, but the existence of the creature is not the problem in Frankenstein. The creature's predicament is not the effect of his birth; his suffering results from a universal consensus that he should be shunned. Although the bulk of recent critical work on Frankenstein is from a cultural studies perspective, and not a Kantian orientation, the scapegoating of Victor Frankenstein relies on a Kantian ethic of personal responsibility. The ease with which this assumption flows through the reception history of Frankenstein shows that we can readily feel culpable for the effects of our own actions but not for effects of power from which we profit only indirectly and accidentally. This intuitively narrow sense of ethical responsibility has a respectable pedigree in the academic study of ethics. As Bernard Williams contends, we "have to take seriously the distinction between my killing someone, and its coming about because of what I do that someone else kills them" ("Critique" 117). This distinction is nearly as effective a shield for Tony Soprano, who rarely commits his own murders, as it is for every citizen of the world who is in a position to extract surplus labor value from others, an extortion that does not occur without the indirect aid of the police or superior military force.

If we were to try to measure our own ethical standards against those of Rousseau's era, we could pick an exemplary figure of his time, someone who embodied an important ethical dilemma of his period—say, Thomas Jefferson—as a figure of comparison. As everyone knows, Jefferson deplored slavery and he owned slaves. There are essentially two ways to assess the contradiction between Jefferson's words and his behavior: either he was a hypocrite who profited from a practice he claimed to abhor, or he was a product of his time who was unable entirely to separate himself from practices that were sanctioned by his culture. What cannot be said about Jefferson is that he was morally exemplary for us. We would not like to say that our highest ethical aspirations are to emulate Jefferson. But we do emulate him. We know that our clothes are made and our food is brought to market by people who work in brutally difficult and degrading conditions. We deplore their exploitation, and we carry on with our everyday lives because we historicize ourselves just as Jefferson historicized himself. Jefferson did not think he was a hypocrite because he told himself that he had not created slavery; that he wished it did not exist; and that if he were to live in a better future in which slavery did not exist, he would willingly forgo the benefits he derived from it. Having reassured himself that this was so, he kept his slaves. We tell ourselves that the world of global inequality is neither one that we have made nor one that we would have made, and our knowledge of the living conditions of migrant farmworkers and sweatshop laborers does not affect what we eat, drink, and wear.

Kantian ethicists continue to reiterate the maxim that it is unforgivable to treat others simply as means to our own ends, without reflecting on the fact that the economic fabric of the lives of propertied subjects is made up of relations in which we do just that. At the other end of structures of inequality from which we benefit are people whose existences are the means of our comfort. When political discourse is informed by Foucault's reminders of the omnipresence of power, it would seem that it should make us more aware of our routine hypocrisies, but it does not. Both the formulation of ethical principles and the futurist orientation of politics allow us to maintain the fiction of the ethical coherence of everyday life. While ethics allows us to restrict our focus of responsibility to the results of our own actions, and narratives of interiority enable us to narrow that focus to those acts which are the effects of abundant intentionality, politics contributes to the legitimating narrative that we are all, at heart, good people by allowing us to believe that we really would be better people in a better world. This rhetoric of the future enabled Jefferson to overlook his daily hypocrisy. Our own legitimating narratives, public and private, are likely to look as threadbare to the future as Jefferson's look to us.

Percy Shelley offered one of the nicest reassurances that practices in the arts would lead, naturally and inevitably, to a general moral improvement when he asserted, "Poetry strengthens that faculty which is the organ of the moral nature of man, in the same manner that exercise strengthens a limb" (*Poetry and Prose* 488). Even those who smile indulgently at Shelley's affective neoplatonism generally harbor the implicit and enabling assumption that, in our own scholarly and pedagogic work, aesthetic appreciation and moral improvement are mutually supportive formations, that learning to love literature is, ethically, different from learning to enjoy chess. But it would be difficult to do a better job of making English prose poetic than this: "I am thinking of aurochs and angels, the secret of durable pigments, prophetic sonnets, the refuge of art. And this is the only immortality that you and I may share, my Lolita" (309). The entire last paragraph of Lolita fulfills Shelley's criterion that "it awakens and enlarges the mind itself by rendering it the receptacle of a thousand unapprehended combinations of thought" (487), but the identification it engenders does not make us better people. And it is very different from Charlotte Brontë's prose when Jane Eyre describes the philanthropy she bestows on Adele Varens after sending her back to boarding school:

> So I sought out a school conducted on a more indulgent system; and near enough to permit of my visiting her often, and bringing her home sometimes. I took care she should never want for anything that could contribute to her comfort: she soon settled in her new abode, became very happy there, and made fair progress in her studies. As she grew up, a sound English education corrected in a great measure her French defects; and when she left school, I found in her a pleasing and oblig-ing companion: docile, good-tempered, and well-principled. By her grateful attention to me and mine, she has long since well repaid any little kindness I ever had it in my power to offer her. (438–39)

Led by Jean Rhys and Gayatri Spivak, we have recovered Bertha Mason, but I think it is fair to say that our current reading practices would find nothing in this passage but a description, on Jane's and Brontë's part, of Jane's gen-erosity. But the overtone of compassion here is subverted in almost every phrase through a persistently unbalanced parallelism. Finding a "school conducted on a more indulgent system" is a middle ground between allow-ing Adele to live in the Rochester household and sending her back to the school she hated; Jane asks the reader to make the second comparison but not the first. The discrepancy between "visiting her often" and "bringing her home sometimes" might, if we could escape the iron control of Jane's dictation, lead us to ask about Adele's desire—how "often" would she like to go "home"? The boundless "anything" that Adele is allowed involves her material comfort, but the time and affection of the Rochesters is, by con-trast, strictly rationed. A word is needed for Adele's new station—it cannot be called a "home"—so it is nearly one, an almost homonymic "abode." Adele is "very happy," but makes only "fair progress," a distinction ex-plained in the next sentence by the difference between her "English educa-tion" and her "French defects." Jane's rigorous assessment of Adele's char-acter is more reminiscent of her own reception at Lowood by Scatcherd and Brockelhurst than by Miss Temple, and Adele finally occupies the place Jane filled in the book's opening—the charity cousin who is never allowed to forget her distance from the inner circle of blood, of "me and mine." Adele fills her marginal place more dutifully than Jane ever did, and the list of her English virtues—"docile, good-tempered, and well-principled"—rings strangely in a book that celebrates the progress of an orphan who disdains docility.

It may seem like an offense against our historical imaginations to think that Charlotte Brontë "the named individual" (Spivak 257) deliberately planted every detail of this paragraph in order to undermine the self-righteousness of her main character, and that we, as readers, have been less sensitive to Adele's deprivations than Brontë was. This is an insult that we will have to get over. If advances in the arts are going to make us more ethical people, this is not going to occur naturally but counterintuitively, as we become sharper, more skeptical readers who are willing to relinquish our own protective narratives: that we hold ourselves to higher standards than people did in the past, that we would behave even more generously in a more perfect future, and that our primary ethical responsibility in the present is not to cause gratuitous harm to others. Politics enables us to imagine a better world, but that prospective vision needs a supplement. Power really is everywhere, and how we respond to that reality is ethics. Ethics is what we do now.

Notes

⋮

Introduction

1   I am making an equation here between deconstruction and literary reading, in accordance with Paul de Man's contention that "Poetic writing is the most advanced and refined mode of deconstruction" (AR 17). The premise that there is a fundamental continuity between New Critical practices and deconstruction was one that de Man was willing to accept; as he said in an interview, when his work was characterized as "just more New Criticism, I can live with that very easily, because I think that only what is, in a sense, classically didactic, can be really and effectively subversive. And I think the same applies there to Derrida" (117). De Man explores the literariness of Derrida's work in "The Rhetoric of Blindness," in which he concludes that "Derrida's text is less radical, less mature than Rousseau's, though not less literary" (140). Derrida does not make similarly explicit claims about literariness, but his assertion in "White Mythology" that metaphor is not "in the text of philosophy" (Margins 209) but that philosophy is in fact metaphoric identifies a relation between figurative language and philosophy that is similar to the one I am arguing here. I have written about deconstruction and literariness in "De Man, Gasché and the Future of Deconstruction" (Symploké 1998: 49–62). I hope readers who disagree with this sketchy reading of Derrida will allow that the granting of priority to literary indeterminacy over iterative principles is a recognizable legacy of deconstruction.

2   A central thesis of D. A. Miller's The Novel and the Police is that realist novels encourage the reader's identification with an omniscient narrator. Autobiographical form, I am arguing, dispels the myth of narratorial omniscience.

3   Edward Said's critique of Derrida in "The Problem of Textuality: Two Exemplary Positions" is that a purely formal deconstruction, which only reveals the inherent instability of knowledge, underestimates the discursive effects of power. As Said argues, "a signifier is an act of will with ascertainable political and intellectual consequences and an act fulfilling a strategic desire to administer and comprehend a vast and detailed field of material." Through this "act of will," "the effective force of knowledge [is] linked systematically ... to power" (Said's emphases; 709). While Foucault and Said focus on public discourses of politics and culture, the personal narratives of legitimation in autobiography follow the same logic of "strategic desire," and they demand the same sort of adversarial close reading.

4   For John Rajchman, "Foucault's way of questioning 'anthropologism' led him to a kind of practical or ethical philosophy whose fundamental category was the category of freedom" ("Ethics After Foucault" 165). Similarly, James Bernauer and Michael Mahon contend that Foucault's ethics are committed to a concept of "radical liberty as the human essence" ("The Ethics of Michel Foucault" 153).

1 Supplements

1   Page citations from the *Confessions* are from *The Confessions and Correspondence, Including the Letters to Malesherbes*, translated by Christopher Kelly. This text contains substantive variants from the Paris manuscript of the *Confessions* in the notes. I have also consulted the Pléiade edition of the *Confessions* and J. M. Cohen's translation, and I have revised Kelly's translation in some cases in order to provide a more literal or colloquial rendering of Rousseau's words or to fit the quotation to the surrounding syntax.

2   Without mentioning Rousseau, Philippe Lejeune dates the origin of modern autobiography as 1770, the date of the completion of *Les Confessions* (*On Autobiography*, 4).

3   Jean Starobinki's influential work has generally assumed an unproblematic coherence across Rousseau's philosophical, political, and autobiographical works. Two of the most recent studies that have followed Starobinski in explicating Rousseau's autobiographical writings through the principles enunciated in his philosophical and political works are Christopher Kelly's *Rousseau's Exemplary Life* and Eugene Stelzig's *The Romantic Subject in Autobiography*. In a contrary vein, Bernard Williams points to the inadequacy of Rousseau's political work to explain his more clearly fictional texts when he argues that "the *Social Contract* is a political romance, except that it is less truthful than some of Rousseau's own fictional writings" (*Truth and Truthfulness: An Essay in Genealogy*, 200).

4   See Goulemot, pp. 32–34, 40–41, 52, 58–59, and 115–18.

5   These terms first appear in explicit opposition when Rousseau describes his adolescent incomprehension of the "genuine" ("*veritable*") object of sexuality and the "bizarre ("*bizarre*") effects" of his deviation (34; Pléiade 41).

6   For triangularity as a structure of desire, see Schwartz 176–77; Williams 54; Grimsley 108–12; Kavanagh 11f.; as an idealized pattern of social organization, see Schwartz 176; Kelly 208.

7   Cranston reports two sources and three stories on the fate of the letters. A neighbor of Mme d'Houdetot reported on two different occasions that she saved either one or four of the letters. D'Houdetot's niece claimed that Sophie saved all of them and that they were burned by her granddaughter (Cranston 72).

8   For example, in *Thérèse Philosophe*, a nun "see[s] Paradise unveiled" through a priest's use of the "cord of St. Francis" (Darnton 262).

2 What Is a Poet?

1   All citations from the *Prelude* are from *The Thirteen Book Prelude*, edited by Mark L. Reed.

2   Paul Magnuson has an incisive discussion of this point in *Coleridge and Wordsworth*, 13–16.

3   This sequence is treated as a unit by Mary Jacobus in *Romanticism, Writing, and Sexual Difference*, 206–15; Lawrence Kramer, "Gender and Sexuality in *The Prelude*"; and Betsy Bolton, "Romancing the Stone: 'Perdita' Robinson in Wordsworth's London." Each of

these analyses notes the opposition between rural purity and urban decadence, and each construes that opposition in terms of Wordsworth's concern with the integrity of his own imaginative power. The epistemological vocabulary of "imagination" and "fancy" is then supplemented by a psychoanalytic vocabulary that purports to show the real stakes of this opposition. Thus Kramer contends that "The preeminent issue of book seven is the survival of the imagination, which for Wordsworth is tantamount to the survival of the ego" (620). The threat to imagination is located in the female figures in this sequence, beginning with Mary Robinson and proceeding through the Sadler's Wells prostitute and the Cambridge road prostitute. As Kramer argues, Wordsworth is compelled to "defend his creative imagination against the very sexuality that she embodies" (620). In Jacobus's analysis, Wordsworth identifies himself with the Blessed Babe in the second part of the sequence, and he deflects the fear of corruption by urbanity and experience onto the mother: "The unstopped boy occupies the same position as the guilty, autobiographically split Wordsworth, who is also subject to growth; but his fall has been displaced on to the forgotten mother" (212–13). Bolton sees the other Mary Robinson, the actress and poet Mary Darby Robinson, as the shadow figure who embodies the urbanized mode of debased representation. All of these analyses impute a deterministic power to unconscious forces, and they describe this passage in the homeostatic terms of the Freudian pleasure principle, which endeavors to subdue the libidinal forces that assault the ego in order to bring the subject to a lower level of excitation. Thus the passage is perceived as defensive in nature (and successfully so) rather than as self-accusatory. In bringing the vocabulary of ethics to bear on this passage, I have presumed that Wordsworth is capable of seeing that the figures with whom he can most easily be identified in this story are not the children but the adult males: John Hatfield and the patrons of the London and Cambridge road prostitutes. If Wordsworth had identified himself with the Blessed Babe, the next story would not be that of the Cambridge prostitute.

4   There is some ambiguity on this point, but I think there is less than meets the eye. Coleridge wrote a series of articles for the Morning Post about the affair, and he never mentions a child; neither does De Quincey in his Post articles. Donald Reiman believes that Mary Robinson did have a child, based on two things: a report in the Morning Post of 18 December 1802, which claimed that "A Paper of Tuesday . . . says—'It is with much sympathy we mention, that poor Mary of Buttermere is with child,'" and a letter sent to the court where Mary's seducer, John Hatfield, was being tried for fraud, which said that Mary Robinson "declines prosecuting Hatfield for the Bigamy, as she is now very advanced in her pregnancy" (Reiman 144). I do not find this evidence persuasive. The Hatfield trial was a highly publicized affair, and newspapers were not above heightening scandal with rumor; the Post's attribution of this information to another, unnamed newspaper functions as a disclaimer of responsibility. Neither is the note sent to the court beyond suspicion; after describing Mary Robinson as "very advanced in her pregnancy," it goes on to complain that "she has been injured by him in every way, as he left a considerable bill for board, lodging, &c. at her father's house." The economic injury to her father is an odd thing for a woman "very advanced in her pregnancy" to focus on. In Mary Lamb's account of the play at Sadler's Wells, the story takes a comic turn as the Maid of Buttermere marries a sailor (Mary Robinson actually married a local farmer). By claiming that Mary Robinson's child died in infancy, Wordsworth evades the problem with the claim of her pregnancy: there is no record of a child. But Wordsworth visited Keswick at the time of

Hatfield's execution, where he saw the adjoining graves of Robert Burns and his son, and he wrote about both graves in the poem "At the Grave of Burns." The real model for Mary Robinson's "nameless babe that sleeps / Beside the mountain chapel undisturbed" would seem to be Burns's son, of whom Wordsworth wrote in 1803: "For *he* is safe, a quiet bed / Hath early found among the dead / Harboured where none can be misled, / Wronged, or distrest; / And surely here it may be said / That such are blest" (*PW* 226).

5 Johnston offers the most extensive speculation on this point; see especially pp. 127–34.

6 After McFarland (1981) come Lucy Newlyn, *Coleridge, Wordsworth, and The Language of Allusion* (1986); Paul Magnuson, *Coleridge and Wordsworth: A Lyrical Dialogue* (1988); Gene W. Ruoff, *Wordsworth and Coleridge: The Making of the Major Lyrics, 1802–1804* (1989); and Richard E. Matlak, *The Poetry of Relationship: The Wordsworths and Coleridge, 1797–1800* (1997). Before McFarland, there was William Heath, *Wordsworth and Coleridge: A Study of Their Literary Relations in 1801–1802* (1970).

3 "Nothing More Unnatural"

1 The 1818 text appears in *The Mary Shelley Reader* (Bennett and Robinson 1990) and in paperbacks issued by Woodstock Books (1993); Broadview Press (1994); Washington Square Press (1995); Norton (1996); Oxford University Press (1998); and Longman (2002). The anthologies that include the 1818 *Frankenstein* are the Harcourt (ed. Mellor and Matlak 1996), the Longman (ed. Damrosch et al. 1998), and the Norton (ed. Abrams and Stillinger 1999).

2 *Frankenstein, or, The Modern Prometheus*, ed. D. L. Macdonald and Kathleen Scherf, 119. Page citations for *Frankenstein* are from this edition, which prints the 1818 version of *Frankenstein* with the 1831 revisions in an appendix. Further references to *Frankenstein* will be cited parenthetically.

3 See Lee Sterrenburg, "Mary Shelley's Monster: Politics and Psyche in *Frankenstein*" in *The Endurance of Frankenstein*.

4 Mellor estimates an average of five to six such emendations per manuscript page (*Shelley* 59).

5 The argument I am making about the 1831 Introduction is similar to that made by Mary Favret about Mary Shelley's notes to her edition of Percy Shelley's poems in "Mary Shelley's Sympathy and Irony: The Editor and her Corpus."

6 (1) Walton revives Victor [58]; (2) Beaufort dies in Caroline's arms [64], (3) Caroline comes to Elizabeth's sickbed [72]; (4) Victor vivifies and abandons the creature [86]; (5) Clerval revives Victor [91]; (6) Beaufort's death, with Caroline in attendance, is memorialized in a painting [106]; (7) Safie nurses her dying servant [154]; (8) the creature revives a nearly drowned young woman [168]; (9) Victor destroys the female creature [197]; (10, 11) Victor tries and fails to revive Clerval [201] and Elizabeth [220]; (12) Alphonse dies in Victor's arms [222]; (13) the creature observes the dead Victor [242].

7 In a letter to a friend, Harriet Shelley reported that Percy Shelley told her that Mary had proposed that the three of them live together, "I [Harriet] as his sister, she as his wife" (*The Letters of Percy Bysshe Shelley*, 1:421).

8 In *A History of a Six Weeks Tour*, Mary Shelley refers to Germans of "the meanest class" as "disgusting" (56, 69). A journal entry of 28 August 1814 speaks of "the horrid and slimy

faces of our companions in voyage" (*MWSJournals* 20), while a letter of 15 August 1822 speaks of the Genovese as "wild savages" (*Letters* 1:249).

9   "Sleeping Beauty in the Wood" is an eighteenth-century French fairy tale written by Charles Perrault. It was sufficiently popular to have undergone several stage adaptations in London during Mary Shelley's childhood.

4 From Jane Eyre *to* Villette

1   A facsimile title page from the first edition of *Jane Eyre* appears in the Norton Critical Edition, edited by Richard J. Dunn, xiii.

2   All page references to the text of *Jane Eyre* are to The Bedford Books edition, edited by Beth Newman.

3   In Bem's revision of Freudian theory (based on a series of studies of sexual orientation), he employs a central premise of the Freudian account of desire—the convertibility of cathexis and identification in the unconscious—but reverses the orthodox Freudian etiology. Bem argues that identification (with coevals, not parents) typically precedes cathexis. To explain the prevalence of hetero- rather than homosexual desire, Bem theorizes that sexual orientation (the path of object-cathexis) is produced dialectically out of, and after, gender identification, so that children who identify with one gender tend to see the members of the other gender as strangely different and exciting. The perception of others as different produces a "nonspecific autonomic arousal" (321) that can be experienced as fear but that can also be culturally coded as erotic attraction. This pattern suggests that "similarity may promote friendship, compatibility, and companionate love, but it is dissimilarity that sparks erotic/romantic attraction and passionate love" (323). It also suggests that ethnic difference can supplement gender difference in intensifying erotic attraction.

5 From Seduction to Fantasy

1   This argument originates with Elizabeth Bruss in *Autobiographical Acts*, 145–46, and is taken up by Christina Tekiner in "Time in Lolita," 463–69; Leona Toker in *Nabokov: The Mystery of Literary Structures*, 208–11; Alexander Dolinin in "Nabokov's Time Doubling," 3–40; and Julian Connoly in "'Nature's Reality' or 'Humbert's Fancy,'" 41–61.

2   For example: The poem "Lilith," which was written in 1928 and translated and published in English in 1970, describes attempted intercourse with "an unforgotten child" (*Poems and Problems*, 53). In a note accompanying the English publication in 1970, Nabokov warns that "intelligent readers will abstain from examining this impersonal fantasy for any links with my later fiction" (55).

Works Cited

⋮

Abrams, M. H. *Natural Supernaturalism: Tradition and Revolution in Romantic Literature.* New York: Norton, 1971.

Abrams, M. H., and Jack Stillinger, eds. *The Norton Anthology of English Literature: Volume Two.* New York: Norton, 1999.

Alexander, Christine, ed. *The Early Writings of Charlotte Brontë.* London: Basil Blackwell, 1983.

Altieri, Charles. *Canons and Consequences: Reflections on the Ethical Force of Imaginative Ideals.* Evanston, IL: Northwestern University Press, 1990.

Anderson, Amanda. *The Powers of Distance: Cosmopolitanism and the Cultivation of Detachment.* Princeton, NJ: Princeton University Press, 2001.

Appel, Alfred A. "Notes." In *The Annotated Lolita,* 321–441. New York: McGraw-Hill, 1970.

Armstrong, Nancy. *Desire and Domestic Fiction: A Political History of the Novel.* Oxford: Oxford University Press, 1987.

Armstrong, Nancy, and Leonard Tennenhouse. "The American Origins of the English Novel." *American Literary History* 4 (1992): 386–410.

Austin, J. L. *How To Do Things With Words.* Ed. J. O. Urmson and Marina Sbisà. Cambridge, MA: Harvard University Press, 1975.

Barker, Juliet, ed. *The Brontës: A Life in Letters.* Woodstock, NY: Overlook Press, 1998.

Bate, Jonathan. *Romantic Ecology: Wordsworth and the Environmental Tradition.* London: Routledge, 1991.

Bem, Daryl J. "Exotic Becomes Erotic: A Developmental Theory of Sexual Orientation." *Psychological Review* 103 (1996): 320–35.

Benjamin, Walter. *Illuminations.* Ed. Hannah Arendt. New York: Schocken, 1969.

Bennett, Betty, and Charles E. Robinson, eds. *The Mary Shelley Reader.* Oxford: Oxford University Press, 1990.

Bernauer, James, and Michael Mahon. "The Ethics of Michel Foucault." In *The Cambridge Companion to Foucault,* ed. Gary Gutting. Cambridge: Cambridge University Press, 1994.

Bolton, Betsy. "Romancing the Stone: 'Perdita' Robinson in Wordsworth's London." *ELH* 64 (1997): 726–55.

Booth, Wayne. "Why Ethical Criticism Can Never Be Simple." In *Mapping the Ethical Turn: A Reader in Ethics, Culture and Literary Theory,* ed. Todd F. Davis and Kevin Womack, 16–29. Charlottesville: University Press of Virginia, 2001.

Boyd, Brian. *Vladimir Nabokov: The American Years.* Princeton, NJ: Princeton University Press, 1991.

——. "Even Homais Nods": Nabokov's Fallibility, or How to Revise Lolita." *Nabokov Studies* 2 (1995): 62–86.

Brontë, Charlotte. *Jane Eyre*. Ed. Richard J. Dunn. New York: Norton, 1971.

——. *Jane Eyre: An Autobiography*. Ed. Beth Newman. Boston: Bedford/St. Martin's, 1996.

——. *The Professor*. Ed. Heather Glen. London: Penguin, 1989.

——. *Villette*. Ed. Margaret Smith and Herbert Rosengarten. Oxford: Oxford University Press, 2000.

Bruss, Elizabeth. *Autobiographical Acts: The Changing Situation of a Literary Genre*. Baltimore: Johns Hopkins University Press, 1976.

Burke, Peter. "Representations of the Self from Petrarch to Descartes." In *Rewriting the Self: Histories from the Renaissance to the Present*, ed. Roy Porter, 17–28. London: Routledge, 1997.

Butler, Marilyn. "Frankenstein and Radical Science." In *Frankenstein: A Norton Critical Edition*, ed. J. Paul Hunter, 302–13. New York: Norton, 1996.

Caruth, Cathy. *Unclaimed Experience: Trauma, Narrative, and History*. Baltimore: Johns Hopkins University Press, 1996.

Centerwall, Brandon. "Hiding in Plain Sight: Nabokov and Pedophilia." *Texas Studies in Language and Literature* 32 (1990): 468–84.

Chitham, Edward. *The Brontës' Irish Background*. London: Macmillan, 1986.

Clark-Beattie, Rosemary. "Fables of Rebellion: Anti-Catholicism and the Structure of Villette." *ELH* 53 (1986): 821–47.

Coburn, Kathleen, ed. *Inquiring Spirit: A New Presentation of Coleridge from His Published and Unpublished Prose Writings*. New York: Pantheon Books, 1951.

Coleridge, Samuel Taylor. *Coleridge's Dejection: The Earliest Manuscripts and the Earliest Printings*. Ed. Stephen Maxfield Parrish. Ithaca, NY: Cornell University Press, 1988.

——. *Collected Letters*. Ed. Earl Leslie Griggs. Oxford: Clarendon Press, 1956–1971. Cited in text as CL.

——. *The Notebooks of Samuel Taylor Coleridge*. Ed. Kathleen Coburn. New York: Pantheon, 1957–.

——. *Samuel Taylor Coleridge: The Oxford Authors*. Ed. H. J. Jackson. Oxford: Oxford University Press, 1985.

Connoly, Julian. "'Nature's Reality' or 'Humbert's Fancy?': Scenes of Reunion and Murder in Lolita." *Nabokov Studies* 2 (1995): 41–61.

Cranston, Maurice. *The Noble Savage: Jean-Jacques Rousseau, 1754–1762*. Chicago: University of Chicago Press, 1991.

Curtis, L. P. *Anglo-Saxons and Celts: A Study of Anti-Irish Prejudice in Victorian England*. Bridgeport, CT: University of Bridgeport Press, 1968.

Damrosch, David, et al., eds. *Longman Anthology of British Literature, Volume Two*. New York: Longman, 1998.

Darnton, Robert. *The Forbidden Best-Sellers of Pre-Revolutionary France*. New York: Norton, 1995.

DeJean, Joan. "The Politics of Pornography: L'Ecole des Filles." In *The Invention of Pornography: Obscenity and the Origins of Modernity, 1500–1800*, ed. Lynn Hunt, 109–24. New York: Zone Books, 1993.

Deleuze, Gilles, and Felix Guattari. *A Thousand Plateaus: Capitalism and Schizophrenia*. Trans. Brian Massumi. Minneapolis: University of Minnesota Press, 1987.

de Man, Paul. *Allegories of Reading*. New Haven: Yale University Press, 1979. Cited in text as AR.

——. "An Interview." In *The Resistance to Theory*. Minneapolis: University of Minnesota Press, 1986.

——. "The Rhetoric of Blindness." In *Blindness and Insight: Essays in the Rhetoric of Contemporary Criticism*. 2nd ed. Minneapolis: University of Minnesota Press, 1983.

de Rougemont, Denis. *Love in the Western World*. New York: Harcourt, Brace, 1940.

Derrida, Jacques. *Margins of Philosophy*. Trans. Alan Bass. Chicago: University of Chicago Press, 1982.

———. *Of Grammatology*. Trans. Gayatri Chakravorty Spivak. Baltimore: Johns Hopkins University Press, 1974. Cited in text as OG.

———. *The Post Card: From Socrates to Freud and Beyond*. Trans. Alan Bass. Chicago: University of Chicago Press, 1987.

De Selincourt, Ernest. *The Prelude, or Growth of a Poet's Mind*. London: Oxford University Press, 1926.

Dolinin, Alexander. "Lolita in Russian." In *The Garland Companion to Vladimir Nabokov*, ed. Vladimir E. Alexandrov. New York: Garland, 1995.

———. "Nabokov's Time Doubling: From *The Gift* to *Lolita*." *Nabokov Studies* 2 (1995): 3–40.

Duclos, Charles Pinot. *Les Confessions du Comte de ***.* Ed. Laurent Versini. Paris: Editions Desjonquères, 1992.

Ellis, Kate. "Monsters in the Garden: Mary Shelley and the Bourgeois Family." In *The Endurance of Frankenstein*, ed. George C. Levine and U. C. Knoepflmacher, 123–42. Berkeley: University of California Press, 1979.

Favret, Mary. "Mary Shelley's Sympathy and Irony: The Editor and Her Corpus." In *The Other Mary Shelley: Beyond Frankenstein*, ed. Audrey A. Fisch, Anne K. Mellor, and Esther H. Schor, 17–38. New York: Oxford University Press, 1993.

Ferenczi, Sandor. "Confusion of Tongues Between the Adult and the Child." In Jeffrey Moussaieff Masson, *The Assault on Truth: Freud's Suppression of the Seduction Theory*, 283–95. New York: Farrar, Straus and Giroux, 1984.

Foucault, Michel. *Discipline and Punish: The Birth of the Prison*. Trans. Alan Sheridan. New York: Vintage, 1995.

———. *Ethics: Subjectivity and Truth*. Trans. Robert Hurley et al. Ed. Paul Rabinow. New York: New Press, 1997. Cited in text as EST.

———. *The History of Sexuality. Volume One: An Introduction*. Trans. Robert Hurley. New York: Vintage, 1980. Cited in text as HS.

———. *The Use of Pleasure. The History of Sexuality: Volume Two*. Trans. Robert Hurley. New York: Vintage, 1985. Cited in text as UP.

Freud, Sigmund. *The Aetiology of Hysteria*, in Jeffrey Moussaieff Masson, *The Assault on Truth: Freud's Suppression of the Seduction Theory*, 251–82. New York: Farrar, Straus and Giroux, 1984.

———. "Beyond the Pleasure Principle." In *The Standard Edition of the Complete Psychological Works of Sigmund Freud*. Trans. James Strachey et al., vol. 18:3–64. London: Hogarth, 1955. Cited in text as SE.

———. "The Ego and the Id." In *The Standard Edition of the Complete Psychological Works of Sigmund Freud*. Trans. James Strachey et al., vol. 19:3–66. London: Hogarth, 1955. Cited in text as SE.

Gaskell, Elizabeth. *The Life of Charlotte Brontë*. London: J. M. Dent, 1913.

Genette, Gerard. *Narrative Discourse Revisited*. Trans. Jane E. Lewin. Ithaca, NY: Cornell University Press, 1988.

Gilbert, Sandra M., and Susan Gubar. *The Madwoman in the Attic: The Woman Writer and the Nineteenth-Century Literary Imagination*. New Haven: Yale University Press, 1979.

Goulemot, Jean Marie. *Forbidden Texts: Erotic Literature and Its Readers in Eighteenth-Century France*. (Translation of *Ces livres qu'on ne lit que d'une main*.) Trans. James Simpson. Philadelphia: University of Pennsylvania Press, 1994.

Green, Martin. "The Morality of Lolita." *Kenyon Review* 28 (1966): 352–77.

Grimsley, Ronald. *Jean-Jacques Rousseau: A Study in Self-Awareness*. Cardiff: University of Wales Press, 1969.

Harpham, Geoffrey. *Shadows of Ethics: Criticism and the Just Society*. Durham, NC: Duke University Press, 1999.

Heath, William. *Wordsworth and Coleridge: A Study of Their Literary Relations in 1801–1802*. Oxford: Clarendon Press, 1970.

Holmes, Richard. *Coleridge: Darker Reflections, 1804–1834*. New York: Pantheon Books, 1999.

Hunt, Lynn, ed. *The Invention of Pornography: Obscenity and the Origins of Modernity, 1500–1800*. New York: Zone Books, 1993.

Jacob, Margaret. "The Materialist World of Pornography." In *The Invention of Pornography: Obscenity and the Origins of Modernity, 1500–1800*, ed. Lynn Hunt, 157–202. New York: Zone Books, 1993.

Jacobus, Mary. *Romanticism, Writing, and Sexual Difference: Essays on the Prelude*. Oxford: Clarendon, 1989.

Jamieson, Dale. "Method and Moral Theory." In *A Companion to Ethics*, ed. Peter Singer, 476–87. Oxford: Blackwell, 1991.

Johnson, Barbara. "My Monster, My Self." *Diacritics* 12 (1982): 2–10.

Johnston, Kenneth. *The Hidden Wordsworth: Poet, Lover, Rebel, Spy*. New York: Norton, 1998.

Joseph, M. K. "Editor's Introduction" to *Frankenstein*. Oxford: Oxford University Press, 1969.

Karlinsky, Simon, ed. *Dear Bunny, Dear Volodya: The Nabokov-Wilson Letters, 1940–71*. Berkeley: University of California Press, 2001.

Kavanagh, Thomas. *Writing the Truth: Authority and Desire in Rousseau*. Berkeley: University of California Press, 1987.

Kelly, Christopher. *Rousseau's Exemplary Life: The Confessions as Political Philosophy*. Ithaca, NY: Cornell University Press, 1987.

———. "Introduction." *The Confessions and Correspondence, Including the Letters to Malesherbes*. Trans. Christopher Kelly. Ed. Christopher Kelly, Roger D. Masters, and Peter G. Stillman. Hanover, NH: University Press of New England, 1995.

Kramer, Lawrence. "Gender and Sexuality in *The Prelude*: The Question of Book Seven." *ELH* 54 (1987): 619–37.

Leiris, Michel. "The Autobiographer as Torero." In *Manhood: A Journey from Childhood into the Fierce Order of Virility*, 153–64. Trans. Richard Howard. Chicago: University of Chicago Press, 1992.

Lejeune, Philippe. *On Autobiography*. Trans. Katherine Leary. Minneapolis: University of Minnesota Press, 1989.

Levinson, Marjorie. *Wordsworth's Great Period Poems: Four Essays*. Cambridge: Cambridge University Press, 1986.

Liu, Alan. *Wordsworth: The Sense of History*. Stanford, CA: Stanford University Press, 1989.

Macaulay, Thomas Babington. *The History of England from the Accession of James II*. Chicago: Bedford and Clarke, n.d. (orig. pub. 1849).

Macdougall, Hugh A. *Racial Myth in English History: Trojans, Teutons and Anglo-Saxons*. Hanover, NH: University Press of New England, 1982.

Magnuson, Paul. *Coleridge and Wordsworth: A Lyrical Dialogue*. Princeton, NJ: Princeton University Press, 1988.

Masson, Jeffrey Moussaieff. *The Assault on Truth: Freud's Suppression of the Seduction Theory*. New York: Farrar, Straus and Giroux, 1984.

——. *The Complete Letters of Sigmund Freud and Wilhelm Fliess, 1887–1904*. Trans. and ed. Jeffrey Masson. Cambridge, MA: Belknap Press of Harvard University Press, 1985.

Matlak, Richard E. *The Poetry of Relationship: The Wordsworths and Coleridge, 1797–1800*. New York: St. Martin's Press, 1997.

McFarland, Thomas. *Romanticism and the Forms of Ruin: Wordsworth, Coleridge, and Modalities of Fragmentation*. Princeton, NJ: Princeton University Press, 1981.

McMahan, Jeff. *The Ethics of Killing: Problems at the Margins of Life*. Oxford: Oxford University Press, 2002.

Mellor, Anne K. "Choosing a Text of Frankenstein to Teach." In *Approaches to Teaching Shelley's Frankenstein*, ed. Stephen Behrendt, 31–37. New York: Modern Language Association, 1990.

——. *Mary Shelley: Her Life, Her Fiction, Her Monsters*. New York: Methuen, 1988.

Mellor, Anne K., and Richard Matlak, eds. *British Literature, 1780–1830*. Fort Worth: Harcourt Brace College Publishers, 1996.

Miller, D. A. *The Novel and the Police*. Berkeley: University of California Press, 1988.

Millett, Kate. *Sexual Politics*. New York: Doubleday, 1980.

Milton, John. *Paradise Lost*. In *John Milton: Complete Poems and Major Prose*. Ed. Merritt Y. Hughes. Indianapolis: Odyssey Press, 1957.

Mitchell, W.J.T. "Influence, Autobiography, and Literary History: Rousseau's *Confessions* and Wordsworth's *The Prelude*." ELH 57 (1990): 643–64.

Moers, Ellen. "Female Gothic." In *The Endurance of Frankenstein*, ed. George C. Levine and U. C. Knoepflmacher, 77–87. Berkeley: University of California Press, 1979.

Morrison, Toni. *Beloved*. New York: Knopf, 1987.

Nabokov, Vladimir. *The Annotated Lolita*. 2nd ed. Ed. Alfred A. Appel. New York: Vintage, 1991.

——. *The Enchanter*. Trans. Dmitri Nabokov. New York: Putnam, 1986.

——. *Nabokov's Dozen*. New York: Popular Library, 1958.

——. *Poems and Problems*. New York: McGraw-Hill, 1970.

——. *Speak, Memory*. New York: Putnam, 1966 (orig. pub. 1951 as *Conclusive Evidence*).

Nagel, Thomas. "Moral Luck." In *Moral Luck*, ed. Daniel Statman, 57–71. Albany, NY: State University of New York Press, 1993.

Newlyn, Lucy. *Coleridge, Wordsworth, and the Language of Allusion*. Oxford: Clarendon Press, 1986.

Nussbaum, Felicity. *The Autobiographical Subject: Gender and Ideology in Eighteenth-Century England*. Baltimore: Johns Hopkins University Press, 1989.

Nussbaum, Martha. "Exactly and Responsibly: A Defense of Ethical Criticism." In *Mapping the Ethical Turn: A Reader in Ethics, Culture and Literary Theory*, ed. Todd F. Davis and Kevin Womack, 59–79. Charlottesville: University Press of Virginia, 2001.

——. *The Fragility of Goodness: Luck and Ethics in Greek Tragedy and Philosophy*. Cambridge: Cambridge University Press, 1986.

——. *Love's Knowledge: Essays on Philosophy and Literature*. New York: Oxford University Press, 1990.

——. *Poetic Justice: The Literary Imagination and Public Life*. Boston: Beacon Press, 1995.

O'Rourke, James. "De Man, Gasché, and the Future of Deconstruction." *Symploké* 1998: 49–62.

Phelan, James. "Sethe's Choice: *Beloved* and the Ethics of Reading." In *Mapping the Ethical Turn: A Reader in Ethics, Culture and Literary Theory*, ed. Todd F. Davis and Kevin Womack, 93–109. Charlottesville: University Press of Virginia, 2001.

Poovey, Mary. *The Proper Lady and the Woman Writer: Ideology as Style in the Works of Mary Wollstonecraft, Mary Shelley, and Jane Austen*. Chicago: University of Chicago Press, 1984.

Rajchman, John. "Ethics After Foucault." *Social Text* (1986): 165–83.

Reiman, Donald. "The Beauty of Buttermere as Fact and Romantic Symbol." *Criticism* 26 (1984): 139–70.

Restif de la Bretonne, Nicolas-Edmé. *Monsieur Nicolas; or, The human heart laid bare.* Trans. Robert Baldick. New York: C. N. Potter, 1967.

Rhys, Jean. *Wide Sargasso Sea.* New York: Norton, 1982. Orig. pub. 1966.

Richardson, Samuel. *Pamela: Or, Virtue Rewarded.* Ed. Peter Sabor. London: Penguin, 1985.

Rorty, Richard. "The Barber of Kasbeam: Nabokov on Cruelty." In *Contingency, Irony and Solidarity,* 141–68. Cambridge: Cambridge University Press, 1989.

Rousseau, Jean-Jacques. *The Confessions.* Trans. J. M. Cohen. New York: Penguin, 1953.

——. *The Confessions and Correspondence, Including the Letters to Malesherbes.* Trans. Christopher Kelly. Ed. Christopher Kelly, Roger D. Masters, and Peter G. Stillman. Hanover, NH: University Press of New England, 1995.

——. *Les Confessons et Autre Textes Autobiographiques.* Ed. Bernard Gagnebin and Marcel Raymond. Paris: Pléiade, 1959.

——. *Emile.* Trans. Barbara Foxley. London: Dent, 1963.

——. *The First and Second Discourses, Together with the Replies to Critics, and Essay on the Origin of Languages.* Trans. Victor Gourevitch. New York: Harper, 1990.

——. *Julie, or The New Heloise: Letters of Two Lovers Who Live at the Foot of the Alps.* Trans. Philip Stewart and Jean Vache. Hanover, NH: University Press of New England, 1997.

——. *Reveries of the Solitary Walker.* Trans. Peter France. New York: Penguin, 1979.

Ruoff, Gene W. *Wordsworth and Coleridge: The Making of the Major Lyrics, 1802–1804.* New Brunswick, NJ: Rutgers University Press, 1989.

Said, Edward. "The Problem of Textuality: Two Exemplary Positions." *Critical Inquiry* 4 (1978): 673–714.

Schwartz, Joel. *The Sexual Politics of Jean-Jacques Rousseau.* Chicago: University of Chicago Press, 1984.

Shelley, Mary. *Frankenstein, or, The Modern Prometheus.* Ed. D. L. Macdonald and Kathleen Scherf. Peterborough: Broadview Literary Texts, 1994.

——. *Frankenstein, or, The Modern Prometheus.* Ed. Jonathan Wordsworth. New York: Woodstock Books, 1993.

——. *Frankenstein or, The Modern Prometheus.* Ed. Anne K. Mellor and Teresa Reyes. New York: Washington Square Press, 1995.

——. *Frankenstein: A Norton Critical Edition.* Ed. J. Paul Hunter. New York: Norton, 1996.

——. *Frankenstein, or, The Modern Prometheus.* Ed. Marilyn Butler. Oxford: Oxford University Press, 1998.

——. *Frankenstein, or, The Modern Prometheus.* Ed. Susan Wolfson. New York: Longman, 2002.

——. *A History of a Six Weeks Tour.* Oxford: Woodstock Books, 1989.

——. *The Journals of Mary Shelley 1814–1844.* Ed. Paula R. Feldman and Diana Scott-Kilvert. Baltimore: Johns Hopkins University Press, 1987. Cited in text as *MWSJournals.*

——. *The Letters of Mary Wollstonecraft Shelley.* Ed. Betty T. Bennett. Baltimore: Johns Hopkins University Press, 1980.

——. "Rousseau." In *Mary Shelley's Literary Lives and Other Writings. Volume 3: French Lives,* ed. Clarissa Campbell Orr, 320–66. London: Pickering & Chatto, 2002. Cited in text as "Rousseau."

Shelley, Percy Bysshe. *The Letters of Percy Bysshe Shelley*. 2 vol. Ed. Frederick L. Jones. Oxford: Clarendon Press, 1964.

———. *Shelley's Poetry and Prose*. Ed. Donald H. Reiman and Sharon B. Powers. New York: Norton, 1977.

Spacks, Patricia Meyer. *Imagining a Self: Autobiography and the Novel in Eighteenth-Century England*. Cambridge, MA: Harvard University Press, 1976.

Spark, Muriel. *Mary Shelley*. New York: Dutton, 1987.

Spivak, Gayatri Chakravorty. "Three Women's Texts and a Critique of Imperialism." *Critical Inquiry* 12 (1985): 243–61.

Starobinski, Jean. *Jean-Jacques Rousseau: Transparency and Obstruction*. Chicago: University of Chicago Press, 1988.

Stelzig, Eugene. *The Romantic Subject in Autobiography: Rousseau and Goethe*. Charlottesville: University Press of Virginia, 2000.

Sterrenburg, Lee. "Mary Shelley's Monster: Politics and Psyche in *Frankenstein*." In *The Endurance of Frankenstein*, ed. George Levine and U. C. Knoepflmacher, 77–87. Berkeley: University of California Press, 1979.

Tekiner, Christina. "Time in Lolita." *Modern Fiction Studies* 25 (1979): 463–69.

Thormahlen, Marianne. *The Brontës and Religion*. Cambridge: Cambridge University Press, 1999.

Toker, Leona. *Nabokov: The Mystery of Literary Structures*. Ithaca, NY: Cornell University Press, 1989.

Trilling, Lionel. "The Last Lover: Vladimir Nabokov's Lolita." *Encounter* 11 (1958): 9–19.

Vendler, Helen. "Tintern Abbey: Two Assaults." In *Wordsworth in Context*. Ed. Pauline Fletcher and John Murphy. London: Bucknell University Press, 1992.

Whiting, Frederick. "'The Strange Particularity of the Lover's Preference': Pedophilia, Pornography, and the Anatomy of Monstrosity in Lolita." *American Literature* 70 (1998): 833–62.

Williams, Bernard. "A Critique of Utilitarianism." In *Utilitarianism: For and Against*, ed. J. J. C. Smart and Bernard Williams, 77–150. Cambridge: Cambridge University Press, 1973.

———. "Moral Luck." In *Moral Luck*, ed. Daniel Statman, 35–55. Albany, NY: State University of New York Press, 1993.

———. *Truth and Truthfulness: An Essay in Genealogy*. Princeton, NJ: Princeton University Press, 2002.

Williams, Huntington. *Rousseau and Romantic Autobiography*. Oxford: Oxford University Press, 1983.

Wolfson, Susan. "Feminist Inquiry and Frankenstein." In *Approaches to Teaching Shelley's Frankenstein*, ed. Stephen Behrendt, 50–59. New York: Modern Language Association, 1990.

Wollstonecraft, Mary. *A Vindication of the Rights of Women*. Ed. Carol H. Poston. Norton: New York, 1988.

Wood, Michael. *The Magician's Doubts: Nabokov and the Risks of Fiction*. Princeton, NJ: Princeton University Press, 1995.

Wordsworth, Dorothy. *The Grasmere Journals*. Ed. Pamela Woof. Oxford: Clarendon Press, 1991. Cited in text as *Journals*.

Wordsworth, William. *Poetical Works*. Ed. Thomas Hutchinson; rev. ed. by Ernest de Selincourt. Oxford: Oxford University Press, 1978. Cited in text as *PW*.

———. *The Thirteen Book Prelude*. Ed. Mark L. Reed. Ithaca, NY: Cornell University Press, 1991.

Wordsworth, William, and Samuel Taylor Coleridge. *Lyrical Ballads 1798*. Ed. W. J. B. Owen. Oxford: Oxford University Press, 1969. Cited in text as *LB*.

Wordsworth, William, and Dorothy Wordsworth. *The Letters of William and Dorothy Wordsworth:*

The Early Years. Arr. and ed. Ernest de Selincourt. 2nd ed. rev. Chester L. Shaver. Oxford: Clarendon Press, 1967. Cited in text as *Letters1*.

———. *The Letters of William and Dorothy Wordsworth: The Middle Years.* Arr. and ed. Ernest de Selincourt. 2nd ed. rev. Chester L. Shaver. Oxford, Clarendon Press, 1967. Cited in text as *Letters2*.

Index